The Belt & Road Initiative in the Global Arena

Yu Cheng · Lilei Song · Lihe Huang
Editors

The Belt & Road Initiative in the Global Arena

Chinese and European Perspectives

Editors
Yu Cheng
Tongji University
Shanghai, China

Lihe Huang
Tongji University
Shanghai, China

Lilei Song
Tongji University
Shanghai, China

ISBN 978-981-10-5920-9   ISBN 978-981-10-5921-6   (eBook)
https://doi.org/10.1007/978-981-10-5921-6

Library of Congress Control Number: 2017948720

This Palgrave Macmillan imprint is published by Springer Nature
The registered company is Springer Nature Singapore Pte Ltd.
The registered company address is: 152 Beach Road, #21-01/04 Gateway East, Singapore
189721, Singapore

Tongji University China Today Book Series focuses on contemporary China studies from an international perspective. Contributors to the book series span different disciplines and constitute a joint team at Tongji University, led by Professor Peiming Lü (Vice President of Tongji University), conducting research and offering courses in English on contemporary China studies. After years of endeavor, these courses, as a package, have received several honors, including *English-taught Exemplary Course for International Students* granted by the Ministry of Education, P.R. China.

The articles published in this book exclusively reflect the points of view of their authors and are not the official standpoint of institutions providing financial support for the research grants. This work was partially sponsored by the following projects:

Jean Monnet Teaching Module Program: European Integration: Experience, Practices, and Policies (No. 2013-3175).

2016 Civil Diplomacy Program of Shanghai Overseas Returned Scholars Association.

Tongji University "The Belt & Road Initiative" Think-Tank Project (Fundamental Research Funds for the Central Universities).

FOREWORD

The "Belt and Road" (OBOR) initiative refers to the "Silk Road Economic Belt" and the "21st Century Maritime Silk Road" initiatives, which were unveiled by Chinese President Xi Jinping in 2013. Together, these initiatives constitute a Chinese framework for organizing multinational economic development, primarily in Eurasia.

The Belt and Road initiative is an inevitable extension of China's comprehensive opening up and the inevitable trend for cultural revival. It includes the demands of globalization, which indicates that China has undergone from participating in globalization to shaping globalization. Since the 1970s, China's "Reform and Opening Up" policy mainly paid attention to opening up to developed Western countries. Through decades of development, however, Western countries have now opened up to China and China is opening up more to developing countries and neighboring countries. China not only exports products, but also exports a sustainable development pattern as its contribution to the world. Today, the Belt and Road initiative is an important public good that China is giving to the world, and is a new proposal from China for enhancing international cooperation after the so-called globalization, also known as Americanization or Westernization, failed to reach its goals.

The Belt and Road initiative is essentially aimed at providing efficient supply, thus stimulating fresh demand, with a focus on infrastructure investment in both developed and developing economies, which covers 4.4 billion people. As the Bloomberg Report said recently, the Belt and Road initiative will help 3 billion Asians grow into the middle class by

2050. China's own research also predicts that China's trade volume with the countries along the Belt and Road will increase to US$2.5 trillion in the next 10 years. The Belt and Road initiative will help generate vitality and further promote China's inland provinces to open up, enabling more exchange with other countries and regions. When I mentioned this to European friends, they were excited and felt there were a lot of opportunities.

Many countries, ranging from the United Kingdom to ASEAN members, have shown interest in endorsing the Belt and Road initiative, highlighting their desire to use innovative means to improve their domestic infrastructure. The Belt and Road initiative welcomes other countries to enjoy the benefits of China's economic development and will consequently strengthen economic and cultural cooperation, while putting aside complicated military and political differences to bring about a win–win situation. Admittedly, some China observers cannot accept China's rise and believe that its participation in global governance is associated with grave security risks. Some have even played up Beijing's so-called challenge to the Washington-led world order, regarding the Belt and Road initiative and the Asian Infrastructure Investment Bank (AIIB) as threats to the environment and the rule of law.

The fact is that China still needs the support of Europe to carry forward its strategic plans, although some European politicians remain suspicious of the intentions and feasibility of the Belt and Road initiative. Therefore, measures have to be taken to convince them that stabilizing global growth is also in China's interest. Both China and Europe should work closely together to improve global infrastructure and economic integration, in a bid to upgrade their bilateral ties and learn from each other to bridge the widening gap between the demand and supply of international public goods, which is exactly what the Belt and Road initiative seeks to achieve. This was the intention of the forum "The Belt and Road to a Better Future: China–Europe Youth Dialogue" hosted by Tongji University in June 2016, which collected truly innovative suggestions by young scholars from Europe and China.

This proceedings of the forum on the One Belt, One Road initiative covers the cultures, religions, languages, political systems, and national interests of the different Eurasian nations, trying to provide answers to questions on the implementation of the Belt and Road initiative, which is likely to encounter numerous challenges. This book aims to be a very useful reference for graduate students and teachers of international relations, in China and in the countries along the proposed Belt and Road. This collection can also be recommended to researchers and government officials who want to know more about the Belt and Road initiative.

Prof. Dr. Yiwei Wang
Renmin University of China
Beijing, China

PREFACE

This book is the proceedings of the international forum "The Belt and Road to a Better Future: China–Europe Youth Dialogue," initiated by Dr. Yu Cheng, Dr. Lilei Song, and Dr. Lihe Huang. This forum was hosted by the International School of Tongji University and supported by the Shanghai Overseas Returned Scholars Association, Shanghai Institute for European Studies, and the Collaborative Innovation Center for Belt and Road Security Issue, Tongji University. Twenty young scholars from both China and Europe presented their research outcomes on the forum and fourteen papers were selected for inclusion in this volume, after peer review.

The forum assembled a package of next-generation ideas for the patterns of regional trade, investment, and infrastructure development. It also discussed the next steps for promotion of enhanced policy coordination across the Eurasian continent and strategic implications for EU, Russia, and other major powers. This new publication is a comprehensive presentation of diverse papers on the Belt and Road initiative from the perspectives of spatial, temporal, geopolitical, economic, cultural, and other dimensions.

The volume mainly focuses on four important themes of the Belt and Road initiative: comprehension and communication, regional cooperation, economic cooperation, and geopolitical challenge.

"Part One, Comprehension and Communication on the Belt and Road Initiative," includes four articles: "Public Opinions on the Belt and Road Initiative: A Cross-Cultural Study" by Yu Cheng. This paper conducts a comparative study to examine cross-cultural differences in shaping the image of the Belt and Road initiative as well as the functions of public opinion and media in this process. Cheng suggests a communication strategy for launching the initiative. In the paper "China's Belt and Road Initiative: Connecting and Transforming Initiative," Dragana Mitrovic discusses China's bold attempt to reshape the existing global order and transform it into something new, more multipolar, and more Sinocentric.

Lihe Huang's paper "Intercultural Education on the Theme of the Belt and Road Initiative: A Multimodality Oriented Pedagogical Design" discusses how to make full use of the Belt and Road initiative to develop Chinese students' intercultural competence using a blended instruction pattern. The main purpose of this paper is to introduce a pedagogical design by using international and domestic affairs for students' intercultural education, which is a practice of "internationalization at home."

Lilei Song and Zhao Qiqi's paper "A Model for the Belt and Road Initiative: China's Cultural Diplomacy Toward Central and Eastern European an Countries" explores the roadmap China has formulated for its cultural diplomacy toward CEE countries and examines the developments and problems of China's cultural diplomacy to CEE countries in recent years.

Part Two mainly talks about regional cooperation in the Belt and Road initiative. Ágnes Szunomár's paper "One Belt, One Road: Connecting China with Central and Eastern Europe" suggests that the One Belt, One Road initiative could provide a new framework for cooperation between China and CEE countries because it offers several opportunities for countries that wish to participate in implementing the strategy. "Determinants and Directions of Polish–Chinese Cooperation in the Context of the One Belt, One Road initiative" is by Piotr Bajor. The author discusses the political and economic cooperation between China and Poland, with particular emphasis on the changes that have occurred in China's relations with CEE countries after the accession of some of them to the European Union. Ikboljon Qoraboyev's paper "One Belt, One Road: A Comparative Regionalism Approach" contributes to efforts at conceptualizing the initiative using alternative theoretical and conceptual frameworks.

Part Three refers to economic cooperation in the Belt and Road initiative. Balázs Sárvári and Anna Szeidovitz use the modern Silk Road concept as an example of China's foreign policy in the wake of globalization and the emergence of a new multipolar world order. Ida Musiałkowska's paper "Subnational Development Policy as the Area of Common Interest Under the One Belt, One Road Initiative? The Case of Regional Policy-Making in Poland" provides an analysis on the evolution and evaluation of regional policy-making (at subnational level) in Poland, one of the 28 EU Member States, in the period just before entry to this organization in 2004 to the present. Dmitry Doronin's paper "Comparative Study of the Labor Markets for Distant High-Profile Specialists in China and Russia" discusses how China and Russia could cooperate within the globally emerging creative economy. It describes the potential that could be exploited by opening the labor market for high-profile specialists and those who work in knowledge-intensive and creative industries. "China–Europe Investment Cooperation: A Digital Silk Road" is written by Mireia Paulo. She explores a specific field, the digital industry, and particularly the fifth-generation (5G) market, which opens a number of doors for the Silk Road and the European Fund for Strategic Investments.

Part Four is "Geopolitical Challenge in the Belt and Road Initiative." The paper "One Belt, One Road and Central Asia: Challenges and Opportunities" is submitted by Filippo Costa Buranelli. He contribute to the debate surrounding the One Belt, One Road project by addressing the views, concerns, political, and economic considerations of the Central Asian governments, thus adding new voices and new perspectives to the current literature (academic and specialized) on the project. Péter Marton's paper "Is Afghanistan in the Way or on the Way of the New Silk Road?" formulates some modest proposals as to what can be accomplished, and within which policy framework, for key actors, including China, to take the idea of a Silk Road connection forward. The paper "China in Central Asia and the Balkans: Challenges from a Geopolital Perspective" by Junbo Jian suggests that China should do much more than reduce questions from other powers while involving the great geopolitical game through the One Belt, One Roadinitiative. Beijing should never pretend that the One Belt, One Road project is only about economy.

In today's academia, young scholars are playing a more pivotal role in contemporary Chinese studies all around the world. Their passion and creativity are the source of the innovation in this book, and inspire the editors to present their ideas to academia. The editors would like to thank all the authors for their active involvement in the forum and their agreement to publish their research in this volume. Anyone interested in the investment, infrastructure development, and policy coordination across Eurasia and strategic implications for the EU, Russia, and China under the Belt and Road initiative is invited to read this publication.

Shanghai, China   Yu Cheng
                                                     Lilei Song
                                                     Lihe Huang

CONTENTS

EDITORS AND CONTRIBUTORS

About the Editors

Yu Cheng Ph.D. is Associate Professor at the International School of Tongji University. She is also the Director of International Curriculum Program of the International School; Deputy Director of the Liaison Office of Confucius Institutes of Tongji University. Her research interests are international education, internationalization of education, and cultural adaption of international students.

Lilei Song Ph.D. is Associate Professor at the School of Political Science and International Relations, Tongji University. She was post-doc at the Corvinus University of Budapest in 2014–2015, and academic visitor at the University of Oxford 2015–2016. Her research interests are China–EU relations, Chinese cultural diplomacy, and the EU's neighborhood policy. Major publications include *European Neighborhood Policy and EU's External Governance* (Shanghai Renmin, 2011).

Lihe Huang Ph.D. is Lecturer and Deputy Head of English Department at the School of Foreign Languages, Tongji University. He has published widely in linguistics and higher education, and undertaken several research projects funded by different institutions. Dr. Huang is a Humboldt Fellow of the Germany-based Alexander von Humboldt Foundation and has conducted research at the University of Cologne and University of Bremen. He is also a member of several academic associations both at home and abroad.

Contributors

Piotr Bajor Ph.D. is Assistant Professor at the Faculty of International and Political Studies, Jagiellonian University in Kraków (Poland). He is also a journalist and columnist for prestigious magazines in Poland.

Filippo Costa Buranelli is Lecturer at the School of International Relations at the University of St. Andrews, UK. Prior to this, he was teaching fellow and research associate at King's College London and UCL. His research interests include international relations theory (especially the English School), global governance and international organizations, and regionalism, with a strong focus on Central Asia and the post-Soviet space. His work has been published in *Millennium: Journal of International Studies*, the *Journal of Eurasian Studies*, and *Global Politics*. He was awarded the *English School Prize for the Outstanding Paper by a Younger Scholar* in 2015 by the International Studies Association.

Dmitry Doronin is Ph.D. candidate at Donghua University, Shanghai, China. The research interests of Dmitry Doronin include the creative industries, performance of virtual teams, and international project cooperation.

Junbo Jian Ph.D. is Associate Professor at the Institute of International Studies, Fudan University. His research interest is China–European relations, European external relations, China's foreign affairs, and international relations theory. In 2011–2012, he visited the London School of Economics.

Péter Marton is Associate Professor at Corvinus University's Institute of International Studies in Budapest, Hungary. His research fields are foreign policy analysis and security studies. Research interests include Afghanistan on which he has published a book, co-authored with Nik Hynek, entitled *Statebuilding in Afghanistan: Multinational Contributions to Reconstruction* (New York and London: Routledge, 2011).

Dragana Mitrovic Ph.D. full time Professor at the University of Belgrade, Faculty of Political Sciences (FPS) is a leading Serbian expert on economy, politics, and the security of modern China and East Asia. She is head of the Centre for Asian and Far Eastern Studies at the FPS. Professor Mitrovic teaches political economy, international political economy, political economy of the PR China and East Asia, geopolitics, and geo-economics. She is head of the Regional Asian Studies masters course. Professor Mitrović is the author of three books and more than 50 papers. She is a member of the Board of Economic Science of the Serbian Academy of Arts and Sciences. Professor Mitrovic is founder and director of the Institute for Asian Studies, Belgrade (ias.rs) and editor of the scientific journal *Asian Issues*.

Ida Musiałkowska Ph.D. is Assistant Professor at Poznań University of Economics and Business, Department of European Studies and director of postgraduate studies on EU funds led by the department. She is an expert in both public and private sectors (regional policy, cohesion policy of the EU, EU funds). Her research interests are regional integration processes in the world, regional (subnational) development, business cycles, and policy transfer.

Mireia Paulo is an expert on EU–China investment relations. She currently works at A&Z Law Firm in Shanghai, China, and is a Ph.D. candidate in the Department of East Asian Politics, Ruhr University Bochum, Germany. She has been awarded several prizes for research work during her graduate years. She collaborates as a researcher for think-tanks, European study centers, and Chinese research institutes. She is often invited to lecture to postgraduate students and to tailor training for companies and governmental agencies. Her research focuses on relations between the European Union and China, including economic and financial matters, political relations, environment, and civil society.

Ikboljon Qoraboyev is Director of the KAZGUU Center for International Law (KCIL) in Astana, Kazakhstan. Before this, he held teaching and research positions in Belgium, France, and Turkey. He holds a Ph.D. in Public International Law from the University of Toulouse 1 Capitole in France. His research interests cover international law, international organizations, and comparative regionalism, with a particular focus on post-Soviet space and Central Asia.

Balázs Sárvári is Teacher Assistant at Corvinus University of Budapest (CUB) and Professor at Saint Ignatius Jesuit College. Previously, he was Junior Research Fellow at the Institute of World Economics in the Hungarian Academy of Sciences. Among his highlighted works is the book the *Political Economics of Globalization* (co-authored with Pál Gervai and László Trautmann; 2015, Typotex Publishing House, Budapest), and the articles "Economic Relevance of the Chinese

Tradition" (*Köz-Gazdaság*, CUB, 2016/4, pp. 191–206) and "Strategic Vision of Brzeziński" (*Köz-Gazdaság*, CUB, 2012/3, pp. 234–242). His major fields of research are the political economics of globalization, Chinese economic development, and cultural heritage.

Ágnes Szunomár Ph.D. is the head of the Research Group on Development Economics at the Institute of World Economics, Centre for Economic and Regional Studies of the Hungarian Academy of Sciences. Her research focuses on China's foreign economic relations, including the relation between China and Central and Eastern Europe. She has also carried out research on emerging markets and on foreign direct investment issues and related policies in CEE, with special attention to developments in Hungary.

Anna Szeidovitz is a research assistant at Corvinus University of Budapest, Hungary.

Zhao Qiqi is a graduate student at the School of Political Science and International Relations Tongji University, Shanghai.

LIST OF FIGURES

LIST OF TABLES

PART I

Comprehension and Communication on the "Belt and Road" Initiative

CHAPTER 1

Public Opinions on the Belt and Road Initiative: A Cross-Cultural Study

Yu Cheng

1.1 Introduction

"For thousands of years, the Silk Road spirit of peace and cooperation, openness and inclusiveness, mutual learning and mutual benefit has been passed from generation to generation, promoting the progress of human civilization, and contributing greatly to the prosperity and development of the countries along the Silk Road" (NDRC, MFA and MC 2015). The Belt and Road initiative also follows the same principles as the ancient Silk Road and thus keeps the heritage in a new way. The "Belt" is the Silk Road Economic Belt, which stretches through Eurasia and mirrors the route of the ancient Silk Road. Just as in ancient times, this road is seen as the belt that joins China and Europe, and is a favored route of exchange. The "Road" is the 21st-Century Maritime Silk Road, which links China to the Mediterranean Sea. This road will be one of the most important international trade routes and will connect important developing markets to Chinese production and investments. The initiative aims to create economic corridors and economic, political, and cultural cooperation with win–win outcomes for all countries, with free trade agreements and opportunities for the excess production of each country to be sold, and free circulation of local currencies.

Y. Cheng (✉)
Tongji University, Shanghai, People's Republic of China

© The Author(s) 2018
Y. Cheng et al. (eds.), *The Belt & Road Initiative in the Global Arena*,
https://doi.org/10.1007/978-981-10-5921-6_1

The Belt and Road initiative was put forward when China's influence in commercial and geostrategic matters grew. The initiative involves more than 60 countries, which represent more than one third of the world global economy and the half of the world population. Therefore, the magnitude of the Belt and Road approach is global and not only regional. The countries along the Belt and Road have different mindsets and agendas, and their images of China are varied. What is the best way to communicate effectively and efficiently with the dozens of relevant countries, who have diversified cultures, political systems, and social conditions? This chapter tries to provide some suggestions based on a cross-cultural study of the perceptions of this initiative in these countries.

1.2   Public Opinion, National Image, and Media

The success of the Belt and Road initiative depends on the successful collaboration of numerous countries. For these countries, the perception of this initiative is related to their image of China and public opinion on whether their governments should join the initiative or not.

Public opinion can be described as the dominating opinion, which compels compliance of attitude and behavior in that it threatens the dissenting individual with isolation (Noelle-Neumann 1974). It is "the aggregate of public attitudes or beliefs about government or politics" (Bianco and Canon 2013). The concept of public opinion is often introduced with a process of democracy or in democratic theory. The opinion should be educated, so that it can be shared and expressed (Bianco and Canon 2013). How is public opinion formed? According to the theories of Paul Lazarsfeld, Elihu Katz, and colleagues (Katz and Lazarsfeld 1955; Lazarsfeld et al. 1968), a small minority of "opinion leaders" act as intermediaries between the mass media and most of society. The internet has accelerated the gain in power of these opinion leaders. In this chapter, the opinions of experts and politicians have been collected to obtain the voice of opinion leaders.

The image of a country or nation is also a kind of public opinion, which can influence opinions on the affairs of the country and determine the way in which the world sees it and treats it (Anholt 2005). According to the results of the Global BAV survey, Ramo (2007) thought "China's problem is more complex than whether or not its national image is 'good' or 'bad,' but hinges on a more difficult puzzle: China's image of herself and other nations' views of her are out of alignment." The Belt and Road initiative is a long-term, global plan launched by China. Its perception is part of the image of China's policy. China's initiative of building the Silk Road Economic Belt and the 21st-Century Maritime Silk Road highlights its concept of peaceful development and will contribute to the win–win cooperation between China and Eurasian countries. But, as Joshua Cooper Ramo (2007) stated, whether China can change its national image will determine the country's future, and the future of the initiative.

Viewing China as a threat is not new in some countries. China has tried to communicate to the world its disinclination to expand and dominate. Although there are still some Samuel Huntington supporters who warn against possible Chinese triumphalism in the twenty-first century in view of the country's huge population, considerable territory, and rapid technological advancement. As the world is varied, so the images of one country and the ways that country has been treated are also varied.

To shape the images of certain nations, however right or wrong they might be, is a very complex communication process that involves various information sources. Radio and TV transmissions of international programs, newspapers, books, news services, and so on are probably the strongest shapers of the image of a country (Kunczik 1997).

The growing prominence of the World Wide Web makes online resources a new and powerful image shaper. The internet is transforming the processes of news and information production and reading (Beam et al. 2016), influencing the content and structure of knowledge about public affairs (Eveland et al. 2004).

More and more traditional newspapers have opened websites with an electronic edition for online reading. Recent studies suggest that more and more people are looking online for their news (e.g., Eveland et al. 2004). Compared with printed news, a benefit of online news is the possibility for online comments, which bring interaction between the news and the readers. Therefore, both online news and online comments have been collected in this study.

In theory, the relationship between public opinion, national image, media, and policy-making can be expressed by the arrows in Fig. 1.1. The following five relationships are shown:

1. Media is the shaper of China's image
2. China's image influences the way in which the world sees it and treats it (public opinion)

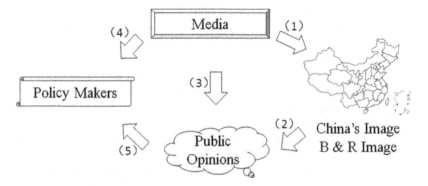

Fig. 1.1   Public opinion, national image, media, and policy-making

3. Media provides the resources for forming public opinion
4. Members of the governmental policy-making system and diplomats rely on mass media to make a map of the world (Cohen 2015)
5. Public opinion is a proximate cause of policy (Page and Shapiro 1983)

1.3   Method

In May 2015, 60 international students of Tongji University from more than 50 countries cooperated with Chinese students from the same university to conduct team studies on the Belt and Road initiative. Each team was set up to target different countries on the Belt or Road. They collaborated in a "1 + 1" approach, which consisted of at least one Chinese student and one international student from the target country. Each team had access to a large number of online documents, online questionnaires, video interviews, and so on. Teams were under the guidance of eight professors, majored in transportation engineering, intercultural communication, and politics and international relations. Each of the 51 studies completed had the following outline:

1. General view of the economy, international trade, foreign affairs, finance, and infrastructure of the target country
2. Analysis of online news and comments and of surveys to show the local people's awareness and view of the initiative

3. Suggestions for the government, enterprises, and other stakeholders on how to participate in the initiative

From September 2016, studies on the second batch of 14 countries were conducted by 14 Chinese students majoring in foreign languages and about 50 international students registered in the course *China Today*. They set up 14 research teams to analyze opinions from governments, online newspapers, academic circles, and the public.

The main research methods adopted by these teams were (1) literature research, (2) analysis of online opinions, and (3) survey. By January 2016, 65 studies had been finished. The results are summarized in Sect. 1.4 and the conclusions discussed in Sect. 1.5.

1.4   RESULTS

1.4.1   Overview of Opinions

The Belt and Road initiative was often mentioned in the news about President Xi Jiping's visits. In addition to such news, which mainly reports facts rather than opinions, opinions from deeper analysis mostly concerned the benefits and risks of this initiative.

The major benefit for countries along the Belt or the Road is the establishment of new and modern infrastructure in the form of ports, roads, railways, and pipelines. This will not only enhance trade and commerce along the route but also greatly improve the economy of the partnering countries. The newly founded Asian Infrastructure Investment Bank (AIIB) agreed to support parent countries financially in setting up new infrastructure. Countries that lack the required financial resources to improve the domestic infrastructure could take the opportunity to benefit from this support. This is yet another accelerator to boost the economy of all countries taking part in this initiative. Several countries announced that they would act as hubs of the Road or the Belt. Competition to be the hub has even appeared in some regions. The increased exchange and flow of information and knowledge is also likely to improve innovation and the development and diffusion of modern technologies to areas where they are needed and can be applied effectively. Modernized infrastructure also facilitates the flow of tourists and students along the route. This not only benefits the local tourism industry of many countries but also offers the chance of an easier and more convenient way of traveling and exploring new cultures and countries, thereby exploiting another form of opportunity of this initiative. More and more countries have begun to view China as one of the most important tourist resource countries. The Belt and Road routes can therefore increase global and regional connectivity and benefit all partners along the way.

Even though opinions reflect awareness of the opportunities offered by this initiative, the opinion leaders also considered the risks it bears. The Belt and Road initiative was initiated by China and it is assumed that China aims to acquire, in addition to economic benefit, a stronger political position in the world and in the regions along the Belt and Road routes. This also led to the conclusion that the increasing presence of China in these regions is a cause for concern for other large nations, such as the USA, India, and Russia. India and Russia might feel increasing pressure from the rise of China, and this initiative might be considered a step to accelerate the "political and economic expansion of China." The Belt and Road initiative also represents a cause of unease for the USA because it is completely left out of this initiative. On the one hand, the opinion leaders worried that these counties might set barriers to the initiative and to countries that are active in it. On the other hand, such discussion reached different conclusions in different countries; for example, some East European countries viewed the initiative as a way to reduce dependency on Russia.

In addition, opinion leaders in some countries worried that the corruption of their government might become more serious when more infrastructure is built. "More dependency on China" was another situation that they thought the initiative might bring about. Some of China's neighbors, especially the smaller ones, feel threatened that the initiative will contribute to "an increasing dependency on an even stronger China." There is also concern that it is too "China-centric" in that China will be the largest beneficiary and other participating countries will reap only marginal benefits. Even when agreeing that it will be a double-win project, they do not want to let China win more.

Another area of concern evolves from the security of the Belt and Road. The maritime route has to be protected from maritime piracy and terrorism. The land road has to pass through unsafe and unstable regions.

There is no doubt that the Belt and Road initiative will be accompanied by great changes in the political and economic environment. However, the public hope that the specific plans of their governments and the outcome will become clearer in the near future.

1.4.2   Comparison of Quantity

The 65 teams conducted research by collecting online news, articles, and comments with a series of key words related to the initiative. It was found that the quantities of documents found, as well as the quantity of information in the documents, varied from country to country. There were four levels considering the quantity:

1. No information at all; mainly in Africa
2. Only a few online news stories, but no analysis articles nor online comments; mainly in central Asia
3. Online news and articles; the main economies in South and Southeast Asia
4. Online news, articles, and online interaction; mainly the European countries, South Korea, and some other developed Asian countries.

The reasons for this situation can be expressed by the following three aspects:

1. *Technical factors.* The internet was the primary means of accessing research data in this project; therefore, the level of information abundance in certain countries is affected by their development of internet technology. The internet provides a convenient way to participate in public affairs, but it is necessary to consider the differences in the stage of technical appliance from country to country.
2. *Economic factors.* When there is more bilateral trade and economic cooperation, there is more attention to this initiative. It is easy to draw this conclusion when comparing neighbors in the same region of the Belt and Road. The level of economic cooperation influenced not only the quantity of attention paid to the Belt and Road initiative, but also to other topics related to China.
3. *Cultural factors.* Cultural factors are reflected in many aspects. For example, there are cultural differences in how people prefer to obtain and absorb useful information Lewis (1996). In Africa, Central Asia, and West Asia, more emphasis is placed on face-to-face communication, whereas Europeans are more reliant on text and data. The latter produces more textual public opinion. In addition, whether people prefer to give their opinions in public (the internet

is a virtual public place) varies between countries, as does whether these public opinions can have an impact on national policy-making.

1.4.3   Comparison of Content

Perceptions of this initiative are linked to specific economic, political, or military conditions. These decide whether a particular country becomes involved in the Belt and Road.

1. *Political factors*: The most significant political factors are ideology and the power game. Ideological factors here include not only the differences from China's ideology, but also whether they are entangled in the ideology difference. China supports countries following their own path of development. If a country cannot agree with China's ideology, there is still a possibility that it can agree with this initiative.

   Discussion of power games is quite normal in the articles of the Belt and Road initiative. Some European countries wish to balance the powers. Reducing dependency on the USA or Russia is a reason for them to join the initiative. Of course, the opposite situation also exists.

2. *Economic factors*: Discussion of the economic impact of the Belt and Road initiative is far more active than discussion of the political impact. When there is more expectation of economic benefit, opinions on the initiative are more positive.

3. *Cultural factors*: Cultural factors are naturally diverse. There are cultures that encourage criticism and cultures that do not. East Asians prefer to avoid being openly critical in public. At this point, China's government need not be upset because of criticism, nor be too satisfied when there is no criticism.

1.5   DISCUSSION

Each of the 65 teams collected and analyzed online news, articles, and comments from one country. Surveys were also conducted when necessary. Based on their reports, some suggestions were made on how to improve communication between China and other countries on the Belt and Road. The following points aim to build international trust and reduce misunderstanding and suspicion.

1.5.1   Communication Tasks

Samuel Huntington (1997) warned against possible Chinese triumphalism in the twenty-first century in view of the country's huge population, considerable territory, and rapid technological advancement. Concern about Chinese triumphalism can reduce mutual trust, which is necessary for cooperation. When the public consider the benefits and risks of the initiative, more risks were found, especially when there was a lack of trust. Consider the following example:

> It seems that the Georgian people are very skeptical of their government and any involvement with foreign entities. The largest worry about the One Belt, One Road initiative for Georgia is the country's vulnerability. The country is underdeveloped, the government is not very powerful, and the country has an abundance of rich natural resources. China will begin to invest in Georgia, create infrastructure, but the Georgian government should not allow itself to become a puppet state to the Chinese government.

This is not only the case in Georgia; other countries, such as Kazakhstan and some of their neighbors, reported similar concerns. Such distrust of China is combined with the distrust of their own governments. If a country that is underdeveloped and in need of international cooperation can maintain a relatively uncorrupt government, then Chinese influence in the country can be a springboard for successful growth of these countries into the future. On the one hand, it should be clearly understood that this initiative will help equip the countries along the Belt and Road with infrastructure, capital goods, and a trading line that will connect countries all across Eurasia. On the other hand, citizens should receive information to confirm that their governments can maintain them as the primary objective and that all will benefit from the initiative. In summary, in addition to disseminating the achievements of the two governments, it is essential to spread information about the benefits to citizens.

Some obvious benefits are that the world-altering initiative will cut travel costs, reduce the prices of certain luxury goods, and increase the availability of rare goods. Arguably, the most important aspect of this initiative is that the world will become more stable because any war or period of unrest will harm the economies of all countries.

1.5.2   Communication Subjects

When discussing the aims of China, writers tend include such issues as seizing natural resources; rebalance of the powers of the USA, Russia, India and China; and transfer of excess production capacity. The public is sensitive to the purpose of energy, and worries that this initiative might result in overexploitation of their country's resources and cause pollution. How to reduce such suspicions? It is counter to the inclusive spirit of the Belt and Road initiative that it is a threat to the power of USA, Russia, or India. Such suspicions have caused communication of this initiative to fall into the whirlpool of power games. When wearing such colorful glasses, some foreign governments and the public prefer to wait and observe, even if they are interested in the potential investment, trade, jobs, and economic growth. Therefore, a risk–benefit analysis is still needed, especially from a range of perspectives. At the same time, the public need more details of what the connecting of Eurasia will bring them. Who will be the next opinion leader, telling an understandable story to the public about the Belt and Road initiative?

The survey results show that foreigners with experience of studying in China have a more positive attitude toward the Belt and Road initiative. If international students in China or foreigners working in China have interest in this topic and are willing to give opinions, they have more chance of becoming opinion leaders because of their experience and knowledge of China.

Chinese scholars should consider the various interests of the audience and possible benefits to them when telling the story of China. In addition, the way to tell this story should also be based on the preferences of the audience. Lectures, conferences, and online articles are necessary; face-to-face communication with governments, enterprises, and public along the Belt and Road are also necessary. In summary, effective communication means to give facts. Data seekers want facts and data, and talk seekers want a conversation.

Chinese overseas workers and Chinese tourists traveling abroad are likely to become communicators. Newspapers, television, radio, and the internet are an extension of human language and cannot be divorced from human thinking.

1.5.3 Communication Content

Implementation of the Belt and Road initiative should take into account the different national conditions of each participating country. The ancient Silk Road in history was the crystallization of the common wisdom and industriousness of China and the Western countries, and so is the current Belt and Road initiative. It cannot be achieved with only the efforts of China and infrastructure projects. The initiative as a symbiotic system can be developed only in an inclusive and cooperative environment that respects the economic, political, cultural, and institutional differences between countries. Therefore, China, who initiated the project, should fully understand each country's specific national conditions and relevant policies. Talented people should be found to promote this initiative, or the educational systems should train students for this work. The two countries should focus on their common interest in motivating both the government and public to participate. In Hungary, for example, China's Belt and Road initiative and Hungary's "Opening to the East" plan have a similar vision. To plan the process of realizing a vision together is much more fruitful than discussing power games. For Hungary, the initiative could be a solution to its economic problems and would take full advantage of Hungary's geographic location and its stable political system and society.

From the point of view of the interests of participating countries along the route, the initiative could be a catalyst for accelerating economic growth, technological advancement, and modernization. Such positive developments could also improve political relations between participating countries. If the "all along the way" initiative is successfully achieved, it will become the foundation and backbone of a strong economic and political network. The network means increasing and improving interoperability between many countries and, to a certain extent, transformation of the world order, as the countries along the modern Silk Road will work together to build a large new alliance.

From the perspective of the public, their focus is on economic improvement rather than politics, such as international cooperation to provide better jobs and reduce unemployment. Such messages are easy to perceive and understand. Because policy coordination does not have an immediate impact on the people, economic changes are more susceptible to perception and understanding.

In addition, some countries have already benefited from the projects of the Belt and Road initiative. The public is often aware of the project without knowing about the initiative. There were cases where local people were familiar with some of these infrastructure projects, but did not know that they were part of the Belt and Road. Therefore, a country's successful project could be used to promote this initiative.

1.5.4   Communication Approaches

With the development of modern technology, more and more traditional forms of media are using the internet for increased diffusion. Online news and social media play an increasingly important role in providing information to the public. Making and diffusing news and opinions online seems to be a common phenomenon. However, when including the technological and cultural factors, such a situation is regional. There is still slow internet connectivity in some counties and many people who trust face-to-face communication more than text. Therefore, methods of transmitting information are bound to be diverse.

In addition, although the news media play a major role in shaping the image of China and the image of the Belt and Road initiative, everything with a "Chinese label" can be a form of transmission. Chinese products, the behavior of Chinese tourists, local Chinese enterprises, and even the Chinese people are likely to become a means of transmission.

As the environment of the Belt and Road initiative, the perceptions and opinions of this initiative have an important influence on its realization. The Belt and Road initiative cannot be achieved solely through China's own enthusiasm and input. In spite of the language barriers and cultural differences, public opinion abroad, especially opinions from neighboring countries, can tell the short board in conducting the initiative, and also give guidance on the communication tasks, subjects, content, and approaches needed to reach the common ambition.

Acknowledgements This work was partially sponsored by the Preparatory Education Research Program (Key Project) "The Status, Trends and Planning of China's Preparatory Education" ([2013] 4482-A) granted by the China Scholarship Council, Higher Education Science Project "International Student Union (Association) in China and Cultural Integration" (2016–2017Y003) granted by CAFSA (China Association for International Education) and Tongji

University "The Belt & Road Initiative" Think-Tank Project "International Students Mobility along the B&R: the Strategy of Education Internationalization" (wx0275020171026, Fundamental Research Funds for the Central Universities).

REFERENCES

Anholt, S. (2005). *Brand new justice: How branding places and products can help the developing world* (p. 105). Oxford: Elsevier Butterworth-Heinemann.

Beam, M. A., Hutchens, M. J., & Hmielowski, J. D. (2016). Clicking vs. sharing: The relationship between online news behaviors and political knowledge. *Computers in Human Behavior, 59*, 215–220.

Bianco, W. T., & Canon, D. T. (2013). Public Opinion. *American politics today* (3rd ed.). New York: W.W. Norton.

Cohen, B. C. (2015). *The Press and foreign policy* (pp. 12–13). Princeton: Princeton University Press.

Eveland, W. P., Marton, K., & Seo, M. (2004). Moving beyond "just the facts" the influence of online news on the content and structure of public affairs knowledge. *Communication Research, 31*(1), 82–108.

Huntington, S. P. (1997). *The clash of civilizations and the remaking of world order* (pp.168–173). London: Simon & Schuster.

Katz, E., & Lazarsfeld, P. F. (1955). *Personal influence; the part played by people in the flow of mass communications.* Glencoe, IL: Free Press.

Kunczik, M. (1997). *Images of nations and international public relations* (p. 1). Mahwah, NJ: Lawrence Erlbaum.

Lazarsfeld, P. F., Berelson, B., & Gaudet, H. (1968). *The people's choice: How the voter makes up his mind in a presidential campaign.* New York: Columbia University Press.

Lewis, R. D. (1996). *When cultures collide: Managing successfully across cultures.* London: Nicholas Brealey.

NDRC, MFA and MC (National Development and Reform Commission, Ministry of Foreign Affairs, and Ministry of Commerce of the People's Republic of China). (2015). Vision and actions on jointly building belt and road [Online]. Available from: http://english.cri.cn/12394/2015/03/29/2941s872030_1.htm. [1 November 2015].

Noelle Neumann, E. (1974). The spiral of silence a theory of public opinion. *Journal of communication, 24*(2), 43–51.

Page, B. I., & Shapiro, R. Y. (1983). Effects of public opinion on policy. *American Political Science Review, 77*(01), 175–190.

Ramo, J. C. (2007). *Brand China* (p. 13). London: Foreign Policy Centre.

CHAPTER 2

China's Belt and Road Initiative: Connecting and Transforming Initiative

Dragana Mitrovic

2.1 New Great Leap Outward: Launching the Belt and Road Initiative

In a speech at Nazarbayev University on 7 September 2013, during his state visit to Kazakhstan, Chinese President Xi Jinping proposed that China and Eurasian countries undertake a grandiose joint project, the Silk Road Economic Belt. The aim is to create a land connection from Southeast Asia over China to Western Europe. On 3 October of the same year, in his address to the Indonesian Parliament, President Xi Jinping proposed the twenty first Century Maritime Silk Road as a new maritime Silk Road connecting China with ASEAN countries, South Asian countries, Africa, and Europe. He used the opportunity to also

D. Mitrovic (✉)
Faculty of Political Sciences, University of Belgrade, Belgrade, Serbia

D. Mitrovic
Institute for Asian Studies, Belgrade, Serbia

© The Author(s) 2018
Y. Cheng et al. (eds.), *The Belt & Road Initiative in the Global Arena*,
https://doi.org/10.1007/978-981-10-5921-6_2

announce establishment of the Asian Infrastructure Investment Bank (AIIB) as a new financial tool that would support regional interconnectivity and further economic integration through network infrastructure.[1]

However, The Belt and Road initiative should not be comprehended or translated geographically. Both the Belt and the Road represent a roadmap for how China wants to become integrated into the world economy and strengthen its political, economic, and cultural influence in the Belt and Road regions while combining its internal and external economic, political, cultural, and security interests. The projected network could take several decades to complete and involve more than four billion people and a market unparalleled in scale and value. The initiative reflects China's vision of effectively implementing its new regional and global role through an economic policy that serves China's internal and external strategic goals. At the same time, it aims to address some of the current, but fundamental, issues and needs of China, Asia, and the world.

At the crossroads of two centuries and two millennia, the numerous and continuous indicators of the growing power of PR China are one of the world's most pronounced phenomena. There is a wide spectrum of areas that demonstrated this, including production and trade, finance, culture, ecology, energy, security, the military, and geopolitics. During the past thirty eight years, China has evolved into one of the most important (sometimes the most important) participant in existing structures, agreements, and relationships at the regional and global level. China is also an initiator, re-constructer, and architect of many new initiatives, which are based on principles substantially different from those that had been dominant in the contemporary world until recently. By doing this, China exercises a huge influence, which is unprecedented for a state that was only a regional power and lacked the main features of a global power—military power and a doctrine formulating the intent to use this power to impose a given ideology and interest-driven discourse of its political, economic, and security reality on others (Mitrovic 2011).

---

[1] In the Third Plenary Session of the 18th Central Committee of the Communist Party of China, held in November 2013, acceleration of the infrastructure networking among the regional countries, as well as pursuing construction of the Silk Road Economic Belt and twenty first-Century Maritime Silk Road were enhanced as priorities at the specific moment of the Reform and Opening Up.

During the period of pursuing the "Reform and Opening Up" policy, China has been consistently promoting, through bilateral and multilateral arrangements, its strategy of international economic cooperation, "mutual benefit, common development" (Xinhua 2010), whose realization should, accordingly, contribute to the creation of a more just international order. This strategy was also named the "win–win strategy." Recently, when speaking of the Belt and Road initiative, Chinese President Xi introduced the concept of "three together" (Wu 2015). During the past few years, Chinese "activism," in some cases seen as assertiveness, has accelerated as a result of internal Chinese and external developments. Some developments were pushed to the surface by the onset of the crisis in the US financial system, which turned into a global financial economic crises, not excluding the Eurozone and the EU. China stepped in as a holder of constructive solutions and expected that the new power of its economy and of others would be recognized within the reforms of the IMF, World Bank, and other crucial global financial institutions. Opposition from Washington obstructed this power sharing and China was pushed toward creating parallel paths and mechanisms for global governance, while pursuing reform of the existing situation from within. A significant part in this process was played by the dominant and creative personality of Xi Jinping, the new Chinese president and CCP Central Committee's general secretary.

2.2   The Belt and Road Initiative: Content and Aims

This strategic initiative has been reshaped and enlarged with new routes and projects. The Belt and Road initiative now concerns 4.4 billion people in sixty five countries with a collective GDP of US$2 trillion. The initiative aims to address primarily the infrastructure investment needs of Asia. The Asian Development Bank (ADB) estimates that about US$8 trillion is needed for infrastructure investment in the Asian region between 2010 and 2020. Based on an implementation guideline for the Belt and Road initiative released by China's National Development and Reform Commission (NDRC) in March 2015, development plans along the Belt and Road routes aim to improve connectivity in five areas: policy, infrastructure, trade, currency, and people. Priority is given to development of transport infrastructure such as roads, railways, and ports. Another area of focus is connectivity of energy infrastructure, such as power grids, oil and gas pipelines, liquified natural gas terminals, high-voltage power lines, nuclear power reactors, renewable energy installations and other energy projects. Construction of communication line networks and IT infrastructure links across Asia, the Middle East, East Africa, and Europe is also important.

East Asia is the fastest growing and most dynamic area of global economy, followed by the strong growth of South Asia. Central Asia lags behind in many aspects, although it is richest in natural reserves. The goals of the Belt and Road initiative address this particular point because Central Asia is probably the first and nearest area where projects regarding energy, transport infrastructure, and introduction of common standards will be implemented. Properly implemented, the projects that comprise the Belt and Road initiative could significantly boost regional economic growth, development, and integration. They can also promote political cooperation, better understanding, and stability, which could reduce the roots of and fields for terrorism and extremism in the region, going hand in hand with set of strategic policies and goals of the Shanghai Cooperation Organization (SCO). On the other side of the continent and China's borders, ASEAN countries have high levels of energy deficiency and a critical need for energy infrastructure investment, coupled with a desire for increased regional energy connectivity. The ASEAN countries are also expected to be high on the agenda of the Belt and Road initiative's list of projects (SIEW 2015). Experience of East Asia's economic rise has shown that economic success has had a positive impact on domestic social and political stability, as well as on regional interstate relations, although there are limitations resulting from historical, ideological, and other invisible and deeply rooted obstacles.

Domestic needs reflected at, and strategic goals and gains coming from, the Belt and Road initiative are numerous. Considering China and her domestic needs, the initiative is intertwined with a range of challenges related to sustainable growth of the Chinese economy. China has been facing many problems in trying to switch to a new model of economic growth, some of the most grave being the need to access resources and markets for final products; reduce or reallocate part of its industrial overcapacity; deleverage some crucial sectors of the economy; and diversify and safely and efficiently deploy its enormous US$3.51 trillion in foreign reserves (Wei 2015).

The Belt and Road initiative is an opportunity to solve some of these problems. By building or upgrading infrastructure relating to transport, energy, and communication along the Road and the Belt and connecting it with existing infrastructure, China can create a new and vibrant network. This brings the opportunity to export technologies, creativity, management skills, materials, and labor, which will reduce the pressure of overcapacity in sectors such as steel and cement manufacture, and maintain high and sustainable economy growth. It can also absorb and diversify China's financial surplus and help increase capitalization and control extensive domestic investment. Economic structural reform is an urgent issue for China in order to overcome the steady decrease in its working-age population and the consequences of excessive domestic investment and overreliance on export-driven growth in recent decades.

Nevertheless, President Xi Jinping said he hoped that annual trade between the countries involved in Beijing's plan to create a modem Silk Road would surpass US$2.5 trillion within a decade (Wei 2015), which shows the importance of revitalizing exports as a growth engine for the Chinese economy. This should ease the process of structural change in the domestic economy. Furthermore, continuing economic growth would give the chance for China's "Reform and Opening Up" program to once again become inclusive. Further results in alleviating poverty confirm the legitimacy of the Communist Party's leading role, proving its continuing ability to provide a share of global wealth to the Chinese nation, more equally distributed than ever in the long history of the Chinese state. In that sense, economic growth is inseparable from national security. Also, China could and should further promote internationalization of the renminbi.

Beijing also hopes that improved connectivity between its less developed southern and western provinces, its richer coast, and the countries involved in the Belt and Road initiative will improve China's internal economic integration and competitiveness and spur more regionally balanced growth. Regarding domestic security in China, the Belt and Road initiative offers an opportunity for central government to intensify its policy of economically upgrading the Xinjiang Uyghur Autonomous Region, which is the epicenter of the country's secessionist and terrorist threats. Xinjiang, which borders Mongolia, Russia, Kazakhstan, Kyrgyzstan, Tajikistan, Afghanistan, Pakistan, and India, is strategically important for the infrastructure network of the Belt and Road initiative, which will pass through the region and connect China with relevant neighbors. This is particularly true for Central Asian countries that will be connected with western China through Xinjiang as the gateway. Such a position has already been provided with several infrastructure projects, such as a high-speed railway between Urumqi and Lanzhou, and initiatives for investing in Xinjiang's banking sector, manufacturing, tourism, transportation and commercial hubs, and other sectors that should create work for locals and stimulate growth of the region's economy and general well being. Beijing is counting on the calming effect that economic development and elimination of poverty should have on ethnic issues and political dissatisfaction on the part of the local Uyghurs.

External goals that China could achieve through the Belt and Road initiative are plentiful and inseparable from domestic goals. There is no doubt among the majority of decision-makers and analysts from the interested sides that implementation of the Belt and Road initiative could assist in deepening regional economic integration. This would come through increased cross-border trade, benefiting from improved transportation and legal infrastructure, simplified procedures, and unified standards for trade and investments. For China, this initiative is the most rational way to exert its growing potential as a rising power and increasingly influential international player, especially because the USA's Asia Pivot has strengthened US military alliances in East Asia and the Pacific. Maritime and border issues in the South China Sea showed China's gained military strength and self-confidence, but were counterproductive in terms of deepening mutual trust and maintaining good neighborly relations. Furthermore, Washington has been pushing two major economic initiatives on both points of its global dominance: the Atlantic and Pacific Oceans. The Trans-Pacific Partnership (TPP) and the Transatlantic Trade and Investment Partnership (TTIP) both exclude China. Certainly, containment of China's rise has so far proved unsuccessful, but it has pushed China toward its western geostrategic vector and perhaps reassured its leaders that "peaceful rise" and "win–win" economic cooperation are better options than security and military pressure or confrontation. The Belt and Road initiative benefits China's geopolitical and security interests by tying other countries into very close and interdependent economic relations.

These relations would strengthen China's importance as an economic partner for its neighbors and, potentially, increase its political and strategic power in the region, including its strong cultural influence. Increased investment in energy and mineral resources, particularly in Central Asia, could also help reduce China's reliance on commodities imported from overseas, including oil transiting the Strait of Malacca, while maintaining energy security.

2.3   EXPECTED OBSTACLES AND CHALLENGES TO THE BELT AND ROAD INITIATIVE

Many of the countries in the mentioned regions have already developed and pursued close economic relations with China, especially in areas such as trade, energy infrastructure investment, and developmental projects, which indicates their ability to deepen that cooperation easily and willingly. However, there have also been examples showing the opposite, which has created a negative image of similar projects at home and internationally.

That is the reason why it is crucial to create and obtain support from the general public and business communities, based on the expected gains, in the countries along the path of the Belt and Road, before making decisions in the relevant countries regarding this multilevel and multipurpose gigantic project. In addition to seeing the mutual benefits, a lot of work needs to be done, bilaterally and multilaterally, related to the necessary harmonization of customs and financial standards and regulations, adjusting and probably lowering tariff and non-tariff barriers, and facilitating trade and investment. Cooperation in dealing with complex and sensitive processes for visa facilitation procedures will be necessary. The legal framework should also be considered for promotion of tourism, education, common research and development projects, cultural exchange, and similar programs that deepen integration and support social and cultural interaction on the people-to-people level. Cooperation between the relevant countries should be an integral part of the Belt and Road initiative, because such cooperation has proved to be the binding force of every lasting bilateral and multilateral cooperation.

Transparency and inclusiveness while developing plans and specific policies and decisions are of the highest importance for the legitimacy and public support of the Belt and Road initiative within partner countries. Many Chinese experts suggest that it is crucial to find mutually beneficial solutions whereby participating countries can map and pursue their particular priorities and development projects along the various planned routes. A truly transparent approach seems to be obligatory for substantially easing the doubts, fears, and reservations of other nations, especially if they enter a joint enterprise with their sovereign soil as an invested resource.

As some Chinese experts have pointed out, it would be wrong for Beijing to assume that gigantic infrastructure projects and growth through huge investment, which have characterized China's economic development, are universally applicable and welcomed by all or even most developing countries, with their individual circumstances. If China ignores the differences and needs of participating countries, it would be repeating the path it has so carefully avoided when leading developing states in many arenas and in bilateral cooperation—the path of "often disastrous mistakes of Western universalism" (Shi 2015).

As already stressed, transparency could reduce possible risk or a wrong approach concerning projects of the Belt and Road initiative that are to be built or financed by the Chinese in the territories of other countries. Some previous projects have been the target of domestic and international criticism on the grounds of being environmentally and socially insensitive or not considerate enough toward local communities. In the past, such projects were not discussed publicly and decisions were made at the top level, without the necessary transparent and publicly oriented procedures for projects that should be beneficial for the majority of people. Some of the most prominent examples are the hydropower dams within the Greater Mekong Subregion, such as the Laotian Xayaburi megadam project on the Mekong river that left fishermen with empty hands and stomachs and threatens the future of the river and local ecosystem (Nijhuis 2014). Other more recent problems emerged with Chinese-financed projects in Sri Lanka, which the new government has put under investigation. Chinese firms had been awarded work on the Colombo Port City project, worth US$1.5 billion,[2] the key Maritime Silk Road project in the Indian Ocean, and another 34 projects. All these projects were concluded with the former government in a bilateral framework, at the top level, financed by a bilateral loan from Beijing. A similar example came with the new Syriza coalition government of Greece, which put on hold the sale of Piraeus Port to COSCO (China Ocean Shipping Company), which had been agreed with the previous government.

Two recent cases occurred in the big and important market of Indonesia, a rising south-Asian power. One project was planned and badly executed during the previous local administration, and another with the new government. In the first case, strongly supported by

---

[2] The Port of Colombo project was agreed in September 2014 when Chinese President Xi visited Sri Lanka as part of his tour through South Asia to promote the One Belt, One Road initiative.

several high officials from the previous Indonesian government, China's Shenhua Guohua Electric Power Co., Ltd. led consortiums that won the bid to build nine out of ten of the largest coal plants on Java during the three years up to 2014. As part of the gigantic Indonesian project to provide 35,000 MW of electricity, the consortium bid to build 10,000 MG stations at a cost of US$700,000 per megawatt, which was about 30% of the average market price. Unlike usual practice, the constructor left the project after the work was completed, but with stations running far below capacity and not even compliant with the power of local coal. The Indonesian state-run power supplier PLN was left with serious maintenance and performance issues with the newly built stations and accused the Chinese consortium of using backward technology boilers and second-hand equipment. After requests by the new administration, the Chinese partners returned to repair some faults, but by mid-2016 only 7000 MW were operating efficiently (McBeth 2016). Even though China's energy corporations remain the most desirable partners for the new Indonesian administration and their ambition energy plan, which is an important project for the sea route of the Belt and Road initiative, PLN remain reluctant to do business with Chinese partners in the future.

In spite of President Widodo's personal push for the project and an official ceremony in January 2016, another huge infrastructure project with crucial Chinese involvement has had numerous issues. The Jakarta–Bandung high-speed rail project, worth US$5.1 billion, has been delayed because of financial, environmental, and land issues that question the viability of the project. Rail experts claim that the proposed 350 km/h speed and four planned stops is highly unsuitable for a distance of only 143 km (McBeth 2016).

The risk that comes from a changed policy toward Chinese companies and their business involvement in locally situated projects could be reduced by avoiding nontransparent deals and pursuing stronger legal procedures. Even more important are the quality of work and the business ethics expressed during the whole process, which are left behind as a legacy that could open or close the door for future engagement of Chinese businesses.

Those negative examples demonstrate that such long-term initiatives might face challenges from the very nature of political processes and from the manner of conducting business. Transparency and inclusion of local stakeholders might help in some cases. In others, the type of political system and tradition might not allow such a "code of conduct." However, smart publicity campaigns explaining the broad-spectrum benefits that projects could bring should achieve more understanding and public support in general. Otherwise, a negative track record in those traditionally friendly countries will diminish the existing positive image that China has in the relevant countries.

Expansion of Chinese political, economic, cultural, and geopolitical influence in the territories that are to be connected by the Belt and Road initiative and its network has already increased tensions in major countries in those regions, such as India and Turkey. Such expansion will also create reaction from major global powers such as Japan, the Russian Federation, and the European Union. In spite of the thoughtful diplomatic initiative of Beijing, which stresses the "win–win" potential of the Belt and Road initiative, the projects will create important foreign and domestic policy implications for all of the mentioned countries, and others. Some argue that China's policymaking process has lacked transparency, leaving uncertainty about China's intentions (Tao and Haenle 2016).

The Maritime Silk Road will inevitably demonstrate China's capacity to project its growing naval power abroad, challenging the dominant power (the USA) and many of the Chinese neighbors along the routes, especially those with maritime border issues with China in South China Sea. In contrast to the previous period when the USA hoped to indirectly control China's rise to the position of a regional power, the global impact of the Belt and Road initiative, together with the founding of the AIIB, have changed Sino-American relations into a competition for dominance in Asia and almost all of its subregions. There is also a concept that China is pivoting toward the West as a response to the US Asia–Pacific Pivot, although this initiative from Washington proved to have poor results.

Regarding the Chinese initiative "16+1" (Sixteen plus One), some politicians and experts speak of China building "a new Great Wall" across the EU and trying to take the Balkan states away from the EU path (Mitrovic 2014). In December 2014, the third Meeting of Heads of Government of China and 16 CEE countries was held in Belgrade, Serbia, with an upgraded and enriched agenda for cooperation. Reviving and intensifying the economic cooperation between China and the crisis-stricken countries of central and southeastern Europe through the "China plus Sixteen" framework is promising and matches interest-based cooperation between these investment- and technology-hungry countries and China. The long history and tradition of cooperation since the birth of the People's Republic and absence of political preconditioning support the issue. In spite of plentiful potential benefits, China's strong initiative toward Central and Eastern Europe (CEE) is viewed with concern in certain offices in Brussels.

Meticulous attention is required in dealing with the issue of how much the Belt and Road initiative will overlap with or compete with other strategic projects and initiatives. These include Shanghai Cooperation Organization (SCO) projects and initiatives; the Eurasian Economic Union and its Eurasian Development Bank (EDB),[3] initiated by Russia; ADB, EU, Indian, Japanese, and US initiatives in Central Asia; the Conference on Interaction and Confidence Building Measures in Asia (CICA); BRICS New Development Bank projects; and others, including China's own initiatives. China's initiatives include construction or bidding for construction of high-speed railways from Russia to Indonesia, the Bangladesh–China–India–Myanmar (BCIM) Economic Corridor, and the China–Pakistan Economic Corridor.

Regional powers such as India, which has its own strategic ideas for developing the Indian Ocean (the "Spice Route of India" and the "Mausam Project") (Aneja 2015), face the initiative with mixed attitudes. China's intention to secure trade routes through the Indian Ocean could be perceived by Delhi as an aggressive move. Some experts claim that bigger challenges for the Maritime Silk Road initiative could come from the existing global shipping system (Ghosh 2015). On the other hand, East Asian neighbors Japan and the Republic of Korea are, so far, not included in the initiative. Tokyo remains reserved and concerned about the hidden strategic agenda of the Belt and Road initiative while Seoul is engaged in connecting its own initiatives into this one. President Park initiated another Eurasian economic and cultural cooperation mechanism in 2013, the "Eurasia Initiative," and wants to connect

---

[3]The EDB was established in 2006 by the Russian Federation and Kazakhstan. The Republic of Armenia and the Republic of Tajikistan became full members of the EDB in 2009, the Republic of Belarus in 2010, and the Kyrgyz Republicin 2011. The aim of the EDB is to promote economic growth in its member states, extend trade and economic ties between them, and support integration in Eurasia. The bank has provided financing totaling more than US$5.3 billion for investment projects in its member states. Retrieved from http://www.eurasianet.org/node/72701.

trans-Korean railways with the Trans-Siberian railway, which is to be part of the Belt and Road initiative.

Projects of the Belt and Road initiative in Central Asia are already burdened with geopolitical tensions. China's growing leverage over the region will naturally create additional concerns in Moscow, which is sensitive to its traditional backyard and areas of high security, economic, and geopolitical interest. Central Asia is abundant in natural resources and strategically located and is therefore also of great interest of the EU. Not to be left behind China and Russia, the EU has established both bilateral and regional mechanisms with the region, most of which have little relative influence compared with Chinese and Russian initiatives, but have not reduced the EU's strategic interest.

With sixty six million people and huge infrastructure needs, Central Asia is a highly attractive market for producers and investors in the EU, China, Russia, Japan, and other countries. Central Asia borders China, Iran, and Russia and is a natural transportation hub connecting Europe with Asia that significantly affects the EU and Euro-Asian energy security. For the same reason, it is also important to Japan and Turkey, which, in pursuing Neo-Osmanism, wants to spread its cultural, economic, and political influence in the region. The expected increase in Chinese involvement in constructing regional IT infrastructure is per se a security challenge because it literarily creates new platforms for Beijing to spread its influence over Central Asia (Kennedy and Parker 2015). Furthermore, Central Asia shares a border with Afghanistan and risks a possible spillover of instability from its southern neighbor, as well as religious, national, and other connections with major transnational threats such as terrorism, organized crime, and trafficking of people, weapons, and drugs. Therefore, the stability of the region is of crucial importance to China, Russia, India, and the EU. The Central Asian states are seen to play the role of key allies in the fight against Islamic extremism (Gast 2014).

Until recently, China's reliance on oil from Central Asia was limited to less than 5% of its needs, compared with 3.5% of Europe's fuel imports. However, the proportion of China's oil and gas imports from Central Asia has grown to over 10%. This has strategic importance because China wants to reduce its dependence on maritime routes controlled by the USA, NATO, and its allies. Competition for access to Central Asian resources is likely to grow between the EU and China, as Russia fulfils its relative goals through its relations with Turkmenistan and the strong ties of Gazprom and its subsidiaries along the Caspian Sea and in the former Soviet Republics.

On the other hand, most of the projects of the Belt and Road initiative directly "call" on neighboring powers to cooperate. When China was engaged in extending the Tibetan railway line from Lhasa to the Indian frontier in the south, it asked India to develop a trans-Himalayan economic zone of cooperation jointly with Nepal and Bhutan. Also, China has invited India to build the BCIM Corridor that would link Yunnan Province with Myanmar, Bangladesh, and eastern India.[4] China has carefully responded to Delhi's concern regarding the Indian Ocean and overlapping of the two initiatives, offering their mutually beneficial cohesion. Additionally, in 2013 during the RIC (Russia, India, China) foreign ministers summit, the Chinese proposed a three-level cooperation strategy, of which the third part is common engagement in "building the Silk Route Economic Corridor and Asia-European Continental Bridge" (The BRICS Post 2013). Furthermore, in February 2014, China's President Xi and Russian President Putin agreed on construction of the Belt and Road initiative and on connection of its rail links with Russia's Euro-Asia railways. Their cooperation within the frameworks of BRICS, SCO, Asia–Europe Meeting (ASEM), and other mechanisms should also have a very positive impact on Belt and Road development.

2.4   Financing the Belt and Road Initiative: Emergence of a New Regional/Global Financial Structure

China has also been working to develop financial institutions and financial structures that can offer financial support for the numerous projects of the Belt and Road initiative and provide opportunities for foreign and private investors to take part in the established financing network. China will try to avoid some of the previous less successful and not well-received patterns of financing business operations abroad.

On 4 November 2014, at the Asia-Pacific Economic Cooperation (APEC) conference in Beijing, China's president announced a plan to

---

[4]Xi raised this issue with Prime Minister Narendra Modi when they met for the first time on the margins of the Brazil, Russia, India, China and Soth Africa (BRICS) summit in Fortaleza, Brazil, July 2014. Please, read more at: http://carnegieendowment.org/2014/08/13/chinese-takeaway-one-belt-one-road

direct US$40 billion from China and welcomed other investors to con-
tribute as "The Silk Road Fund will be open ... and the fund's managers will welcome investors from Asia and beyond to actively take part"
(Zhang 2014). The State Council will forward the nation's foreign currency reserves for about 65% of the Silk Road Fund's initial amount.
The rest of the fund's assets will come from the government's sovereign
wealth fund, China International Trust and Investment Corporation
(CITIC), and the two policy banks, the Export-Import Bank of China
and the China Development Bank Capital Co. (CDB). CITIC's share
will be 15%, and the two banks will contribute 15 and 5%, respectively.
Future investments may be ordered if needed, according to the State
Council sources.

In May 2015, at the ASEM Industrial Dialogue, Chinese vice-premier, Zhang Gaoli, announced that six economic corridors with countries along the Belt and Road's trade routes connecting Asia and Europe
will be funded by the AIIB, the Silk Road Fund, Chinese banks and corporations, and other interested investors. According to Zhang, corridors
are set to run through China–Mongolia–Russia, the New Eurasian Land
Bridge, Central China and West Asia, the China–Indochina Peninsula,
China–Pakistan, and Bangladesh–China–India–Myanmar (He 2015).
Meanwhile, the CDB announced that it would invest more than US$890
billion in more than 900 projects in 60 countries as part of its efforts
to bolster the Belt and Road initiative (*China Daily* 2015). So far,
according to Li, the bank's vice-president, over US$10 billion has been
invested in projects covering coal and gas, mining, electricity, telecommunications, infrastructure, agriculture, and so on.

The Silk Road Fund projects (for example, projects within the Belt
and Road initiative) include some recent major Chinese investment initiatives. These projects will increase similar multibillion-dollar funds
financed by China (or bilaterally) in recent years to support development
in Africa, Latin America, southeastern Europe, and Southeast Asia.

Repeating the same pattern as elsewhere around the globe, China has
moved toward multiplying and strengthening its presence in Europe.
Since the global financial crisis, Mediterranean, eastern, and southern European countries have become very attractive to the Chinese
business community, supported by the Chinese government. In April
2012, Prime Minister Wen Jiabao met high envoys from 16 central and southeastern European countries in Warsaw at the economic
forum (announced a year before in Budapest) and introduced "Twelve

Measures" for development within the 16+1 cooperation. Measures include a credit line worth US$10 billion for support of future projects, of which 30% of the amount would be financed under preferential conditions for Third World countries. Projects in the area of infrastructure, high technology, and renewable energy were prioritized. China intends to stimulate 16+1 trade to double in value and achieve US$100 billion by 2015 and to build one economic development high-technology zone in each of the 16 countries in the following five years. In recent years, cooperation in "industrial capacity" speeded up and became a very important element of the cooperation between China and the 16 CEE countries (Mitrovic 2016a and Mitrovic 2016b).

Another important institution formed to financially support this specific branch of the Belt and Road initiative is the China–CEE Investment Cooperation Fund, "a government-backed, adhering to market-oriented and commercial operation" (The Silk Road News, June 24, Xinhua 2016). It is an equity fund and Mitrovic 2016 registered in Luxembourg that has US$500 million for investment in CEE countries (US$470 million coming from the Export-Import Bank of China and US$30 million from Eximbank Hungary) and a special credit line of US$10 billion dollars at the disposal of fund management to invest in relevant projects in the 16 CEE states. Three projects in Poland have already been approved. According to The Silk Road News and Xinhua, the fund's first investment went to Polish Energy Partners S.A. (Jakobowski, cited in Mitrovic 2016c).

The Silk Road Fund Co Ltd. has a special role in financing projects of the Belt and Road initiative. The fund was set up in December 2014 with an initial capital of US$10 billion, with 65% coming from the China's foreign exchange reserves. Its capital later grew to US$40 billion. It is equity investment, where the Belt and Road initiative will be innovative by involving public and private investors, as well as international organizations such as the ADB, IFC, and AIIB. According to the governor of China's Central Bank, Zhou Xiaochuan, it could become a model of public–private cooperation, operating like a private equity fund but with a longer investment prospect.

Chinese state-owned conglomerate CITIC Ltd. announced in June 2015 that it will invest up to US$113 billion in the One Belt, One Road initiative. The money will come from its banking, securities, trust, and construction divisions, and will help finance the completion of approximately 300 projects from Singapore to Turkmenistan (Zhang and Miller 2015).

One of China's biggest foreign policy successes and strategic wins occurred in Beijing on Monday, 29 June 2015 when delegates from fifty seven countries signed an agreement on the Asian Infrastructure Investment Bank (AIIB). Currently, fifty seven countries from Australia to Germany are AIIB stakeholders, of which thirty seven come from the Asia–Pacific region, while the other twenty come from Europe, Africa, the Middle East, and Latin America; Fourteen are EU Member States. The AIIB began with authorized capital of US$50 billion, which will eventually be raised to US$100 billion. Asian countries are expected to own up to 75% of the bank, with European and other nations owning the rest. Each Asian member is allotted a share of that 75% quota based on economic size. China is about to hold a 25–30% stake.

Founding the AIIB could certainly be seen as an attempt by China, Russia and other BRICS countries, as well as numerous emerging economies, to change the existing order by taking part of the global power cake from the USA, EU, and the global financial oligarchy. BRICS and other emerging economies obtain their "relational power" from their relative position as big regional or global importer or exporter, or as a trader with scarce resources (such as oil, gas, or rare earths). However, what is even more important and new in this process is that the AIIB brings "structural power," which is based on a system of building, controlling, and making rules by the founders. By definition, these rules should give the biggest gain to members.

2.5   Conclusion

If China encourages inclusion and equal possibilities for all stakeholders, and abides by dominant and agreed legal norms and rules, the Belt and Road initiative will give very positive impetus to global markets and efficient allocation of capital investment. It will create an unprecedented scope of opportunities for direct investment and wake up sleepy markets.

The One Belt, One Road strategy underlines China's bold and powerful move forward to a bigger role in global economic and political affairs and shows the way it would like to participate in shaping the world and its future. This is the one of the two most strategic and leadership-expressive initiatives of the PR China. It also reenforces the policies of "reclaiming national pride and enhancing personal well-being" while realizing "China's Dream." Some analysts even see the future network of the Belt and Road initiative as "an economic empire centered in China" (Lo 2015).

REFERENCES

Aneja, A. (2015). China's Silk Road diplomacy willing to enmesh India's projects. *The Hindu.* Retrieved from http://www.thehindu.com/news/international/china-silk-road-india-mausam-spice-route/article7073804.ece.

The BRICS Post. (2013). *China asks India, Russia to join economic Silk Road.* Retrieved from *TheBRICSPost.*

Carnegie Endowment for International Peace. (2014). Retrieved from http://carnegieendowment.org/2014/08/13/chinese-takeaway-one-belt-one-road.

China Daily. (2015, May 28). http://usa.chinadaily.corn.cn/business/2015-05/28/content_20845687.html.

"China CEE Investment Cooperation Fund", (2016, June 24). Xinhua. *The Silk Road News.* Retrieved from http://silkroad.news.cn/2016/0624/2686.shtml.

Dai B. (2010, December 6). Zhongguo guowu weiyuan jianchi zou heping fazhan zhi lu. *Waijiaobu wangzhan.* Beijing: Xinhua.

Gast, A. (2014). A shift in the EU strategy for Central Asia? *Carnegie Moscow Center.* Retrieved from http://carnegie.ru/publications/?fa=55483.

Ghosh, P. K. (2015). Daunting realities: Territorial disputes and shipping challenges to China's maritime Silk Road. *Global Asia, 10*(3).

He, Y. (2015). China to invest $900 billion in Belt and Road Initiative. *The Telegraph.* Retrieved from http://www.telegraph.co.uk/sponsored/china-watch/business/11663881/china-bi1lion-doIlar-belt-road-ini.

Kennedy, S., & Parker, D. (2015). Building China's "One Belt, One Road". *Center for Strategic & International Studies.* Retrieved from http://csis.org/publication/building-chinas-one-belt-one-road.

Lo, C. (2015). The economics and politics of China's New Silk Road. *South China Morning Post.* Retrieved from http://www.scmp.com/comment/insight-opinion/article/1829384/economics-and-politics-chinas-new-silk-road.

McBeth, J. (2016, December 11). Why does Indonesia cling to its plagued Chinese projects? *South China Morning Post.* Retrieved from http://www.scmp.com.

Mitrovic, D. (2011). Izvori i granice kineske moci. *Analiza politike.* Belgrade: FPN.

Mitrovic, D. (2014). China in the West's East and beyond: Politics and economics of the China Plus Sixteen Cooperation Framework. *Serbian Political Thought.* Belgrade: Institute for Political Studies. *10*(2):19–50.

Mitrovic, D. (2016a). The Suzhou Summit: Upgrading of the 16+1 cooperation. Islam, S. (Ed.). *EU-China relations: new directions, new priorities,* Discussion paper. Brussels: Friends of Europe, 2016, pp. 139–141.

Mitrovic, D. (2016b). The belt and road: China's ambitious initiative. *China International Studies.* ISSN 1673-3258, 2016, (No. 59, July/August, pp. 76–95).

Mitrovic, D. (2016c). "Sixteen Plus One" in 2015/2016—Upgrading, framing and stepping up cooperation. *Asian Issues* (Vol. 2, No. 1/2016, pp. 7–23). Belgrade: Institute for Asian Studies.

Nijhuis, M. (2014). Dam projects Ignite a legal battle over Mekong River's future. *National Geographic*. Retrieved from http://news.nationalgeographic.com/news/special-features/2014/07/140711-mekong-river-laos-thailand¬dams-environment/.

Rickleton, K. (2015, March 25). By Opposing SCO Development Bank, Is Russia biggest loser? *Eurasianet*. Retrieved from http://www.eurasianet.org/node/72701.

SIEW. (2015). http://www.siew.sg/programme/roundtables/china-one-belt-one-road-initiative-opportunities-for-asean-energy-rnarket.

Shi, Y. (2015). China must tread lightly with its 'one belt, one road' initiative. *South China Morning Post*. Retrieved from http://www.scmp.com/print/comment/insight-opinion/article/1850515/china-must-tread-lightly-its-one-belt-one-road-initiative?utm_source=edm&utm_medium=edm&utm_content=20l50819&utm_campaign=scmp-today.

Tao, X., & Haenle, P. (2016, January 19). Is China's Belt and Road a strategy? *Carnegie–Tsinghua Center for Global Policy*. Retrieved from http://carnegietsinghua.org.

Wei, S. L. (2015). China's Xi: Trade between China and Silk Road nations to exceed $2.5 trillion. *Reuters*. Retrieved from http://www.reuters.com/article/us-china-economy-oneroad-idUSKBN0MP0J320150329#v4VXHRrEmC7I2GIc.99.

Wei, L. (2015). China's foreign exchange reserves drop $43.26 billion in September. *The Wall Street Journal*. Retrieved from http://www.wsj.com/articles/chinas-foreign-exchange-reserves-drop-43-26-billion-in-september-1444199770.

Wu, J. (2015). One Belt, One Road, far reaching initiative. *China & US Focus*.

Zhang, Y. (2014). With new funds, China hits a Silk Road Stride. Caixin Online. Retrieved from http://english.caixin.com/2014-12-03/100758419.html.

CHAPTER 3

Intercultural Education on the Theme of the Belt and Road Initiative: A Multimodality Oriented Pedagogical Design

Lihe Huang

3.1 Introduction

With the increasingly important role China is playing in the world, it is becoming more proactive in regional and global affairs. The launch of the Belt and Road initiative is a reflection of the new shift in China's international positioning, and thus an important concern is cultivation of internationally competitive talents with global insight and domestic understanding. In this future-oriented process of cultivating talented students, Chinese educators should consider how to make good use of international and Chinese hot issues to develop college students' international capability in this internet age. The Chinese government clearly states in its official document *Outline of China's National Plan for Medium and Long-term Education Reform and Development (2010–2020)* that "a large number of talents shall be cultivated that are imbued with global vision, well-versed in international rules, and capable of participating in international affairs and competition." This consideration is a prompt response

L. Huang (✉)
Tongi University, Shanghai, China

© The Author(s) 2018
Y. Cheng et al. (eds.), *The Belt & Road Initiative in the Global Arena*,
https://doi.org/10.1007/978-981-10-5921-6_3

to today's economic globalization and internationalization of higher education, which should be implemented in China's higher education sector.

Before the internet age, intensive intercultural exposure and interaction were only available through experience abroad. However, with the advancement of internet technologies and increasing internationalization at universities, the indispensable and accessible role of internet technologies as input, output, and social environment for intercultural learning and exchange is now widely recognized (Belz and Thorne 2006; Liaw 2006). It is now commonplace to exploit the internet for intercultural exploration and exchange (see Müller-Hartmann 2000, 2006; Furstenberg et al. 2001; O'Dowd 2004; O'Dowd and Eberbach 2004; Belz and Thorne 2006). In this internet-bound society, educators are practicing an increasing interface of new internet-mediated technologies and intercultural learning, which is particularly interesting and significant for development of students' intercultural competence. Meanwhile, the importance of integrating intercultural competence development into foreign language education is well realized, yet few empirical studies have been reported in terms of course development and activity design (Wang and Coleman 2009), especially with internet mediation.

The main purpose of this paper is to introduce a pedagogical design for intercultural education, on the theme of the Belt and Road initiative, to help students in developing and assessing their intercultural competence. It is believed that this pedagogical design and its practice are feasible and accessible to students in both the Chinese context and international arena.

3.1.1   The Belt and Road Initiative and Its Communication in the Internet Age

More than 2000 years ago, the ancient people of Eurasia opened up several routes of trade and cultural exchange that linked the major civilizations of Asia, Europe, and Africa, collectively called the Silk Road by later generations. These exchange routes symbolize communication and cooperation between the East and West, in which ancient China played an indispensable and important role.

The Belt and Road initiative embraces the trend of a multipolar world in which economic globalization and cultural exchange are flourishing in this internet era. It is also an endeavor to seek a more proactive role for

China in international cooperation and global governance, with increasing expectation of China's involvement in global affairs and the rapid rise of its comprehensive strength.

This initiative also embraces the trend toward a world with greater application of information technology. The internet and other technologies facilitate international communication and cooperation among the countries and regions along the Silk Road Economic Belt and the Twenty First-Century Maritime Silk Road. The developing internet technologies prompt dialog between people, especially the younger generation (as internet natives) in the different civilizations alongside the Belt and Road. This dialogue promotes cultural exchange and economic cooperation on the principles of seeking common ground and drawing on each other's strengths, while putting aside differences in this multipolar world.

With such a background, information and communication technologies in the Web 2.0 era offer further involvement of internet technology in students' development. Internet mediation connects students from different regions of the world and provides them with an authentic and source-rich environment for learning and interaction. Within such a setting, students can experience all the rewards and opportunities of the process of interacting with people from diverse cultural backgrounds and can easily access information and knowledge for offline peer interaction.

Therefore, Chinese educators should see and exploit the intersection between cultural exchange in the Belt and Road initiative, internet mediation in the digital age, and intercultural competence in future-oriented cultivation of talented students.

3.1.2   *Internet Mediation and Multimodal Interaction for Development of Intercultural Competence*

With the increasing role of online learning and assessment in higher education, attention should be paid to internet-mediated resources for intercultural competence. Fortunately, educators have realized the necessity and feasibility of developing intercultural competence by making good use of internet resources. Some practice provides evidence for the effectiveness of the online environment in promoting student interaction. The "International Leadership in Education Technology" (ILET) program is an example. This project contained three strategies, including "a sojourn abroad, a summer academy, and an online reading group"

(Davis and Cho 2005). The research shows that in a fully text-based and online environment, students felt they were encouraged to become more flexible in unfamiliar situations and be open to new people and their ways of thinking and expressing themselves (Davis and Cho 2005). Similar results were found by Liaw (2006).

However, some previous studies have shown that, regarding internet-mediated learning of languages and cultures, "textbooks remain the predominant authority, while internet tools are used as a source of information rather than a means of communication" (Wang and Coleman 2009). In this situation, the problem is not the accessibility of Web 2.0 communication tools (such as blog, podcast, audio or video conferencing, QQ, Wechat, and other synchronous applications), but rather the existence of a well-designed project or learning activity that promotes participants to actively interact by using these internet communication tools.

Why is internet-mediated interaction helpful for development of intercultural competence and is there any theory to back this practice? The author believes that multimodality theory and its related practice can provide the possible explanation.

In recent decades, the term "multimodal" or "multimodality" has become quite familiar to academia, and has been applied to various contexts and disciplines, including linguistics, psychology, semiotics, artificial intelligence, and education studies. In the field of human neuropsychology, modality refers to a sensory modality, and multimodality to multiple sensory modalities. In social semiotics, multimodality refers to multiple modes of semiotic resources. Although there are two different versions and connotations of "multimodality" here, they are bridged by the fact that multimodal communication in humans ultimately relies on their sensory modalities and the construction of meaning by different modes of semiotic resources is therefore based on the working of multiple sensory modalities.

Kress (2009, p. 54) claims that "*Mode* is a socially shaped and culturally given resource for making meaning. *Image, writing, layout, music, gesture, speech, moving image, soundtrack* are examples of modes used in representation and communication" (italics are original). Kress' theory of multimodal meaning making can help us understand the constraints and potentials of internet-mediated interaction with regard to language and intercultural learning. In today's media-saturated society, we can conceptualize multimodality as a pool of multiple semiotic resources that are constructively integrated in a communicative artifact for the user/writer's multimodal production and the user/reader's multimodal

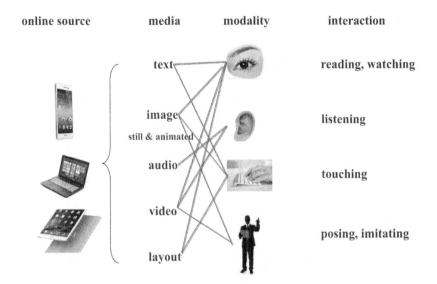

Fig. 3.1 Relationship between online source, media, and modality

consumption. For example, a web page can include still and animated images, orthographic texts in varied color fonts, music, sophisticated design patterns, and so on. The whole layout of the webpage constructs meaning in a multimodal way.

Multimodality is also related to the effectiveness of learning. Many scholars have discussed how to make good use of multimedia resources to promote students' multimodal learning, which is believed by some researchers to be more effective than monomodal learning if the material and approaches are scientifically arranged (Gu 2007). In the digital era, online resources accessed by computers, smart phones, PDAs, tablets, or other mobile electronic devices can offer many different types of media, which carry rich information. The information from online resources is accessed and processed by students in a multimodal way. Figure 3.1 illustrates the relationship between online sources, related media, involved modalities, and interaction processes.

In this sense, internet mediation is an ideal and practical approach that can promote learning and development for students in this multimedia-saturated and multimodality-activated context. It can be utilized for the development of intercultural competence.

3.2   Internet-Mediated Intercultural Interaction: Organization Model and Task Design

In the practice of internet-mediated intercultural learning, many scholars have already defined the role of internet mediation in foreign language education. In this paper, internet-mediated intercultural training is defined as follows (Debski 2006):

> The training project based on well pedagogical design with a certain theme for students, in which internet is used as the information access channel and social communication environment, offering rich possibilities for communication, self-expression and collaboration.

Internet information and communication tools have been developed to support intercultural dialogue, learning, debate, and research. These tools facilitate intercultural interaction between people from different backgrounds, which also provides students with a wealth of opportunities for development of intercultural competence. With such technological advancement, some patterns already exist for such internet-mediated intercultural foreign language projects, such as "telecollaboration" and "tandem learning," which has received significant attention in recent years.

The telecollaboration model is very well-known to North American language educators. This model is featured as an international class-to-class partnership within an institutionalized setting (Belz 2003; Kinginger 2004). By definition, telecollaboration occurs within a teacher-instructed environment and offers a wide range of interactional possibilities such as pair work, small-group work, or even whole class exchanges (Thorne 2006, p. 7). However, this model is also related to a high level of coordination, curricular design, and institutional location. The platform *Cultura* developed by the Massachusetts Institute of Technology is noteworthy for its significant infrastructure development of web-based materials and activities (Furstenberg et al. 2001). The system includes asynchronous interaction, web-based questionnaires, sentence completion, and question responses.

Another frequently used model is tandem learning, the pairing of individuals in a mini-group where each is interested in learning the other's language (Kötter 2002; O'Rourke 2005). Tandem learning is most related to noninstitutional learning configurations and usually requires students to work on certain topics and keep a balance between overt pedagogical and conversational activity (Thorne 2006, p. 8).

The two most frequently exploited approaches are fully autonomous learning and significant teacher mediation and intervention, but there is a substantial middle ground shared by telecollaboration and tandem learning. In practice, these two approaches are functionally indistinguishable from one another (Thorne 2006).

It is beyond the scope of this paper to introduce all the different models of internet-mediated intercultural education, but we advocate a successfully launched project targeting internet-mediated intercultural education. Huang (2017) reports an internet-mediated research project for college students based on tandem learning together with some organizational features from telecollaboration. Figure 3.2 illustrates such an idea.

Although appropriate choice of an organizational model for internet-mediated intercultural learning is very necessary, the pedagogical design of intercultural education that integrates internet technologies is also an important aspect. Internet-mediated activities, like those in other language learning contexts, can be divided into non-interactive activities (working with materials such as online newspapers) and interactive activities (working with other people, for example, completing tasks using email or video conferencing) (Wang and Coleman 2009). In practice, most of the activities are limited to information searching, using online audiovideo and graphic resources, online reading etc. Engagement in online collaboration and interaction still needs further exploration.

Wang and Coleman (2009) observed that teachers and students are enthusiastic and supportive of developing intercultural competence by incorporating internet technologies into traditional classroom instruction. Correspondingly, the project is grounded in classroom instruction and oriented in international and domestic issues by utilizing internet technologies. These internet technologies lead to a practice of "internationalization at home" (Nilsson 2003), which means bringing an intercultural and global dimension to students' educational experiences in their home institutions.

Following these principles, the author's university integrates both traditional classroom courses and internet-mediated interaction into the curriculum, taking the issues of global insight and China's concern as topics. The aim is to develop students' intercultural competence with an understanding of both international and domestic affairs. The approach and content are believed by the university to give an all-round intercultural education with updated insights.

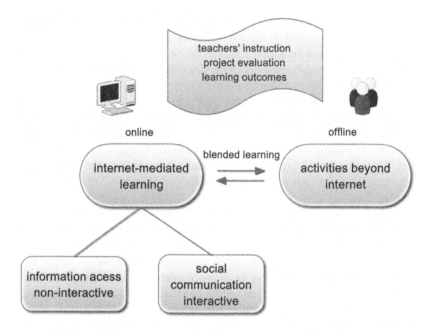

Fig. 3.2   Blended learning

3.3   PROJECT PRACTICE ON THE THEME OF THE BELT AND ROAD INITIATIVE

3.3.1   *Why Is the Theme Called the "Belt and Road Initiative"?*

The Belt and Road initiative is a major strategy introduced by China in response to emerging trends in economic globalization. It is far more than an economic initiative, but a comprehensive regional and even global cooperation project, with emphasis on cultural interaction and human exchange between the relevant countries and regions.

The initiative is a reflection of the new shift in China's international positioning, and requires the country to cultivate more intercultural talents for global cooperation and competition. A growing number of Chinese scholars and officials have begun to discuss how to implement cultural exchanges effectively in the long-term development of the Belt and Road initiative, because the soul of the initiative is to promote mutual trust and economic benefit across the countries and regions.

In this sense, the implementation of such an initiative can improve China's regional or even global cultural diffusion, promote more people-to-people exchange, deepen strategic ties with the countries along the Belt and Road, and produce a chain reaction to expand China's influence in the international community.

Incompatible with China's international status and the role it plays in today's world, the number and the rank of Chinese employees in international institutions such as the UN, UNESCO, and some important NGOs are relatively constrained compared with employees from other major powers (Wen et al. 2011). This situation impedes China's expansion of international influence and more proactive participation in global affairs.

To resolve such a problem, a large number of international talents should be cultivated, a priority being intercultural competence or international capability. Therefore, developing students' intercultural competence is an important task in today's foreign language education in China, especially from the perspective of the national strategy for China's further rise.

In such an international and domestic context, Chinese educators are considering how to cultivate internationally competitive talents with global insight and all-round understanding of China, with an adequate exploitation of internet technologies to facilitate international communication and cooperation among the young generation in the countries and regions along the Belt and Road. The Silk Road in ancient China, on both land and sea, symbolized openness, inclusiveness, cooperation, and peace. These spirits and values are inherited by the Silk Road Economic Belt and the Twenty First-Century Maritime Silk Road, which are indispensable in today's globalization process. Undountedly, these values should be included in intercultural competence and international capability.

With such a background, the concern of educators at Tongji University is how to design a pedagogical project on current international and national issues (for example, the Belt and Road initiative) to develop students' international capability in the internet age. In this Belt and Road initiative-related project, we focus on content but leave sufficient space for participants to develop their own subtopics within the thematic strands. As a very current world-concerned and China-related theme, it encourages students to generate their own ideas from social, cultural, economic, educational, and political perspectives based on their own interests and abilities.

3.3.2   Blended Pedagogical Design of the Project

We firmly believe that intercultural competence is gradually developed from social interaction rather than from mere accumulation of knowledge. Intercultural education, therefore, should offer students more activity-based opportunities instead of constraining them to a traditional indoor classroom teaching environment (Huang 2015, p. 202).

However, providing students with a platform that integrates synchronous interaction does not automatically lead to efficient and constructive interaction. Researchers discovered that many different factors can affect the interaction taking place (Hauck 2007; Hauck and Youngs 2008; Berglund 2009). Qualitative analysis showed that students do not always fully use the communicative facilities of various tools, despite the employment of multimodal strategies (e.g., Berglund 2009). Correspondingly, it is always important to discuss how to implement an efficient design for the task and the best tools for constructive development of intercultural competence. To solve this problem, the concept of "blended learning" is believed by the author to be complementary and indispensable to such an intercultural education.

Blended instruction means the integration of technology-mediated instruction with traditional forms of practice or learning, such as face-to-face communication. However, little research has been conducted on the interplay of technology-mediated and non-technology-mediated instruction. Furthermore, the relationship of various configurations to learners' effective development remains underexplored (Belz and Thorne 2006). With a firm belief in the effectiveness of intercultural competence training using a blended learning method, we initiated a project that integrates both online tandem research and offline traditional teaching together with face-to-face discussion.

In the practice of intercultural education, some educators discuss different approaches, locations, or patterns for implementing the training. Byram (1997, pp. 64–70, 73) mentions three possible locations for the acquisition of intercultural communicative competence: classroom, fieldwork, and an independent learning environment. Huang (2015) introduced a practical pattern for fieldwork in intercultural training. Based on previous discussion and the author's experience, the internet-mediated intercultural training approach in this paper constructs an independent learning environment for students. In this environment, students are provided with the opportunities of both learning independent of teachers and learning from teachers.

The practice at Tongji University has selected the theme "China's Belt and Road initiative from the perspective of the community of common destiny," which asks participants to make a project study on the opportunities, challenges, and media responses for different countries and regions after the announcement of the Belt and Road initiative.

The project involved 60 international students from the countries and regions along the Belt and Road, together with 57 Chinese students. At the end of the project, 51 research reports were submitted. The participants were asked to form pair-groups to conduct collaborative research, and to write a complete report based on literature retrieval from the internet and offline resources and from their own study. In this process, participants were encouraged to make good use of Web 2.0 communication tools, face-to-face discussion, and online group work. Researchers agreed that task-oriented groups can perform better if their computer-mediated communication is interspersed with face-to-face interaction, whether occasionally or regularly (Lin 2007; Kennedy et al. 2010). Interaction between participants from local and international backgrounds shaped an authentic internet-mediated communication environment for development of intercultural competence.

The research outline provided by the educators was a reminder for participants to acquire all-round knowledge, develop intercultural awareness, and conduct intercultural reflection.The provided outline was world-concerned and China-related, which encouraged students to generate their own ideas from social, cultural, economic, educational, and political perspectives based on participants' own interests and abilities. Sufficient space was left for participants to develop their own subtopics within the thematic strands. Specific content included the following:

- General view on the countries and regions along the Belt and Road, including economy and finance, politics and diplomacy, culture and education, and infrastructure construction.
- Public opinion and media response on the Belt and Road initiative from the related countries and regions
- Suggestions on participation in the Belt and Road initiative for governments, corporations, and educational institutions

At the beginning of the project, the participation protocol was explicitly explained to all participants. Supervisors were available when any questions arose or any help was needed. Students were scheduled to provide an oral presentation, written report, and online presentation at the middle and end of the project.

The languages involved in this project were usually trilingual (English, Chinese, and the mother tongue of the international student in the pair group). English was used as the dominant language to mediate the research and write the research report. Although English is not the first language in most countries or regions along the Belt and Road, it is the *lingua franca*. The dominant status of English teaching in China's universities determined the pragmatic adoption of English as the mediation language in the intercultural competence education. It is clear that English as a global language can promote communication between different peoples. In many situations, therefore, English is utilized not only to communicate with English native speakers, but also to communicate with speakers of many other native languages (Huang 2016). Chinese was used as the complementary language to search for information in China, because a large amount of information on the Belt and Road initiative is available in this language. The task of Chinese reference retrieval was mainly undertaken by Chinese students in the pair group. Meanwhile, international students could also improve their Chinese proficiency in this process. Most of them take Chinese learning as an important mission during their stay in China. In the project, international students in the pair groups were required to carry out an in-depth search on public opinion and media response after announcement of the Belt and Road initiative. Their mother tongues provided an advantage for this task. The trilingual pattern in the project enabled participants to shift the language in accordance with different needs, and thus further improve their comprehension of intercultural communication (Fig. 3.3).

3.3.3   *China Today Course Package in Intercultural Education*

In the last eight years, the author's university has offered English-taught general education courses entitled *China Today*. These English-taught courses focus on a general introduction to China from both diachronic and synchronic perspectives in a global context. Through these courses, students gain an overall understanding of China's history, culture, society, economy, foreign relations, environmental protection, urban

International Students   Chinese Students

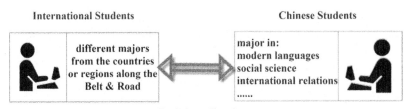

English mediated

distance & face-to-face interaction

Fig. 3.3 Interaction relationship between international and Chinese students during the project

development, and intellectual property and can shape an objective view of China's development, philosophy, social phenomena, and events from a more global perspective. This course package is mainly at the introductory level of contemporary China studies, although deep theories are introduced when necessary. Generally, the highlight of the courses is not the theory or academic value but novelty in terms of the content and perspective (Cheng and Lü 2013). In addition to traditional classroom teaching, experiential and participatory learning is encouraged. Various learning activities such as collaborative assignments, team projects, mini-research, and field trips are recommended and financially supported. In this blended learning, students are provided with both theoretical learning and practical opportunities to improve their knowledge of China and its strategies.

To provide a more profound understanding of China and its international positioning, participants in the Belt and Road initiative-themed project are encouraged to take part in the courses. An indispensable part of the Belt and Road initiative is the enhancement of people-to-people and cultural exchange. These exchanges embrace the global trend toward cultural diversity. The content of the *China Today* course package can lead students to a more profound understanding of the initiative and other related issues.

In addition to traditional lecturing, the *China Today* course package pays much attention to internet platform building. Each individual course has its own website for course information and student–teacher interaction. Multimedia in the package website is utilized with the intention of facilitating students' multimodal interaction for intercultural competence. With the aid of information and communication technology, these courses are more accessible to students and encourage proactive participation in learning. Currently, the teaching team is producing some exemplary courses using massive open online courses (MOOCs), which can benefit more students and equip them with adequate understanding of the wisdom of ancient China and experience of today's China on the road to modernization.

3.4   PROJECT OUTCOMES AND FURTHER SUGGESTIONS

3.4.1   Evaluation and Outcomes of the Project

Because of the multifaceted nature of intercultural competence, there are a large variety of assessment instruments that claim to assess some or all elements of intercultural competence. To reflect the multifaceted nature, some scholars recommend a multidimensional mode of assessment (Zou and Shek-Noble 2014). Multidimensional assessment comes in the form of tests, interviews, and surveys, with the types of assessment being expert, reciprocal, peer, or self-evaluative.

Huang (2016) advocates some principles or approaches in the assessment of the development of students' intercultural competence. According to Huang, assessment should include various components of intercultural competence, both formative and summative evaluations, use of a variety of assessment instruments, and critical reflection.

As mentioned previously, assessment in this project was multidimensional. At the middle and end of the project, an oral presentation, written report, and online presentation measure the performance and outcome of both individuals and groups. In addition to these approaches, a clearer picture of the participants' outcomes was explored using pre-test and post-test. According to the Intercultural Communicative Competence Self-Report Scale (ICCSRS) for Chinese students, as developed by Zhong et al. (2013), the participants' strategic competence, awareness, knowledge, and skills were significantly improved ($P < 0.05$), but linguistic competence, sociolinguistic competence, discourse competence, and intercultural skills were not significantly changed ($P > 0.05$). Meanwhile, most participants reported in their reflection that they benefited a lot in both intercultural competence and collaborative research capability (refer to Huang (2017) for detailed discussion).

3.4.2   Further Suggestions from the Practice

In today's higher education sector, development of intercultural competence should shift from an added-value side effect to an all-persuasive motive (Huang 2016), which is a direct response to UNESCO's belief that "Intercultural education cannot be just a simple 'add-on' to the regular curriculum" (UNESCO 2006, p. 19).

From our previous experience, pedagogical design and project implementation are key factors in improving the effectiveness of such an intercultural competence project. Huang (2011, 2014a, b, 2016) has provided a series of suggestions on organizing intercultural activities and implementing the related curriculum.

In addition to traditional teaching and field trip activities, internet-mediated intercultural training with a blended pattern is a novel approach appropriate for today's digital age. From previous experience, two approaches seem viable for internet-mediated intercultural teaching and learning: task-based (Corbett 2003; Müller-Hartmann 2000, 2006) and project-based (Gu 2005; Debski 2006) approaches. Debski (2006, p. 10) points out that a project can be broken up into tasks, so a combined approach is feasible. In a well-designed project, students are assigned different tasks within one general theme and the whole project can last for several semesters, allowing continuous work on the initial training goal.

At the institutional level, systematic support should be made available, including resources, administration, and staff (Wang and Coleman 2009; Huang 2011). Sometimes students are unclear about the difference between exchanging information and exploring or contrasting different cultural perspectives (O'Dowd 2004, p. 367). In this sense, internet-mediated intercultural training should be included in the academic curriculum and teachers are encouraged to implement adequate pedagogical interventions to ensure project effectiveness. Consequently, some expanded roles for teachers should be developed, which will help to advance students' autonomous and independent learning skills.

Belz (2003, pp. 92–93), Huang (2011, 2014a) and some other scholars have explored the role of teachers in intercultural education activities. Belz (2003) argues that "the teacher in telecollaboration must be educated to discern, identify, explain, and model culturally contingent patterns of interaction in the absence of paralinguistic meaning signals. Otherwise it may be the case that civilizations ultimately do clash—in the empirical details of their computer-mediated talk." Teachers tend to take on the role of facilitators, who scaffold and monitor the process, and provide guidance and feedback (Walker and vom Brocke 2009, p. 221). In the author's understanding, supervisor, consultant, and evaluator are appropriate roles for teachers in this process (Huang 2011, 2014a):

- Teachers, as supervisors, should coordinate all learning resources to inspire students' passions and interests and guide them in the acquisition of intercultural competence.
- The consultant helps teachers by providing academic suggestions relating to the design and organization of activities and by offering professional and individualized help as needed.
- The evaluator assesses the effectiveness of students' participation and decides whether certificates of intercultural competence should be issued.

3.5   Conclusions and Further Agenda

Implementation of the Belt and Road initiative provides rich opportunities for students to develop intercultural competence, in addition to the presence of a growing number of international students in China and exchange programs between universities in Eurasia. In turn, development of students' intercultural competence will provide adequate trained personnel for China's proactive participation in regional and international cooperation, including the Belt and Road initiative.

In today's intercultural education, a variety of options that integrate the internet into teaching have been put into practice.The aforementioned project integrates many updated concepts in learning and teaching, including student-oriented, content-based approaches, in this technology-rich and internet-bound environment.

Internet-mediated intercultural training is a pragmatic approach for students in countries where face-to-face experiential intercultural interaction with people from different cultural backgrounds is relatively less accessible. Because internet-mediated communication offers new opportunities for increased participation for this young generation as digital natives, the author firmly believes that technology-facilitated collaboration for learning and research can be exploited in the development of students' intercultural competence in the background internationalization of higher education. The effectiveness of this project is largely dependent on multimodal interaction between participants for attaining global insight, on which development of internet-mediated intercultural competence is based.

Despite the fact that much attention has been paid to development of internet-mediated intercultural competence, some areas that could lead to more profound theoretical investigation and more efficient practice remain underexplored. These issues include but are not limited to the following:

- Efficiency of pedagogical design and technology usage
- Relationship between activities beyond the classroom and traditional teaching
- Changing role of teachers during project implementation
- Use of less commonly taught foreign languages as project-mediated languages
- Recording and assessment of students' outcomes
- Recognition of credits for participation
- Position of such a project in the whole curriculum

Educators should make good use of current national strategies and international trends to facilitate students' intercultural education. Practically, intercultural education should be included as an important part of English education in universities (further discussion see He and Huang 2017) because China has a large number of students learning English in higher education. At present, Chinese educators are endowed with new strategic opportunities, and the Belt and Road initiative is an excellent educational resource to exploit. Although these aforementioned aspects still need further exploration and the author's report is based on the endeavors of one Chinese university, the findings and suggestions are believed to be significant and applicable to higher education in the global arena.

Acknowledgements This work was partially sponsored by 2016 China Foreign Language Education Foundation Project "Promoting the Development of International Talents at Chinese Universities: Based on English-Taught General Education Program" (No. ZGWYJYJJ2016B05), 2017 Tongji University Teaching Reform Project "Intercultural Competence and International Orientation: A Reformed English Majors' Syllabus" (No. 1100104108/003) and Tongji University "The Belt & Road Initiative" Think Tank Project "Developing Students' International Competence under the Background of the Belt & Road Initiative: Teaching and Practice" (No. wx0110020171025).

REFERENCES

Belz, J. A. (2003). Linguistic Perspectives on the Development of Intercultural Competence in Telecollaboration. *Language Learning & Technology, 7*(2), 68–117.

Belz, J. A., & Thorne, S. L. (2006). Internet-mediated Intercultural Foreign Language Education and the Intercultural Speaker. In J. A. Belz & S. L. Thorne (Eds.), *AAUSC 2005: Internet-mediated intercultural foreign language education,* (pp. x–xxv). Thomson, Heinle.

Berglund, T. Ö. (2009). Multimodal student interaction online: An ecological perspective. *ReCALL, 21*(2), 186–205.

Byram, M. (1997). *Teaching and assessing intercultural communicative competence.* Clevedon: Multilingual Matters.

Cheng, Yu., & Lü, Peiming. (2013). English-Taught general education courses in Mainland Chinese Universities: The present and the future. In Chen Yiyi & M. Raevaara (Eds.), *Proceedings of the First International Symposium on Pedagogical Research (October 14–15).* Shanghai: Tongji University Press.

Corbett, J. (2003). *An intercultural approach to English language teaching.* Clevedon: Multilingual Matters Ltd.

Davis, N., & Cho, M. O. (2005). Intercultural competence for future leaders of educational technology and its evaluation. *Interactive Educational Multimedia, 10,* 1–22.

Debski, R. (2006). *Project-based Language Teaching with Technology.* Sydney: National Centre for English Language Teaching and Research.

Furstenberg, G., Levet, S., English, K., & Maillet, K. (2001). Giving a virtual voice to the silent language of culture: The *CULTURA* project. *Language learning & technology, 5*(1), 55–102.

Gu, Peiya. (2005). Multilingual Momentum: Danger and Opportunity. *Essential Teacher, 4*(2), 12–13.

Gu, Yueguo. (2007). On Multimedia Learning and Multimodal Learning. *Computer-assisted Foreign Language Education, 114*(2), 3–12.

Hauck, M. (2007). Critical success factors in a TRIDEM exchange. *ReCALL, 19*(2), 202–223.

Hauck, M., & Youngs, B. L. (2008). Telecollaboration in multimodal environments: The impact on task design and learner interaction. *Computer Assisted Language Learning, 21*(2), 87–124.

He, Jihong, & Huang, Lihe. (2017). *English education in an integrated and diversified pattern.* Shanghai: Tongji University Press.

Huang, Lihe. (2011). A Study on New Second Classroom Pattern for College English Education. *Education and Teaching Research, 25*(3), 90–92.

Huang, Lihe. (2014a). English Education and Development of Cross-cultural Communicative Competence for College Students, *Journal of Cheng-Shiu University for General Education, 11,* 135–150.

Huang, Lihe. (2014b). A Multimodal Approach to the Design of Extended Learning System for College English, *Language Education, 6* (3), 11–16, 21.

Huang, Lihe. (2015). Improving Intercultural Education at Chinese Institutions from German Experience. *Journal of International Students, 5*(3), 201–203.

Huang, Lihe. (2016). Co-curricular activity-based intercultural competence development: Students' outcome of internationalization at Universities. *Innovations in Education and Teaching International.* doi:10.1080/147032 97.2016.1184098.

Huang, Lihe. (2017). A Tandem Research Pattern for College Students' Intercultural Education and its Effect. In Yu. Cheng (Ed.), *The "Belt and Road" Initiative in the Eyes of International Students in China.* Shanghai: Tongji University Press.

Kennedy, D. M., Vozdolska, R. R., & McComb, S. A. (2010). Team decision making in computer-supported cooperative work: How initial computer-mediated or face-to-face meetings set the stage for later outcomes. *Decision Sciences, 41*(4), 933–954.

Kinginger, C. (2004). Communicative Foreign Language Teaching through Telecollaboration. In O St John, K. van Esch, & E. Schalkwijk (Eds.), *New Insights into Foreign Language Learning and Teaching* (pp. 101–113). Frankfurt: Peter Lang.

Kress, G. (2009). What is mode? In C. Jewitt (Ed.), *The Routledge Handbook of Multimodal Analysis* (pp. 54–67). New York: Routledge.

Kötter, M. (2002). *Tandem Learning on the Internet: Learner Interactions in Online Virtual Environments.* Frankfurt: Peter Lang.

Lin, H.-F. (2007). The role of online and offline features in sustaining virtual communities: An empirical study. *Internet Research, 17*(2), 119–138.

Liaw, M. (2006). E-learning and the development of intercultural competence. *Language Learning & Technology, 10*(3), 49–64.

Müller-Hartmann, A. (2000). The Role of Tasks in Promoting Intercultural Learning in Electronic Learning Networks. *Language Learning & Technology, 4*(2), 129–147.

Müller-Hartmann, A. (2006). Learning how to teach intercultural communicative competence via telecollaboration: A model for language teacher education. In J. A. Belz & S. L. Thorne (eds.), *AAUSC 2005: Internet-mediated intercultural foreign language education,* (pp. 63–84). Thomson, Heinle.

Nilsson, B. (2003). Internationalization at home from a Swedish perspective: The case of Malmö. *Journal of Studies in International Education, 7*(1), 27–40.

O'Dowd, R. (2004). *Network-based Language Teaching and the Development of Intercultural Communicative Competence.* PhD dissertation, University of Duisburg-Essen, Standort Essen.

O'Dowd, R., & Eberbach, K. (2004). Guides on the side? *Tasks and challenges for teachers in telecollaborative projects, ReCALL, 16*(1), 5–19.

O'Rourke, B. (2005). Form Focused Interaction in Online Tandem Learning. *CALICO Journal, 22*(3), 433–466.

Thorne, S. L. (2006). Pedagogical and Praxiological Lessons from Internet-mediated Intercultural Foreign Language Education Research. In J. A. Belz & S. L. Thorne (Eds.), *AAUSC 2005: Internet-mediated Intercultural Foreign Language Education* (pp. 2–30). Boston: Thomson Heinle.

UNESCO. (2006). *UNESCO guidelines on intercultural education*. Paris: United Nations Educational Scientific and Cultural Organization.

Walker, U. & vom Brocke, C. (2009). Integrating content-based language learning and intercultural learning online: An international eGroup collaboration, In A. Brown (ed.) *Proceedings of CLESOL 2008*.

Wang, Liang, & Coleman, J. A. (2009). A survey of Internet-mediated intercultural foreign language education in China. *ReCALL, 21*(1), 113–129.

Wen, Q. F., Su, J., & Jian, Y. H. (2011). A Model of National Foreign Language Capacity and Its Trial Use. *Foreign Languages in China, 41*(8), 4–10.

Zhong, H., Bai, L., & Fan, W. (2013). Construction of Intercultural Communicative Competence Self-Report Scale for Chinese college students: A Pilot Study. *Foreign Language World, 156*(3), 47–56.

Zou, P., & Shek-Noble, L. (2014). Developing Students' Intercultural Competence. In J. Wang (Ed.), *Proceedings of the 17th International Symposium on Advancement of Construction Management and Real Estate* (pp. 1047–1056). Berlin: Springer-Verlag.

CHAPTER 4

A Model for the Belt and Road Initiative: China's Cultural Diplomacy Toward Central and Eastern European Countries

Lilei Song and Zhao Qiqi

China strives to achieve more regional cooperation. Its China's Belt and Road Initiative will not only drive domestic development but also boost the global economy. Under the initiative, more highways, railways, and air routes will be established, and Chinese regions will further integrate resources, policies, and markets to connect with the outside world. The governments of more than 50 countries have signed a memorandum with the Chinese government for cooperation on the Silk Road Economic Belt and the 21st-Century Maritime Silk Road. However, this grand strategy has increased the international public's suspicion of China's intentions. To promote further cooperation by countries along the Belt and Road, China must increase international understanding of Chinese willingness to conform to the twenty-first century norms of promoting peace, development, and cooperation and adopting a win–win

L. Song (✉) · Z. Qiqi
Tonjii University, Shanghai, China

© The Author(s) 2018
Y. Cheng et al. (eds.), *The Belt & Road Initiative in the Global Arena*,
https://doi.org/10.1007/978-981-10-5921-6_4

strategy for all. To convince the international public that the idea carries forward the spirit of the ancient Silk Road, which was based on mutual trust, equality, mutual benefit, inclusiveness, mutual learning, and win–win cooperation, the Chinese government should promote cultural diplomacy along the Belt and Road. Experience can be gained from its cultural soft power activities in the countries of Central and Eastern Europe (CEE) under under the "16+1" cooperation framework begun in 2012.

4.1   Aims of China's Cultural Diplomacy Toward Central and Eastern Europe

The increasing importance of China in the foreign economic and trade agenda of CEE countries provides opportunities for China to strengthen soft power tactics in this region. China needs to create a real economic win–win situation under the 16+1 cooperation framework, and also take the opportunity to bring a benefit more valuable than economic benefit—the intangible asset of a good image of China in CEE countries. Chinese scholars think that cultural diplomacy toward CEE countries may be the breaking point of Chinese cultural diplomacy in Europe.[1] It is important to implement China's cultural diplomacy strategy toward CEE countries, which already has a clear roadmap, and to channel it into real projects. The long-term goal of Chinese cultural diplomacy is to build a good image of China among the CEE public. The medium-term goal is to cooperatively build a better Sino-European strategic partnership through making CEE countries the "bridge" between China and the EU. The short-term goal is to defensively counteract "China-bashing" sentiments in the media of CEE countries, which see China as a threat to Europe.

---

[1] Chinese scholars deal with the development or political problems of the region in general theoretical analyses. These types of different country studies and comparative studies are not very sufficient. Many of them focus on the historical lessons of the fall of the Soviet Union and Eastern Europe, with a general introduction on the transformation and restructuring of the region. Recent research is more concentrated on the revival of left-wing forces in the region after the drastic changes in 1989. Kong Tianping. (n.d.). Review of Chinese Research on Central and Eastern Europe 2001–2010. Retrieved from http://ies.cass.cn/Article/cbw/zdogj/201107/4109.asp.

The most common misunderstanding is that China has been pursuing a strategy that clearly asserts its own interests. The main criteria are seen as the successful export of its goods, protection of its own domestic market, access to western high technology and weapons through purchase, getting the world to accept the unitary, single China, and silencing (or at least dividing) uniform criticism on human rights.[2] Because of the doubts and misunderstandings of CEE countries regarding China, Chinese cultural diplomacy to CEE countries is now focused on its short-term aims, which means using cultural communication to improve circumstances for investment, paying special attention to some key countries in CEE regions.

At the official level, Chinese promotion of its soft power influence has been an important part of the relations between China and CEE countries since 2012, followed by the establishment of a secretariat for cooperation between the countries included in China's "Twelve Measures for Promoting Friendly Cooperation" and the CEE countries' institutional counterparts.[3] Premier Wen Jiabao also appealed for closer cultural and people-to-people exchanges, especially among youth and the media.[4] Song Tao, the secretary-general of the Secretariat for Central and Eastern Europe and China's vice foreign minister, said that China and CEE countries have steadily pushed forward pragmatic cooperation in the fields of economy, culture, education, tourism, and others. Strengthening cooperation between China and CEE countries is conducive to realizing a more comprehensive and balanced China–Europe relationship, as well as helping to overcome the current difficulties in Europe.[5]

---

[2] David, S. (2013). *China Goes Global - The Partial Power.* (pp. 77–78). Oxford University Press, USA.

[3] Ministry of Foreign Affairs of the People's Republic of China.(2012). *China's Twelve Measures for Promoting Friendly Cooperation with Central and Eastern Europe*an Countries. Retrieved from http://www.fmprc.gov.cn/eng/zxxx/t928567.htm.

[4] In Chinese Premier Wen Jiabao's speech at a Chinese and CEE leaders' meeting in Warsaw, Poland. (2012, April 26). He put forward a four-point proposal on further promoting relations and deepening cooperation between China and CEE countries. Retrieved from http://news.xinhuanet.com/english/china/2012-04/27/c_123044233.htm.

[5] China to enhance cooperation with Central and Eastern Europe. Retrieved from http://news.xinhuanet.com/english/china/2012-09/06/c_131832154.htm.

4.2   DEVELOPMENT OF CHINA'S CULTURAL DIPLOMACY TOWARD CENTRAL AND EASTERN EUROPE

Chinese cultural diplomacy toward CEE refers to all cultural activities led by the Chinese government and participated in by the Chinese public that target the public in CEE countries in order to promote China's image and enhance their understanding of China. To realize these goals, China has launched a series of cultural diplomacy activities toward CEE countries. Many government agencies, including the Ministry of Foreign Affairs, the Ministry of Education, the Ministry of Culture, the Information Office of State Council, some other chambers of the central government, companies, media, and think-tanks, have created programs related to the topic.[6]

The first activity is media diplomacy. The press, publishing, radio, television, movies, and the internet have all been widely employed by China to promote its achievements in the period of "Reform and Opening-Up" to improve its national image, and to enhance understanding by Central European countries and change their negative perceptions of China. China Radio International (CRI) has launched new channels targeting CEE countries in seven languages, including Czech, Serbian, Romanian, Albanian, Bulgarian, Hungarian, and Polish, which account for nearly one-sixth of all CEE languages.[7] At the same time, the CRI Online website introduces various political, economic, and cultural aspects of China in 48 languages, encompassing the majority of CEE languages.[8] When Ralph Jon, the secretary of Albania's Socialist Movement for Integration party, visited CRI, he said that he was very honored and happy to know that CRI continues to spread the Albanian language.[9]

---

[6] During the 11th Foreign Diplomats Conference in 2009, then Chinese President Hu Jintao only briefly noted the need to improve cultural diplomacy. Instead of accrediting it into a particular department, many departments assumed cultural diplomacy to be one of their tasks.

[7] Description of China Radio International (CRI). (2013, March 26). Retrieved from http://gb.cri.cn/cri/gk.htm.

[8] China Radio International (CRI).(2013, March 26). Retrieved from http://english.cri.cn/.

[9] CEE youth politician visited China Radio International. (n.d.). Retrieved from http://cpc.people.com.cn/n/2015/1030/c164113-27757934.html.

To promote public understanding of Europe and Sino-European relations, on 24 August 2012, the Ministry of Foreign Affairs of the People's Republic of China opened an official microblog through a Sina Weibo account named '@Zhongou Xinshi' (meaning "Sino–Europe messenger" in English). According to the author's statistical analysis, the contents of posts focused on the CEE region occupy about 17.8% every year, which suggests that the new developments in cooperation between China and CEE countries was the hottest topic during that period.[10]

Second, promoting China's image through daily commercial exchange is an important aspect of Chinese public diplomacy. The China Council for the Promotion of International Trade (CCPIT) generally sets up a special zone to introduce China to the local people when it holds exhibitions in CEE countries. For example, at the 2015 exhibition of Chinese exports to CEE countries in Budapest, magazines such as *China Trade News, China's Foreign Trade, China Business Guide, China's Exports of Goods,* and other publications were provided.[11] Trade and investment information was published on the English website of CCPIT, and consulting services were provided, which can be seen as China's cultural diplomacy regarding CEE in the economic realm. In addition, the Chinese government carries out cultural diplomacy programs with CEE business organizations in China. The Prahova Chamber of Commerce and Industry of Romania, the Trade and Investment Chamber of Commerce of Poland and other similar organizations all have offices in China.

The third activity is increasing the number of cultural exhibitions overseas. China regards construction of its cultural soft power as a matter of national strategic importance and, in recent years, has been striving to increase its cultural influence in the world. Since 2009, Chinese cultural festivals have been organized in Poland, Bulgaria, and other CEE countries, including the Chinese Culture Festival Concert, Exhibition of Contemporary Art and Ink Painting, China National

---

[10]Song Lilei & Bian Qin. (2016). The EU through the eyes of Chinese social media: A case study of the official micro-blog of Chinese Foreign Ministry.*International Communication Gazette, 78*(1–2).

[11]Chinese exports in Central and Eastern EuropeExhibition. (2015). Retrieved from http://www.ccpit.org/Contents/Channel_3360/2015/0625/469156/content_469156. htm.

Day Photo Exhibition, China Film Week, and other cultural activities.[12] Many Chinese embassies and consulates in CEE countries held a series of cultural diplomacy activities named "Happy Spring Festival" to make the public aware of Chinese New Year and Chinese culture. For example, in 2013, the ambassador of Albania, Ye Hao, held a New Year Reception Festival for Sinologists and people who are friendly to China. The Chinese Embassy in Bulgaria held a large Chinese culture exhibition "Happy Spring" in the newest Bulgarian shopping mall to celebrate Chinese New Year, which became a hot topic among Bulgarians.[13]

The fourth element is promoting the study of China abroad. The Chinese government plans to provide 5,000 scholarships to the 16 CEE countries, supports the Confucius Institutes and Confucius Classrooms program in the 16 countries, invites 1,000 students from relevant countries to study the Chinese language in China, enhances interuniversity exchanges and joint academic research, and will send 1,000 students and scholars to the 16 CEE countries in the five years from 2012 to 2017.[14] By the end of 2015, 25 Confucius Institutes and 58 Confucius Classrooms had been established in 12 CEE countries.[15] Nearly one-fifth of the 45 languages used by Online Confucius Institutes are CEE languages.[16] This makes it convenient for people of CEE countries to learn the Chinese language and understand China. In September 2012, the Bulgarian–Chinese Language and Culture Intercollegiate Alliance was established to promote the Chinese language and culture in secondary schools in Bulgaria. Representatives from nine leading model schools have expressed the wish to set up Chinese language courses so that Bulgaria middle school students can have the opportunity to understand and learn Chinese language and culture. The Ministry of Education of China plans to host education policy dialogues with CEE countries, such as the second meeting of the China–Central and Eastern

---

[12]The Chinese culture bloom overseas. Retrieved from http://www.cnr.cn/all-news/200912/t20091228_505819393.html.

[13]Enjoy China's New Year in the Bulgarian large shopping malls. (n.d.). Retrieved from http://bg.chineseembassy.org/chn/zbjwhzxx/t1016349.htm.

[14]China's Twelve Measures for Promoting Friendly Cooperation with Central and Eastern European Countries. (2012, April 28). *People's Daily.* p. 9.

[15]Confucius Institutes and Confucius Classrooms. (n.d.). Retrieved from http://www.hanban.edu.cn/confuciousinstitutes/node_10961.htm.

[16]Confucius Institutes online. (n.d.). Retrieved from http://english.chinese.cn/.

European Federation of National Universities and the third China and Poland University Presidents Forum held in Warsaw, with representatives from more than 160 colleges and universities.[17] At the Second China (Ningbo)–CEE countries event on educational cooperation and exchange held in Ningbo in June 2015, representatives of educational institutions from Poland, Estonia, Bulgaria, Romania, and China jointly issued the "Declaration of Ningbo."[18]

The fifth element is intercity diplomacy. China has 59 pairs of sister provinces/states relationships and 41 pairs of twin cities arrangements with 100 provinces, states, and cities from 14 CEE countries (not Montenegro and Estonia).[19] The economic and trade delegation of Amoy visited the Czech Republic, Hungary, and Romania in 2012; organized two investment promotion meetings in Budapest and Bucharest; and communicated with the Czech Chamber of Commerce, Fujian Chamber of Commerce, Fujian Chamber of Commerce in Hungary, Mingxi Chamber of Commerce, Romania Fujian Association, the Chamber of Commerce and Industry of Romania and China, and the China Cultural Exchange Association of Romania.[20] As twin cities, Shanghai and Zagreb held alternately "Shanghai Day" and "Zagreb Day" to promote cultural, educational, economic, and trade exchanges.[21]

In 2011, nearly 200 thousand residents of CEE countries traveled in China, while more than 60,000 Chinese tourists chose CEE countries as their first stop. According to China's "Twelve Measures," the China Tourism Administration will coordinate with civil aviation authorities, travel agencies, and airline companies of the two sides.[22] The

---

[17] The third China–Central and Eastern European countries education policy dialogue was held in PolandRetrieved from http://world.people.com.cn/n/2015/0922/c157278-27618696.html.

[18] China–Central and Eastern European countries Ningbo Declaration released. Retrieved from http://news.xinhuanet.com/world/2015-06/12/c_1115596527.htm.

[19] List of sister city relationships between China and countries in the world. (n.d.). Retrieved from http://www.cifca.org.cn/Web/WordGuanXiBiao.aspx.

[20] Xiamen Municipal Government, P. R. China. Strengthen economic and trade cooperation and cultural exchanges. Retrieved from http://www.xm.gov.cn/zt/gclsgwygyzc/xmdt/201209/t20120925_538718.htm.

[21] Shanghai–Zagreb exchange information. Retrieved from http://gb.cri.cn/27824/2010/05/20/1545s2857286.htm.

[22] Ministry of Foreign Affairs of the People's Republic of China: China's Twelve Measures for Promoting Friendly Cooperation with Central and Eastern European

purpose is to enhance mutual business promotion and joint tourist destination development, and explore the possibility of opening more direct flights between China and the 16 CEE countries. The China Tourism Administration co-organized promotion of tourism products for China and CEE countries during the China International Tourism Mart held in Shanghai in 2012.[23] A special promotion of tourism products for China and Visegrad (V4) countries (Czech Republic, Hungary, Poland, and Slovakia) was held in Shanghai 2014, co-organized by China and the V4 Tourism Administration to present products for the Chinese to experience "Medieval Europe."[24]

China's practice of cultural diplomacy in CEE countries, through a variety of channels and patterns, has different targets. On the political level, the target is to improve communication techniques in order to promote public understanding in CEE countries of the Chinese political system and policies. On the economic level, the aim is to unfold cultural diplomacy in the process of economic and trade cooperation in order to maintain the stable, reliable, and responsible commitments of an emerging economic power. On the cognitive level, relying on the charm of the traditional and modern cultures, the aim is to show the CEE public that China is a reliable and capable member of the international community, who is willing to contribute to world peace.

4.3   Challenge of China's Cultural Diplomacy in Central and Eastern Europe

China has invested heavily in its cultural diplomacy toward CEE countries in recent years, but the outcome has not been very encouraging. Western scholars believe that the influence of China on global cultural trends, its soft power, is very weak and that its international image is

---

Footnote 22 (continued)

Countries. (2012, April 26). Retrieved from http://www.fmprc.gov.cn/eng/zxxx/t928567.htm.

[23]Expanding cooperation in tourism has practical significance in promoting the economic development of China and Central and Eastern European countries. Retrieved from http://gb.cri.cn/27824/2012/11/16/6651s3928962.htm.

[24]V4 countries to propose tourism offers. (n.d.). Retrieved from http://shanghai.kormany.hu/v4-countries-to-propose-tourismoffers.

mixed or even negative at the moment.[25] China's cultural diplomacy is also constrained by a cognitive gap between China and the CEE countries. The specifics are described next.

First, Chinese cultural diplomacy in CEE countries is not well received because of the CEE countries' experience of their communist past. China has utilized information technology to enhance traditional propaganda efforts in public understanding and acceptance of China's political system and foreign policy in Central Europe, but the citizens of these countries often link today's China with the Soviet Union in the Cold War. A common ideology could help them understand the domestic politics of China, the largest socialist country; however, after transition from the former socialist system, it seems that CEE countries showed stronger antisocialist stances than Western countries. Because of fear of the Stalinist socialist period and the Brezhnev Doctrine, it is often easy for CEE countries to form a negative impression when observing China. An example is the impression held by CEE public that Chinese investments are controlled by the Chinese government, which means expansion of the Chinese State. Central European public also tend to believe that Western norms and values are useful for transforming China. In their eyes, a rising China is still one of the "others" that differs from Western values.[26]

Second, the public in CEE countries hold a relatively unfavorable attitude toward China's cultural diplomacy methods. Because most Central Europeans learn about China from their own media and publications, they are suspicious of Chinese messages issued by Chinese official sources. Since the 1990s, CEE countries have been actively building their civil societies. They are more willing to accept the information distributed by civil groups and non-governmental organizations. These attitudes deepen the negative impression that China's propaganda system is trying to carefully construct "what is appropriate to be known" for Europeans.[27] Europeans generally believe that the propaganda sponsored

---

[25] David, S. (2013), *China Goes Global - The Partial Power,* Oxford University Press, USA.

[26] Larson, D.W., & Shevchenko, A. (2010). Status Seekers: Chinese and Russian Responses to U.S. Primacy. *International Security, 34* (4), 64.

[27] D'Hooghe, I. (2007). The Rise of China Public Diplomacy. Clingendael Diplomacy Paper 12, The Hague: Clingendael Institute.38.

by a government is not the mainstream outlet of soft power.[28] Merely providing more information cannot bridge the value gulf between China and Europe. China's cultural diplomacy must be changed from "what Europeans should know" to "what Europeans want to know." As the ancient Chinese saying goes, "amity between people holds the key to sound relations between states." Harmony is built on the basis of mutual understanding and cooperation between people. On the one hand, the people of CEE lack basic knowldge of the situation in China. Information mainly comes by the authority of Western European media and publications in an indirect way. Therefore, when Europe criticizes China's domestic and foreign policy with headlines such as "Chinese manipulation of its currency" or "Chinese African diplomacy is neo-colonialism," clarification by relevant Chinese departments, media, and scholars is delayed and not exactly conveyed to the peoples of CEE. Thus, the transfer from informing to influencing each other through cultural diplomacy requires diplomatic wisdom.

Third, the limited understanding of opinions in these transition countries hinders China from carrying out suitable cultural diplomacy. According to the author's interviews with some intellectuals of the CEE countries, people are most concerned about China's political reform, foreign policy adjustment, and common peoples' lives and social problems. The problem is a lack of relevant poll data focused on the public opinion of China in CEE countries. Western think-tanks on China cognitive surveys often focus on Western European countries. Only the Pew Research Center poll "Respondents opinion of China" includes Poland and the Czech Republic.[29] Both the 2010 BBC poll, with respondents in seven European countries (Russia, UK, Portugal, France, Spain, Germany, Italy), and the German Marshall Fund's "Trans-Atlantic Trends 2010" showed a downward trend in the favorability of Europeans toward China

---

[28] David, S. (2007). China's propaganda system: institutions, processes and efficacy. *The China Journal*, 57, 25–58.

[29] According to Pew research poll, 37% people held a favorable view of China in Poland in 2005, 39% in 2007, 33% in 2008, 43% in 2009, 46% in 2010, 51% in 2011, 50% in 2012. Retrieved from http://www.pewglobal.org/database/?indicator=24&survey=14&response=Favorable&mode=chart.

in 2006–2010. However, these surveys did not cover the public impressions of CEE countries regarding China.[30]

Similar to the European public, Chinese people also have cognitive problems regarding Europe. According to a survey by the Chinese Academy of Social Sciences in Europe, the level of Chinese understanding of CEE is still low, awareness of EU-related knowledge is less than half, and negative evaluation of Europe started to rise from 2008. The majority of Chinese scholars believe that the public of Europe have limited understanding of China and Chinese people, and vice versa.[31] The cognitive gap objectively brings difficulties for China in carrying out cultural diplomacy in CEE countries. For example, according to the aid agreement signed in early 2011, China offered 23 school buses in response to a request by the Macedonian government, which aroused heated discussion by the Chinese public. The Negotiation Foreign Ministry official responded in its Weibo that "the Chinese government is to fulfill its international obligations."[32] In order to enhance Chinese knowledge and understanding of CEE countries, especially for young students, launch of the "2015 Central and Eastern Europe Quiz" was held at Beijing Foreign Studies University in September 2015, with support from the CEE Secretariat.[33]

Fourth, the Chinese do not have enough soft power instruments to promote its image to the CEE public. The information passed to the public of CEE countries through Chinese official channels is still mainly about economic achievements and traditional Chinese culture. Amplifying the development of China exacerbates the pressure of "China's responsibility." Publicity of traditional culture is an important

---

[30] Gallup poll, China's Leadership Unknown to Many - Europe only region where residents more likely to disapprove than approve. (2008, April 18). Retrieved from http://www.gallup.com/poll/106621/chinas-leadership-unknown-many.aspx. Views of US Continue to Improve in 2011 according to BBC Country Rating Poll. Retrieved from http://www.worldpublicopinion.org/pipa/pdf/mar11/BBCEvalsUS_Mar11_rpt.pdf.

[31] Dong, Lisheng. (2011). Cognitive and influencing factors of Chinese scholars on China–EU relations - based on how the Chinese people see the EU 2010 survey. *Foreign Affairs Review*, 28(5), 72–85.

[32] Netizens survey on Netease's blog forum shows 2762 votes expressed dissatisfaction, understandable only 285 votes, accounting for 9%. Retrieved from http://blog.163.com/hot/252/.

[33] CEEC Knowledge Contest launching ceremony was held in Beijing Foreign Studies University. Retrieved from http://gb.cri.cn/42071/2015/09/21/8011s5109781.htm.

tool of cultural diplomacy by China, yet language, arts, and other cultural exchanges cannot eliminate the negative impact of the "China threat theory." As Joseph Nye points out, if a country's culture, values, or policies lack inherent attractiveness, the cultural diplomacy efforts of that country may create an undesired negative image, rather than creating effective soft power.[34] The transfer from informing to influencing each other through cultural diplomacy toward Europe requires more diplomatic wisdom. As Western scholars have commented, the presence of China's influence in Europe is because Europeans expect to expand and deepen their relations with China for political and economic interests. There is still quite a long way to go from this point to be attracted by the ideas and values of China.[35]

Last but not least, China's cultural diplomacy in CEE still suffers setbacks due to sensitive issues in bilateral relations. A few politicians or political parties in CEE countries ignore the great efforts made by the Chinese government to promote social and economic progress in Tibet, often in contact with the Dalai Lama, and even use the Tibet issue as a card to play in bilateral contacts with China. For example, the Polish media and NGOs linked the Tibet issue and human rights with their beliefs against the communist regime and established the so-called "Poland-Tibetans Friendship Association" and "Tibet Solidarity Day." Slovenia issued a presidential statement on the identity of the EU rotating presidency, welcoming dialogue with representatives of the Chinese government and the Dalai Lama in 2008.[36] The Dalai Lama was invited by the authorities of Maribor, Slovenia, to give a lecture called "Young peoples' values in local universities and secondary schools." Also, former Prime Minister Janez Janša and others met with the Dalai Lama in 2010. Attitudes on the issue of Tibet became a major point of conflict in relations between China and Slovenia. To make the Slovenian government better understand the reality of Tibet, China invited Slovenian President Drnovsek to visit Tibet when he came to attend the Boao Forum for

---

[34] Nye, Joseph. (2008). Cultural diplomacy and Soft Power, *The Annals of the American Academy of Political and Social Science, 616*(1). 89–102.

[35] D'Hooghe, I. (2008). Into High Gear: China's Public Diplomacy. *The Hague Journal of Diplomacy, 3*(1). 37–61.

[36] EU Presidency statement on the People's Republic of China's announcement of dialogue with a representative of the Dalai Lama. (2011, March 18). Retrieved from http://www.eu2008.si/en/News_and_Documents/Press_Releases/April/0425KPV_tibet.html.

Asia in 2006. However, so many protests, declarations, and notes from the Chinese government cannot effectively deliver the truth of Tibet to the public of CEE countries. As one Chinese diplomat commented, "We deal with other counties' governments fairly effectively, with communication of politicians at all levels of government, including senators and members of the army, but suffer from lack of experience and tradition in dealing with the media and the public."[37] China needs to properly handle negative comments about China, providing constantly updated, coherent, and constructive information to CEE countries and make it clear what can be obtained for the peoples involved from economic and trade cooperation with China.

4.4 FUTURE OF CHINA'S CULTURAL DIPLOMACY TOWARD CENTRAL AND EASTERN EUROPE

The increasing importance of China's position in foreign economic and trade relations with CEE countries provides opportunities for China to operate its cultural diplomacy in this region. The long-term, medium-term, and short-term goals, together with the political, economic, and cognitive goals of China shape and develop each other and finally formulate a blueprint for China's cultural diplomacy toward CEE countries. The urgent goal of China's cultural diplomacy in this region is to consolidate existing diplomatic achievements, create mutual understanding, and—with the support of local governments and civil institutions—help Chinese domestic enterprises to enter their markets. However, the effect of China's cultural diplomacy in CEE countries is still limited. China needs time and patience to evaluate whether its influence in CEE countries goes beyond the economic level. After all, CEE countries are the "bridge" between China and the EU. The EU suffers debt and refugee crises, while CEE countries are confronted with additional financial difficulties. They find themselves in need of a new, reliable economic partner, and China may prove to be a good alternative.

The experience of China's cultural diplomacy to CEE countries has also inspired China's communication with the public in countries along

---

[37]Fu Ying. (2010, Sept. 11). The public diplomatic weaknesses and how to strengthen the public diplomacy. Retrieved from http://www.china.com.cn/international/txt/2010-09/11/content_20909708.htm.

the Belt and Road. However, there is a cognitive gap when China passes its identity information initiatives to the international public. Therefore, China must realize that if she wants to build long-term cooperation with so many countries, she needs to create a "national identity" that is universally recognized by the international community. This is the necessary precondition to establish a "community of destiny." From most outside observations, it is difficult to answer the question "what is China?" There seems to be incompatibility between China's self-image and the conception of others. The current perception of China's image has not been widely accepted by the international community.

Cultural diplomacy has become one of the fundamental approaches of China's diplomatic strategy for the foreseeable future. The Belt and Road initiative provides a strategic orientation for China's foreign policy as well as a conceptual umbrella under which multiple and, until now, disparate Chinese attempts at cultural diplomacy can be unified and promoted.

Acknowledgements The work was partially sponsored by MOE (Ministry of Education in China) Youth Project of Humanities and Social Sciences (No. 17YJCGJW008).

PART II

Regional Cooperation in the "Belt and Road" Initiative

CHAPTER 5

One Belt, One Road: Connecting China with Central and Eastern Europe?

Ágnes Szunomár

5.1   INTRODUCTION

When some of the countries of Central and Eastern Europe (CEE) became members of the European Union, China developed an interest in strengthening ties with the region, attracted by CEE's dynamic, largely developed, and less saturated economies directly connected to the EU common market. Chinese outward investment flows and stock as well as trade volumes have steadily increased over the last decade and a half, particularly after 2008 as a result of the global economic and financial crisis. If we examine the motivations of the CEE countries, we see that their "eastern awakening" dates back to the same time. As China became a major player in the world economy and politics, CEE countries became more interested in developing relations with the eastern power. The economic and financial crisis was an additional impetus as CEE governments started to seek out new opportunities in their recovery from the recession. Since establishing the "16+1" framework in Warsaw, in April 2012,

Á. Szunomár (✉)
Institute of World Economics, Center for Economic and Regional Studies of the Hungarian Academy of Sciences, Budapest, Hungary

© The Author(s) 2018
Y. Cheng et al. (eds.), *The Belt & Road Initiative in the Global Arena*,
https://doi.org/10.1007/978-981-10-5921-6_5

the CEE region's importance has been further confirmed by China, and China–CEE cooperation has entered a new stage.

Although the relationship is developing well, there is still untapped potential for cooperation. The Silk Road Economic Belt could provide a new framework for cooperation between China and CEE as it offers opportunities for countries that wish to participate in implementing the strategy. The importance of Europe, particularly CEE countries, to the project was emphasized long ago by China and welcomed by several CEE countries, including Hungary, the first European country to sign a memorandum of understanding with China on promoting the Silk Road Economic Belt and the twenty first-Century Maritime Silk Road. The railway line from Chengdu to Łodz in Poland and construction of the Budapest–Belgrade railway are good examples of growing CEE interest in the new Chinese grand strategy. This chapter examines the evolution of China–CEE relations by presenting its main stages of the past 15 years and discusses the potential of closer cooperation in the framework of the One Belt, One Road (OBOR) initiative.

After the introductory section, we briefly present the scientific literature available on China–CEE relations. The section provides a detailed overview of the relations between China and the CEE region, with special emphasis on China's cooperation with its main partners from the region, especially the countries of the Visegrad Four (V4). The next section introduces the potentials of this cooperation in the context of the OBOR initiative. The conclusion summarizes China–CEE relations and contains some recommendations for the future.

5.2   Literature Review

The number and depth of available international scientific publications and other resources on China–CEE relations is very limited; however, we can see growing interest and a growing number of publications in recent years as a result of intensification of political and economic relations. Most of these publications (e.g., Turcsányi et al. 2014; Szunomár 2015; Éltető and Szunomár 2015; Szunomár et al. 2014; Matura 2012, 2013; Pleschová 2015; Semerák 2015). are from CEE, more precisely from V4 authors, which is line with the level of the relationship between China and the V4 countries. Regarding publications outside the CEE region, there are several Chinese contributions to the scientific literature, such as Chen Xin (2012), Shang Yuhong (2012), Song Lilei (2013, 2014), and Liu Zuokui (2013, 2014). These publications provide a comprehensive picture of political and/or economic relations between China and CEE countries. Some authors try to estimate the future evolution of the relationship and give some policy recommendations on how to enhance cooperation. Overall, these papers view the strengthening relationship positively but see untapped potential. Western scholars also discuss this relationship, although to a lesser extent (e.g., Jacoby 2014); however, their views are more critical.

Most of the above-mentioned publications also list some of the main obstacles to the deepening of relationships. These barriers are often related to the mutual (mis)understanding of each other. As a result, there have been some new attempts to gather data on each other's views and understanding, for example to assess relations between the CEE region and the PRC with special emphasis on public perceptions of China. To this end, Matura and Szunomár (2016) carried out a public opinion survey among university students in the most relevant CEE countries in order to understand their views of the present and to predict the potential future of bilateral relations. According to their findings, CEE university students have a rather neutral opinion vis-à-vis China when it comes to trust and and cooperation. Beijing is mostly considered as a partner of their respective countries. The economic role of Beijing and bilateral economic relations between China and CEE countries seems to be more important than politics. We compared individual V4 countries with each other and found that the Czech Republic and Slovakia were somewhat more critical, whereas Poland and Hungary were a bit more tolerant toward China. According to the authors' assumptions, the views of university students are more positive than the opinion of the elderly population of CEE countries, which means that the next generation of CEE leaders is expected to be even more positive toward China.

Regarding the literature on the OBOR initiative, numerous studies and articles have been published since the initiative was announced (e.g., Godehart 2014; Kaczmarski 2015; Minghao 2015). Most of these publications typically focus on details of the OBOR initiative and examine its impact at the global level. Some, however, try to analyze OBOR's potential effects on various regions, Casarini (2015), for example, focuses on how Europe could benefit from China's OBOR initiative and outlines some implications for the EU. A comprehensive analysis is still missing on how the OBOR initiative could enhance cooperation between China and the countries of the CEE region. This chapter represents the very first step in analyzing the opportunities in this regard.

5.3   CHINA AND CENTRAL AND EASTERN EUROPE: A RELATIONSHIP OF GROWING IMPORTANCE

Exchanges between China and the CEE region date back to ancient times, when the Silk Road closely linked these regions together over 2000 years ago. Now, after a long break, the relationship is about to revive. Of course, there were connections between China and the countries of the region during the Cold War and in the 1990s. Some countries had better ties and some had a less friendly relationship, but, in general, the region had no special role from either the Chinese or CEE point of view. Attitudes gradually began to change after the millennium. On the one hand, the transformation of the global economy is responsible for growing Chinese interest in CEE; on the other hand, CEE represents new challenges and new opportunities for China. The growth potential, institutional stability, and market size make the CEE region an attractive place for Chinese investment. As China became a major player in the world economy and politics, CEE countries became more interested in developing relations with China. China also became increasingly interested in the CEE region with the launch of the process for EU accession of CEE countries.

Initially, Chinese companies treated the region as a "back door" to European markets, but recently their motivations have expanded toward efficiency and strategic asset-seeking. Chinese outward flow of investment and stock (as well as trade volumes) has steadily increased in the last 15 years, particularly since 2008. Although most of the countries of the region have indicated interest in developing relations with China, some of them can be considered frontrunners. As can be seen from Fig. 5.1, six countries provided more than 90% of CEE exports to China in 2014—the V4 countries plus Romania and Bulgaria. Figure 5.2 shows that CEE exports to China increased significantly after 2000, the global crisis of 2008 being an important accelerator. On the import side, the situation is similar. In 2014 the same six countries received 80% of total Chinese exports to CEE.

The economic and financial crisis of 2008 was an additional impetus for both China and the CEE countries to strengthen their economic relations. CEE countries started to search for new opportunities in their recovery from the recession. There has been increased interest of the CEE governments in boosting trade relations and attracting Chinese investors. For example, Hungary's "Eastern Opening" policy was

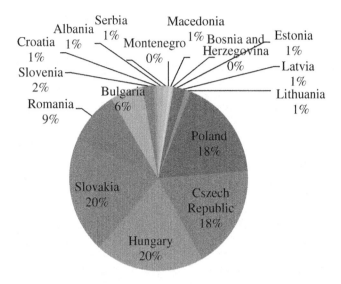

Fig. 5.1 Percentage exports from 16 CEE countries to China in 2014. *Source* National Bureau of Statistics of China (NBSC)

initiated after (and partly as a result of) the crisis, but the crisis also made Poland and, more recently, the Czech Republic look eastward. In parallel, the crisis brought more overseas opportunities for Chinese companies to raise their share in the world economy because the number of ailing or financially distressed firms has increased. China took these opportunities, which is the reason for the wider sectoral representation of Chinese firms in CEE countries in recent years.

The role of Chinese capital in CEE countries is still very small compared with all invested capital, but in the last few years this capital inflow has accelerated significantly and plays an important role in the region's recovery from the crisis. There has been a growing CEE interest in attracting Chinese companies in recent years, especially since the crisis. Similarly, Chinese outward foreign direct investment (FDI) is on the rise in every CEE country, but some stand out. The V4 countries, together with Romania, Bulgaria, and Serbia are the most popular investment destinations (Fig. 5.3).

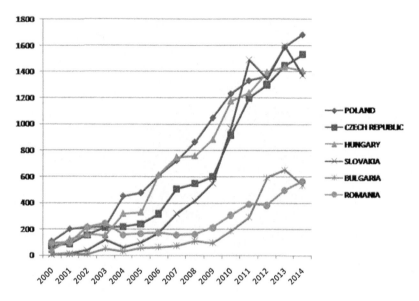

Fig. 5.2 Development of selected CEE exports to China (million euros). *Source* Eurostat Comext

Xi Jinping's European tour as vice-president in 2009 signaled a shift in the Chinese leadership's attitude toward the CEE region and marked the beginning of a new stage in their bilateral relations. Xi made an extended tour of Europe, visiting Belgium, Germany, Bulgaria, Romania, and Hungary, spending the most time in Budapest. This tour was framed as a visit to consolidate and develop cooperation in economic relations between China and the five countries, but Xi's visit to the CEE countries told more about China's evolving "go-out" investment strategy, indicating that the Chinese are eager to accelerate their diversification strategy through the emerging countries in the region.

In 2011, Chinese Premier Wen Jiabao further highlighted the growing importance of Chinese–CEE relations in his speech at the initial 16+1 business forum, the "China–Central and Eastern European Countries Economic and Trade Forum",[1] held in Budapest. He said

---

[1] Wen Jiabao: Strengthen Traditional Friendship and Promote Common Development. Speech at the China–Central and Eastern Europe an Countries Economic and Trade Forum, Budapest, 25 June 2011, http://www.gov.cn/english/2011-06/26/content_1892994.htm.

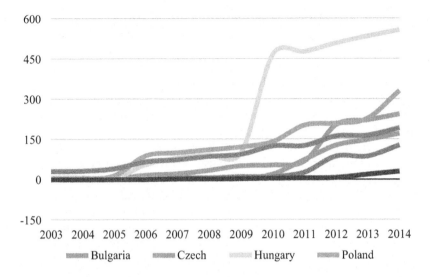

Fig. 5.3 Development of Chinese foreign direct investment in selected CEE countries (million dollars). *Source* CEIC China Premium Database (based on statistics of NBSC)

that China and the CEE countries are not just good friends who stand by each other through thick and thin, but also good partners that draw on each other's strengths and pursue win–win cooperation. Wen also emphasized how cooperation areas have been expanding. Indeed, CEE countries more than doubled their exports to the PRC between 2009 and 2014 and have attracted more investment than ever before. Additionally, in recent years, China and the CEE countries have signed a series of bilateral agreements on a wide range of economic, industrial, scientific, and technological cooperation, including agreements on investment protection and avoidance of double taxation.

In addition to the traditional fields of trade and investment, the cooperation in finance, tourism, legal services, green economy, and infrastructure have steadily increased. The two sides have held various kinds of business forums, product exhibitions, and trade fairs for entrepreneurs, providing important platforms for the business community to intensify exchange and cooperation. Dozens of high- or medium-level diplomatic delegations have also visited China and the CEE countries in recent years. Three years after Wen's visit to Budapest, Warsaw hosted the first summit of the heads of CEE governments,[2] where the 12-measure initiative was presented. This step marked the official beginning of the 16+1 platform, which created a complex framework of contacts between the two sides (Szczudlik-Tatar 2013, 2014).

In fact, Beijing perceives the CEE region not only as one of its new frontiers for export expansion, but also as a strategic entry point for the wider European market. China chose this region because CEE countries have dynamic, largely developed, less saturated economies, which are directly connected to the EU common market. Chinese corporations can cut their business costs significantly in the CEE countries and become integrated into the EU industrial system, but with less political expectations and fewer (or more silent) economic complaints compared with Western Europe. Of course, Beijing's growing interest toward CEE markets cannot be disconnected from some longstanding political and economic goals of China, such as ending the EU arms embargo and granting market economy status to the PRC.

Examining the motivations on the CEE side, their "eastern awakening" also dates back to the same time. As China became a major player in world economy and politics, CEE countries became more interested in developing relations with it. The economic and financial crisis was an additional impetus, as CEE governments started to search for new opportunities in their recovery from the recession. Before the global economic and financial crisis of 2008, many CEE countries had mixed feelings about closer economic ties with China. On the one hand, they actively wanted to attract Chinese FDI and were anxious about losing out on trade and business opportunities with China. On the other hand, there were fears about the unreliability of Chinese firms (as exemplified by the failure of Chinese company COVEC in Poland to complete a section of a highway project) or human rights issues such as the supposed exploitative labor conditions in Chinese-owned workplaces. More and more countries of the CEE region are deciding to put their doubts aside

---

[2]In 2013, the 16 +1 summit took place in Bucharest, Romania. In 2014 the summit was held in Belgrade, Serbia and in 2015 it was held in Suzhuo, PRC.

and even the coolest relations (for example, Czech–Chinese relations) have started to warm. However, despite the above-mentioned developments, most CEE governments lack a unified strategy toward China or Chinese companies. Hungary is one of the few exceptions; in the spring of 2012, the government launched a new economic policy with special emphasis on the "Eastern Opening."[3]

5.4   OBOR: Motivations and New Potentials for Cooperation

As China's economic growth has begun to slow, its economy is facing new challenges and its economic strategy is transforming, with changes in the country's global trade and investment position and strategies. New challenges evoke new answers. China has not chosen to stimulate its economy by turning inward but has chosen diplomacy, trade, and investment to broaden China's sphere of interest and business opportunities. In this way, it can promote economic relations, people-to-people links, and political influence and, at the same time, strengthen its own legitimacy. Therefore, the focus on Beijing's OBOR (*yi dai yi lu*) initiative has domestic, political, geopolitical, historical, and economic rationales.

However, the OBOR initiative is not only a new Chinese grand strategy but also an economic and infrastructural cooperation covering the whole of Eurasia. In fact, it is a set of instruments to facilitate connectivity in terms of trade, investment, finance, and flow of tourists and students (Summers 2015). Connected to this initiative, the "New Silk Road" project, comprising the Silk Road Economic Belt and the twenty first-Century Maritime Silk Road, has become a cornerstone of China's public diplomacy. Furthermore, China has made the 16+1 cooperation part of the OBOR strategy, which not only ensures the durability of the China–CEE cooperation but grants new and more opportunities for the countries involved. As a result, it provides opportunities for CEE countries that want to cooperate in implementing the strategy. The railway line from the Chinese city of Chengdu to Łodz, Poland has been in

---

[3] This strategy puts emphasis on developing trade (and technology) relations with China and other emerging countries. Rapidly growing Asian countries are considered able to provide several business opportunities and China is considered as an alternative source of external financing.

operation for some years and the Pupin bridge has already been built in Belgrade, Serbia. Budapest and Belgrade have also shown great interest in infrastructure (a railway line) from the very beginning (Liu 2014).

When examining interests on both sides, the motivations of China are easy to understand because the OBOR project expands their political and economic sphere of interest. They can counterbalance the Trans-Pacific Partnership, they will be in a more favorable strategic position as a result of the completed alternative transport routes, and they will be able to work off some of their industrial overcapacity accumulated in recent years. In addition, projects such as the Budapest–Belgrade railway or the Pupin bridge can serve as references for further Chinese investment in the CEE region and in the broader region, including Western European countries, which are usually more suspicious of Chinese infrastructure projects.

The importance of Europe, particularly CEE countries to the OBOR initiative was emphasized long ago by China and welcomed by several CEE countries. Hungary was the first European country to sign a memorandum of understanding with China on promoting the Silk Road Economic Belt and the twenty first-Century Maritime Silk Road, during Chinese Foreign Minister Wang Yi's visit to Budapest in June 2015. The Hungarian government was committed to the Budapest–Belgrade railway project when they signed the construction agreement in 2014. Hungarian Prime Minister Orbán even called it the most important moment in cooperation between the EU and China (Keszthelyi 2014). Although this is slightly excessive, it is a good reflection of the country's commitment and the fact that infrastructure development is a hot topic in all CEE countries.

As Casarini (2015, p. 3) highlights, to date, southeastern Europe and the Mediterranean (especially Greece) have been the main beneficiaries of the OBOR initiative. Through them, China can create a land–sea express route that links China, through the Greek port of Pireaus and the Budapest–Belgrade railway, with Eastern and Western Europe (Fig. 5.4). The good geographic position of both Hungary and Serbia makes them suitable for handling the transit traffic between China and Europe and grants an important role for them in implementation of the Chinese grand strategy. Consequently, at the end of 2014, the prime ministers of Hungary, Serbia, China, and Macedonia signed an

Fig. 5.4 Rail route between Piraeus and Budapest, via Skopje and Belgrade. *Source* People's daily online. Available online: http://en.people. cn/n/2014/1218/c90883-8824383.html (accessed 15 September 2015)

agreement in Belgrade, at the third CEE–China 16+1 summit, on the construction of a rail link between Budapest and Belgrade.[4]

New or reconstructed railway lines, highways, or other infrastructural investments are definitely necessary for the CEE region and useful for China, because through them they can reach several markets, not only within CEE but also in Western Europe. Moreover, these roads and lines are not the only advantage CEE countries could gain from such infrastructural projects. Along the railway lines and highways, CEE countries, with (or without) Chinese capital and assistance, could build up

---

[4]Regarding practical issues, the cost of investment for the whole section is around US$3 billion, which will be financed from Chinese loans. The Hungarian section costs around 472 billion HUF (US$1.67 billion/1.5 billion euros) The Hungarian section of the railway line is 166 kilometers long and the Serbian section will be 174 km. According to government information, a double track will be created and the railway line will be electrified. After completion of the railway, trains will be able to travel at speeds of up to 160 kilometers per hour. (See: http://www.kormany.hu/en/ministry-of-foreign-affairs-and-trade/news/modernisation-of-the-budapest-belgrade-railway-line-may-start-this-year).

a support infrastructure to serve as a logistic and/or assembly center. Factories, logistic centers, industrial areas, or economic zones along these lines would help to attract more Chinese investment to these countries, which would further strengthen the cooperation between the countries of the CEE region and China and turn the whole CEE region into a Chinese hub for trade with Europe. This strategy would not only better exploit the potential of the OBOR initiative for CEE and China, but could create further jobs and production in the CEE countries.

5.5   CONCLUSION: OPPORTUNITIES AND CHALLENGES AHEAD

During the past 15 years, CEE governments have committed themselves to the development of relations with China, but especially after the global economic and financial crisis of 2008. Although all of the countries in the region recognize the growing importance of China and the opportunities it can offer, some stand out as frontrunners of the relationship. The countries of the Visegrad Cooperation (the Czech Republic, Hungary, Poland and Slovakia) together with Romania, Bulgaria, and Serbia are among the most active countries of the region in terms of diplomatic relations, trade and investments ties, and people-to-people contact with China.

Although diplomatic visits are on the rise, political dialogues such as the 16+1 format have been established, and most of the countries of the CEE region welcome the OBOR initiative, there are still some unexploited opportunities in China–CEE relations. Regarding economic interaction, a healthy balance needs to be found between CEE needs and Chinese plans because CEE expectations are often excessive. Instead of high demands, CEE countries should have more specific and patient expectations, with more of their own initiatives. People, including decision-makers and politicians in the CEE, still lack proper knowledge of China, Chinese habits, Chinese needs, or "business as usual."

As mentioned, increasing Chinese investment and infrastructure projects can provide a lot of opportunity for CEE countries, but could offer much more for the CEE region as whole. However, the main obstacles to this idea are competing economic interests and lack of consultation about this within the CEE region, especially dialog about attracting Chinese investment and increasing exports to the Chinese market. As a result, the future of cooperation between China and CEE (especially between China and V4 countries, Romania, Bulgaria, and Serbia) is linked to the dynamism within the region and depends on the region to tackle those competing interests. To build a common international position vis-à-vis China, the countries of CEE need to work together to improve both political links and material connections, including roads, railways, and energy networks (Kugiel 2016). China is open to such cooperation; therefore, the ball is now back in the court of the CEE countries. Hopefully, China will be patient enough to wait for them.

Acknowledgements This paper was supported by the Hungarian OTKA Fund project no. K112450, titled "Shift in the world economy: from export orientation towards domestic demand-led growth?"

BIBLIOGRAPHY

Casarini, N. (2015). Is Europe to benefit from China's Belt and Road Initiative? (IAI Working Papers, 15/40). Roma: Istituto Affari Internazionali.

Chen, X. (2012). Trade and economic cooperation between China and CEE countries. Working Paper Series on European Studies, Institute of European Studies, Chinese Academy of Social Sciences, Vol. 6, No. 2.

Éltető, A., & Szunomár, Á. (2015). Ties of Visegrád countries with East Asia—trade and investment (Working Paper No. 215). Budapest: Institute of World Economics, Centre for Economic and Regional Studies, Hungarian Academy of Sciences.

Godehardt, N. (2014). Chinas "neue" Seidenstraßeninitiative: regionale Nachbarschaft als Kern der chinesischen Außenpolitik unter Xi Jinping. *SWP-Studie*, S 9/2014. Berlin: Stiftung Wissenschaft und Politik.

Jacoby, W. (2014). Different cases, different faces: Chinese investment in Central and Eastern Europe. *Asia Europe Journal, 12,* 199–214.

Kaczmarski, M. (2015). The New Silk Road: A versatile instrume CES Commentary, No. 161. Warsaw: Centre for Eastern Studies.

Keszthelyi, C. (2014, December 17). Belgrade-Budapest rail construction agreement signed. *Budapest Business Journal.* Retrieved from http://bbj.hu/budapest/belgrade-budapest-rail-construction-agreement-signed_89894 (accessed on 18.01.2016).

Kugiel, P. (Ed.). (2016). *V4 goes global: Exploring opportunities and obstacles in the Visegrad   Countries' cooperation with Brazil, India, China and South Africa.* Warsaw: Polski Instytut Spraw Międzynarodowych.

Liu, Z. K. (2013). An analysis of China's investment in Central and Eastern European countries under the new situation. *International Studies,* No.1, 108–120.

Liu, Z. K. (2014). The role of Central and Eastern Europe in the building of silk road economic belt. CIIS. Retrieved from http://www.ciis.org.cn/english/2014-09/18/content_7243192.htm (accessed on 18.03.2016).

Matura, T. (2012). The pattern of Chinese investments in Central Europe. *International Journal of Business Insights and Transformation.* ITM Business School, Vol.

Matura, T. (2013). China's economic expansion into Central Europe. In T. Matura (Ed.), *Asian Studies* (pp. 138–151). Budapest: Hungarian Institute of International Affairs.

Matura, T., & Szunomár, Á. (2016). Perceptions of China among Central and Eastern European university students. In J. Wardega (Ed.), *China—Central and Eastern Europe: Cross-cultural dialogue* (pp. 103–120). Cracow: Jagellonian University Press.

Minghao, Z. (2015). China's New Silk Road Initiative (IAI Working Papers). Roma: Istituto Affari Internazionali.

Pleschová, G. (2015). China's engagement in Central and Eastern Europe: Regional diplomacy in pursuit of China's interests. *International Issues & Slovak Foreign Policy Affairs, 24*(3), 15–26.

Semerák, V. (2015). Fututre of trade relations within the 16+1 group: Risks and opportunities. *International Issues & Slovak Foreign Policy Affairs, 24*(3), 27–48.

Shang, Y. H. (2012). A characteristic analysis of good trade structure between China and Middle East European countries. *Theoretical Exploration, 6*, 77–79.

Song, L. (2013). From rediscover to new cooperation: The relationship between China and Central & Eastern Europe. *EU-China Observer,* Issue 5, Bruges: College de l' Europe.

Song, L. (2014). China's public diplomacy toward Visegrad countries: Beyond economic influence? In Á. Szunomár (Ed.), *Chinese investments and financial engagement in Visegrad countries: Myth or reality?* (pp. 108–126). Budapest: Institute of World Economics, Centre for Economic and Regional Studies, Hungarian Academy of Sciences.

Summers, T. (2015). What exactly is 'one belt, one road'? *The World Today, 71*(5), Catham House.

Szczudlik-Tatar, J. (2013). China's charm offensive in Central and Eastern Europe: The implementation of its "12 Measures" strategy. *PISM Bulletin,* No. 106 (559).

Szczudlik-Tatar, J. (2014). China and the CEE look for new development opportunities. *PISM Bulletin,* No. 134 (729).

Szunomár, Á. (2015). Blowing from the East. *International Issues & Slovak Foreign Policy Affairs, 24*(3), 60–77.

Szunomár, Á., Völgyi, K., & Matura, T. (2014). Chinese investments and financial engagement in Hungary (Working Paper No. 208). Budapest: Institute of World Economics, Centre for Economic and Regional Studies, Hungarian Academy of Sciences.

Turcsányi, R. Q., Matura, T., & Fürst, R. (2014). The Visegrad countries' political relations with China. In Á. Szunomár (Ed.), *Chinese investments and financial engagement in Visegrad countries: Myth or reality?* (pp. 127–141). Budapest: Institute of World Economics, Centre for Economic and Regional Studies, Hungarian Academy of Sciences.

CHAPTER 6

Determinants and Directions of Polish–Chinese Cooperation in the Context of the One Belt, One Road Initiative

Piotr Bajor

6.1 China in Polish Foreign Policy

Polish policy toward China and the bilateral relations between the two countries have significantly evolved over the past 10–20 years. The most important factors that affect their mutual perceptions and ties include the dynamic growth of economic cooperation between Beijing and Warsaw, the strong position of China in the world economy, and the latter's growing importance in the international arena.

A breakthrough in Polish–Chinese bilateral relations came with the accession of Poland to the European Union in 2004. Since that landmark moment, Polish policy toward China has taken on three separate dimensions: European, regional, and bilateral. (Szczudlik-Tatar 2015c).

The European dimension is determined by treaties and shaped at the EU level. At the regional level, a new formula for institutionalized contacts between China and Central Europe arose in 2012 in the framework of the "16+1" initiative (Jakóbowski 2015), whose objective is

P. Bajor (✉)
Jagiellonian University, Kraków, Poland

© The Author(s) 2018
Y. Cheng et al. (eds.), *The Belt & Road Initiative in the Global Arena*,
https://doi.org/10.1007/978-981-10-5921-6_6

to intensify economic cooperation between China and the whole region and carry out trans-border infrastructure projects.

Four 16+1 summits have taken place so far. The first was organised in Warsaw in 2012, followed by sessions in Bucharest (2013) and Belgrade (2014).[1] The fourth summit took place in Suzhou (China) in November 2015 and focused on intensifying this form of multilateral cooperation. National leaders adopted a program of cooperation for 2016 (the "Suzhou Guidelines"), as well as a document laying down the principles of cooperation up until 2020. Its priorities include actions aimed at developing projects in the area of infrastructure and transportation, as well as stimulating cooperation in agriculture and logistics. Based on these goals and the declarations of Chinese leaders and regional representatives, the main directions of cooperation will be realized within the One Belt, One Road initiative (Kaczmarski et al. 2015).

During the meeting, Prime Minister Li Keqiang announced that Chinese companies wished to invest US$5 billion in various projects throughout the region. He also underscored the openness of the Chinese economy to CEE capital and vowed to create appropriate conditions for investment (Europa Środkowo-Wschodnia ma ogromne znaczenie 2015). As a key barrier to investment in China, this issue was an important subject in talks aimed at reducing disproportion in the trade balance between partners.

The initiatives described above supplement direct bilateral relations between Poland and China. In recent years, both countries have talked about the need to intensify and take cooperation to a higher level. These declarations have been reflected in increased political and economic cooperation.

A landmark moment in the evolution of Polish–Chinese relations came with the first visit of the Polish head of state to China since 1997. President Bronisław Komorowski visited the country in December 2011. Several major economic agreements were signed during his visit, but it

---

[1] Alongside China, the "16+1" group consists of the following countries of Cental and Eastern Europe: Poland, Lithuania, Latvia, Estonia, the Czech Republic, Slovakia, Hungary, Romania, Bulgaria, Croatia, Slovenia, Serbia, Bosnia and Herzegovina, Montenegro, Albania, and Macedonia. The groups is diverse in terms of economic development, as well as membership and cooperation with the European Union. It should be noted that Austria, Ukraine, and Belarus, though part of the region, do not belong to the group (Kaczmarski 2015; Szczudlik-Tatar 2014).

also marked an important political breakthrough. President Komorowski and the Chinese leader, Hu Jintao, signed an important declaration on establishing a strategic partnership between the two countries (Prezydent podsumował wizytę w Chinach 2011; Wizyta prezydenta w Chinach 2011).

The document stated that both countries highly value their cooperation and wish to strengthen it even further. Because fostering and developing mutual relations is in their shared interest, "both parties decide to raise their bilateral relations to the level of strategic partnership" (Wspólne oświadczenie 2011).

The declaration also addressed differences between the social and political systems of the two countries. It emphasised that Poland and China would adhere to the principles of equal treatment and mutual respect, vowing to "rise above the differences in politics and ideology, respect and support each other's paths of development, as well as the domestic and foreign policies dictated by their specific conditions" (Wspólne oświadczenie 2011).

The document also pointed to the need to intensify contacts and high-level intergovernmental visits, as well as establish the mechanisms of strategic dialogue. As a consequence, the way was paved for brand new structures of dialogue and cooperation aimed at tightening mutual relations and mobilizing trade and investment exchanges between Poland and China. Table 6.1 shows the most important cooperation mechanisms currently in place.

It should be noted that, despite the deep political divisions in Poland, the development of political and economic cooperation with China has enjoyed a broad political consensus. Some politicians point to the need for foreign policy to address political differences and human rights issues; Polish authorities maintain that these aspects are raised in bilateral talks but emphasize that the national interest requires that we tighten our political and economic ties with China nonetheless.

The priorities of Polish foreign policy are redefined by each new government in an address delivered by the prime minister and fleshed out by the minister of foreign affairs at the beginning of each new year. In 2012, the previous Polish government adopted a multi-year strategy for the Polish role in the international arena, entitled "Polish Foreign Policy Priorities 2012–2016" (Priorytety Polskiej Polityki Zagranicznej 2012).

The document laid down the main tasks and objectives for Polish diplomacy and was designed as a strategic approach to Polish foreign policy. The previous government pointed to the growing role and

Table 6.1   Major mechanisms of bilateral cooperation between Poland and China

Cooperation mechanism	Important information and tasks
Poland–China Intergovernmental Committee	Established in 2012, the committee provides the key mechanism for the coordination and development of bilateral relations between Poland and China. Its first session took place in Beijing in June 2015
Committee for Bilateral Economic Cooperation	The committee is in charge of coordinating and developing economic cooperation between the two countries. It meets annually at the level of deputy ministers of the economy
Committee for Scientific and Technological Cooperation	The committee is responsible for developing bilateral cooperation in the field of science and technology. It is composed mainly of scientists; its most recent session took place in June 2015
Steering Committee for Infrastructure	The committee is responsible for bilateral cooperation in the area of infrastructure. It was established based on a cooperation agreement for sustainable infrastructural development. The first session of the committee took place in May 2015 in Warsaw
Steering Committee for Industrial Cooperation	The committee is designed to increase investment cooperation. Chinese Prime Minister Wen Jiaba first called for it in 2012, but the committee has not yet been formally inaugurated. Talks are still underway to determine its composition
Poland–China Strategic Dialogue	Strategic dialogue involves annual meetings between state undersecretaries at the ministries of foreign affairs that cover a comprehensive approach to bilateral relations and their multilateral dimension. Regular sessions have been organized since the first meeting in Warsaw in 2012. The most recent session took place on 13 May 2016 in the Polish capital. It brought together Polish Deputy Minister of Foreign Affairs, Katarzyna Kacperczyk, and the Chinese Deputy Minister of Foreign Affairs, Liu Haixing

Source Based on "Najważniejsze istniejące i planowane mechanizmy" (2016) and "Wiceminister spraw zagranicznych Chin" (2016)

position of China in the international arena. The importance of China in the global economy, it argued, will continue to grow; the country is about to catch up with the EU in innovation rankings, and has already overtaken the USA and the EU in terms of investment flows to regions such as Latin America and Africa (Priorytety Polskiej Polityki Zagranicznej 2012).

The document also focused on the increasing importance of the Asia–Pacific region in the world, arguing that economic cooperation with China, the largest economic partner in Asia, takes on a special significance in this context. Economic contacts should be further developed in various areas such as infrastructure, the financial sector, and tourism. ("Priorytety Polskiej Polityki Zagranicznej 2012).

With that in mind, the previous Polish government tried to implement the above-mentioned strategy toward China and took various measures aimed at tightening bilateral cooperation. These included active political dialogue and intense high-level contacts. Table 6.2 presents data on bilateral dialogue and the most important state visits between 2011 and 2015.

Table 6.2 lists the visits of previous authorities, who lost power in the presidential and parliamentary elections of 2015. On 24 May 2015, the run-off to the presidential election pitted Bronisław Komorowski against the opposition candidate, Andrzej Duda, and the latter was elected as the new president of Poland with 51.55% of the vote. This was followed by parliamentary elections (in two chambers, the Sejm and the Senate) in the fall of the same year, in which the opposition Law and Justice Party won a landslide victory and replaced the governing coalition of the Civic Platform and the Polish People's Party.

This radical overhaul of the political scene, however, will not affect Polish–Chinese relations in a significant manner. The current government is determined to continue the political course of its predecessors, tighten bilateral ties, and expand economic cooperation. This is attested to by the first declarations and steps taken by the new authorities.

Soon after taking office, President Andrzej Duda announced China as the destination of one of his first international visits. The landmark visit took place in November 2015 and opened an important chapter in Polish–Chinese relations; it was also an element in a strategy aimed at strengthening mutual ties (China, Poland agree on better cooperation 2015; China, Poland pledge 2015; Prezydent Duda z przywódcą Chin 2015).

Table 6.2   High-level visits between Poland and China between 2011 and 2015

Year	Type of visit
2011	President Bronisław Komorowski visits China Chinese Foreign Minister Yang Jiechi visits Poland
2012	Polish Foreign Minister Radosław Sikorski visits China Polish Deputy Prime Minister Waldemar Pawlak visits China Chinese Prime Minister Wen Jiabao visits Poland
2013	Speaker of the Sejm, Ewa Kopacz, visits China Deputy Speaker of the Senate, Bogdan Borusewicz, visits China
2014	Member of the Politburo of the Communist Party of China, Sun Zhengcai, visits Poland Chinese Minister of National Defense Wanquan Chang visits Poland
2015	Polish Foreign Minister Grzegorz Schetyna visits China Polish Deputy Minister of Foreign Affairs, Katarzyna Kacperczyk, visits China twice Speaker of the Sejm, Małgorzata Kidawa Błońska, visits China President Andrzej Duda visits China Deputy Chief-of-Staff of the Chinese People's Liberation Army, Sun Jiaunguo, visits Poland Chinese Deputy Foreign Minister Wang Chao visits Poland twice Chinese Foreign Minister Wang Yi visits Poland

Source Based on "Dialog polityczny" (2016)

Additionally, in a speech on 29 January 2016, which presented the priorities of Polish foreign policy, Minister of Foreign Affairs Witold Waszczykowski described Polish–Chinese cooperation in the framework of strategic partnership as successful. He also emphasised the importance of cooperating with the whole CEE region within the 16+1 formula. Minister Waszczykowski also expressed his hope that further cooperation within the One Belt, One Road initiative and the Asian Infrastructure Investment Bank (AIIB) project would bring multiple economic benefits resulting from increased investment flow and trade exchange (Informacja ministra spraw zagranicznych 2016).

6.2   Asymmetric Economic Cooperation

As mentioned, the active development of Polish–Chinese bilateral ties involves increased economic cooperation as the basis of mutual relations. The authorities of the two countries indicate that they are interested in

Table 6.3 Trade between Poland and China in 2009–2014 (in million US$)

Year	2009	2010	2011	2012	2013	2014	2015
Exports	1,469.6	1,627.5	1,860.9	1,747.3	2,119.7	2,250.6	2,017,344
Imports	13,914.3	16,703.3	18,386.4	17,620.4	19,446.8	23,502.2	22,655,330
Total turnover	15,383.9	18,330.8	20,247.3	19,367.7	21,566.5	25,752.8	24,672,674
Trade balance	−12,444.7	−15,075.8	−16,525.5	−15,873.1	−17,327.1	−21,251.5	−20,637,986

Source "Stosunki dwustronne: Chiny" (2015). Data from 22 October 2015 provided by the Main Statistical Office, quoted by the Polish Ministry of Foreign Affairs (Współpraca handlowa i inwestycyjna 2015) further intensifying and tightening their bilateral ties in this area. An analysis of economic cooperation data demonstrates dynamic growth in Polish–Chinese trade in recent years. Details are shown in Table 6.3.

As shown in Table 6.3, trade turnover between Poland and China has risen by 60% in the past six years, with particularly high growth observed for Chinese imports, which increased systematically to achieve record levels in 2014. It is important to note the huge disproportion in the trade balance. Despite their growth, Polish exports to China continue to be significantly lower than imports, which is reflected in the high trade deficit. In 2015, the Chinese share in Polish imports amounted to 11.6%, whereas Polish exports to China accounted for only 1% of the total value of Polish exports. China ranked 21st among the key destinations for Polish products (Wymiana handlowa 2016). Various economic and investment programs are now underway to reverse this negative trend and boost Polish exports to China.

In terms of individual sectors and key products, Polish exports primarily include copper, copper products, furniture, confectionery, car parts and accessories, engines, and automobile components. Key imports include computer devices, phone equipment, radio and TV parts, components for machines and office equipment, textiles, shoe industry products, and mass consumption products (Chiny: Informator ekonomiczny 2016).

It is also worth comparing the cooperation between Poland and China with that of other EU countries. China is the largest exporter to the EU and the second largest (after the USA) EU partner in terms of imports (Countries and regions: China 2016). Eurostat data indicate that the value of trade between the EU and China amounted to 467.1 billion euros in 2013. The trade balance consisted of 164.7 billion euros of EU exports to China, and 302.5 billion euros of imports from China (Chińska Republika Ludowa. Informacja o stosunkach gospodarczych 2015; Facts and figures on EU-China trade 2014).

In 2014, European countries with the largest imports from China included Germany (60.9 billion euros), the Netherlands (57.3 billion euros), the UK (45.8 billion euros), France (25.4 billion euros), and Italy (25.1 billion euros). The list of top exporters looked similar. Germany led with 75 billion euros of exports to China in 2014, followed by the UK (19.6 billion euros), France (16.2 billion euros), Italy (10.5 billion euros), and the Netherlands (8.5 billion euros). Eurostat ranked Poland eighth in terms of imports and twelfth in terms of exports

(Chińska Republika Ludowa. Informacja o stosunkach gospodarczych 2015; Facts and figures on EU-China trade 2014).

As shown above, economic cooperation with China is also vital for the EU as a whole. Current economic trends led to a round of important negotiations aimed at liberalizing mutual trade, and official talks on a comprehensive EU–China Investment Agreement were launched during the 16th EU–China Summit on 21 November 2013. Once signed, the agreement is expected to liberalize and facilitate mutual investment, as well as reduce restrictions and barriers to trade. It is also designed to stimulate investment and ensure compliance with the standards of the World Trade Organization, human rights, and intellectual property protection, which, according to EU negotiators, should have a major impact on the competitiveness of European companies in cooperation with Chinese entities (EU and China begin investment talks 2014; Countries and regions: China 2016; EU and China agree on scope 2016).

6.3   Prospects of Cooperation Within the One Belt, One Road Project

The Chinese One Belt, One Road initiative is another important element in the economic cooperation between China, Poland, the CEE region, and the EU. The project announced by President Xi Jinping in 2013 is a new instrument of Chinese foreign policy, designed to tighten economic ties with various countries on different continents.

The original proposal was to create a land-based economic belt, later accompanied by a maritime belt. The former was initially restricted to China's western neighbors, and the latter to the countries of Southeast Asia. In 2014, following a series of analyses and consultations, President Xi presented an expanded draft proposal. Still far from detailed, it indicated the major objectives and tasks of the project (Szczudlik-Tatar 2015b; Dollar 2015).

Briefly, One Belt, One Road is a comprehensive initiative to create appropriate transport and infrastructure conditions for closer economic cooperation with various regions of the world. It is designed to help China maintain current output markets and secure new ones, which, in turn, is expected to strengthen its overall position in the world economy.

The project forms an important part of Chinese foreign and economic policy, particularly emphasized by Chinese authorities. With transport routes spanning three continents, if successful, the initiative is likely to boost economic growth in participating countries, but also increase the political clout of China in those regions (Szczudlik-Tatar 2015b; Winter 2016; Cheung and Lee n.d.). For this reason, it can be viewed as an element of Chinese soft-power and a broader geopolitical strategy to strengthen China's role in the global power system (Tao 2015).

The One Belt, One Road initiative is also likely to help tighten the economic ties between China and Poland. The previous Polish government repeatedly declared its willingness to join the initiative, and the new authorities continued to champion Polish accession to the project (Rząd za współpracą 2015; Chinese FM discusses Warsaw's role 2015). High-level talks continued and the special agreement was finally signed during President Andrzej Duda's visit to China, reasserting the express interest of both parties in the implementation of this comprehensive initiative.

The Polish government, it should be noted, sees the project as an opportunity to develop Polish foreign cooperation and increase the role of Poland as a transit country and logistics node in the region. During his visit to China, President Duda emphasized that the initiative provides an enormous development opportunity for both countries, as well as for the broader regions of Asia and Europe. Because of its geographical location and business experience, he argued, Poland has an important role to play in the process. He declared that our serious interest in the project confirms Poland's accession to the AIIB (Chcemy współpracować z Chinami 2015) and added that the country would take an active part in the realization of the One Belt, One Road initiative, providing China with "the gateway to Europe" and acting as a logistics center for further Chinese investment (Chcemy współpracować z Chinami 2015; Polish President: Poland can act as ambassador 2015; Prezydent o partnerstwie z Chinami 2015).

The issue of Polish–Chinese cooperation within the framework of the One Belt, One Road project was also discussed in April 2016 during the visit to China of Polish Foreign Minister Witold Waszczykowski. Talks addressed possible future measures in this area. Minister Waszczykowski reaffirmed that Poland is interested in the project and has an important role to play, not only because of its geographical location, but also thanks to its infrastructure and logistics base, including its sea, air, and land routes (Szef MSZ: możliwości współpracy z Chinami 2016; Poland eyes enhanced ties 2016).

An important step in the development of mutual relations also involves the implementation of projects financed through the AIIB.

Polish authorities emphasize that our participation in this initiative reasserts our economic priorities and shows our willingness to become involved in various forms of cooperation.

The AIIB was formally established in January 2016. On 19 April 2016, President Duda ratified its founding document, making Poland one of its 57 founding countries. The bank is expected to have US$100 billion of capital and will mainly finance large projects in the areas of energy, rail, road, and port infrastructure. These will be realized mainly in Asia, but Poland reiterated that opportunities also exist for investment cooperation in the territories of the European members of the bank (Rozmowa ministra 2016).

6.4   Conclusions

Recent years have witnessed the strengthening of mutual ties between Poland and China, especially with respect to economic cooperation. The latter will continue to be the most important factor shaping bilateral relations, the multilateral approach within the 16+1 formula, and EU–China relations. The intensity and development of future cooperation will depend on the economic situations in China, the CEE, and the EU.

Importantly, the tightening of mutual ties will involve implementation of the One Belt, One Road initiative, whose objectives outline important prospects for the further growth of economic cooperation. If successful, the initiative will fuel economic growth in individual countries and enable the implementation of large projects in the field of infrastructure and logistics throughout CEE countries (Szczudlik-Tatar 2015a; Dollar 2015). For this reason, like other countries of the region, Poland is interested in tightening its cooperation with China in this area. The authorities hope that active Polish participation in the initiative will boost the growth of trade and, above all, enhance the role of Poland as a key country for logistics and transit along the regional transportation routes of the One Belt, One Road project.

It is also important, however, to consider the geopolitical consequences of the initiative. If successful, the One Belt, One Road project will strengthen the importance and standing of China in the global arena. This, in turn, will significantly affect its relations and competition with the USA in the global system of power. The USA has already taken a dim view of the Chinese initiative, treating it as an instrument to secure long-term geopolitical objectives (Szczudlik-Tatar and Wnukowski 2015;

Dollar 2015). Because the USA is a key ally of Poland and its pillar of safety, this factor needs to be taken into account when participating in any long-term Chinese initiatives (Marcinkowski 2015). The Polish government needs to run a well-considered policy in this area, so that it maintains its strategic partnership with the USA while reaping the economic and political benefits from the One Belt, One Road project.

REFERENCES

Chcemy współpracować z Chinami dla rozwoju Polski i Europy. (2015). Retrieved from http://www.prezydent.pl/aktualnosci/wizyty-zagraniczne/art,34,prezydent-otworzyl-polsko-chinskie-forum-gospodarcze-w-szanghaju.html. Last accessed on 7 May 2016.

Cheung F., Lee A., *A brilliant plan One Belt, One Road.* (n.d.). Retrieved from https://www.clsa.com/special/onebeltoneroad/. Last accessed on 7 May 2016.

China, Poland agree on better cooperation. (2015). Retrieved from http://news.xinhuanet.com/english/2015-11/24/c_134849798.htm. Last accessed on 6 May 2016.

China, Poland pledge to boost strategic partnership. (2015). Retrieved from http://news.xinhuanet.com/english/2015-11/25/c_134855120.htm. Last accessed on 6 May 2016.

Chinese FM discusses Warsaw's role in building "Belt and Road" with Poland's highest officials. (2015). Retrieved from http://news.xinhuanet.com/english/2015-10/16/c_134717795.htm. Last accessed on 7 May 2016.

Chiny: Informator Ekonomiczny. (2016). Retrieved from http://www.pekin.msz.gov.pl/pl/wspolpraca_dwustronna/wspolpracagospodarcza/gospodarka_chin/. Last accessed on 6 May 2016.

Chińska Republika Ludowa. Informacja o stosunkach gospodarczych z Polską. (2015). Retrieved from http://www.mg.gov.pl/files/Chiny_16_06_2015.doc. Last accessed on 6 May 2016.

Countries and regions: China. (2016). Retrieved from http://ec.europa.eu/trade/policy/countries-and-regions/countries/china/. Last accessed on 6 May 2016.

Dialog polityczny. Wizyty najwyższych władz + konsultacje MSZ. (2016). Retrieved from https://www.msz.gov.pl/pl/polityka_zagraniczna/inne_kontynenty/azja_i_pacyfik/stosunki_dwustronne_azja_pacyfik/chiny;jsessionid=5F8AD1E3AD733B9601139FFE63496F61.cmsap1p. Last accessed on 6 May 2016.

Dollar, D. (2015). *China's rise as a regional and global power: The AIIB and the 'one belt, one road',* Horizons, Summer 2015, Issue no. 4., p. 166.

EU and China agree on scope of the future investment deal. (2016). Retrieved from http://trade.ec.europa.eu/doclib/press/index.cfm?id=1435. Last accessed on 6 May 2016.

EU and China begin investment talks. (2014), *Brussels,* retrieved from http:// europa.eu/rapid/press-release_IP-14-33_en.htm. Last accessed on 6 May 2016.

Europa Środkowo-Wschodnia ma ogromne znacznie dla rozwoju stosunków z Chinami. (2015). Retrieved from http://www.prezydent.pl/aktualnosci/ wizyty-zagraniczne/art,36,europa-srodkowo-wschodnia-ma-ogromne-znacznie-dla-rozwoju-stosunkow-z-chinami.html. Last accessed on 5 May 2016.

Facts and figures on EU-China trade. (2014). Retrieved from http://trade. ec.europa.eu/doclib/docs/2009/september/tradoc_144591.pdf.   Last accessed on 6 May 2016.

Informacja ministra spraw zagranicznych o zadaniach polskiej polityki zagranicznej w 2016 roku. (2016). Retrieved from http://www.msz.gov.pl/pl/ polityka_zagraniczna/priorytety_polityki_zagr_2012_2016/expose2/ expose2016/. Last accessed on 6 May 2016.

Jakóbowski, J. (2015), *Chińskie zagraniczne inwestycje bezpośrednie w ramach „16+1": strategia, instytucje, rezultaty,* Komentarze OSW, No. 191, November 27, 2015.

Kaczmarski, M., *China on Central-Eastern Europe: '16+1' as seen from Beijing,* Commentary, Centre for Eastern Studies, Number 166, 15.04.2015. Retrieved from http://www.osw.waw.pl/en/publikacje/osw-commentary/2015-04-14/china-central-eastern-europe-161-seen-beijing.   Last accessed on 5 May 2016.

Kaczmarski, M., Jakóbowski, J., & Hyndle-Hussein, J. (2015), *The China/Central and Eastern Europe summit: a new vision of cooperation, old instruments,* Retrieved from http://www.osw.waw.pl/en/publikacje/analyses/2015-12-02/china/central-and-eastern-europe-summit-a-new-vision-cooperation-old. Last accessed on 5 May 2016.

Marcinkowski, B. (2015). *Zanim Polska zachłyśnie się zwrotem ku Chinom,* Retrieved from http://biznesalert.pl/marcinkowski-zanim-polska-zachlysniesie-zwrotem-do-azji/. Last accessed on 7 May 2016.

Najważniejsze istniejące i planowane mechanizmy współpracy dwustronnej. (2016). Ministerstwo Spraw Zagranicznych RP, Retrieved from https://www.msz. gov.pl/pl/polityka_zagraniczna/inne_kontynenty/azja_i_pacyfik/stosunki_ dwustronne_azja_pacyfik/chiny;jsessionid=5F8AD1E3AD733B9601139FFE 63496F61.cmsap1p. Last accessed on 5 May 2016.

Poland eyes enhanced ties, cooperation with China: FM. (2016). Retrieved from http://news.xinhuanet.com/english/2016-04/22/c_135304096.htm. Last accessed on 7 May 2016.

Polish President: Poland can act as ambassador in relations between China, Europe. (2015). Retrieved from http://news.xinhuanet.com/english/2015-11/23/c_134846723.htm. Last accessed on 7 May 2016.

Prezydent Duda z przywódcą Chin o współpracy i partnerstwie. (2015). Retrieved from http://www.prezydent.pl/aktualnosci/wizyty-zagraniczne/ art,37,spotkanie-z-przewodniczacym-chinskiej-republiki-ludowej.html.   Last accessed on 6 May 2016.

Prezydent o partnerstwie z Chinami ws. "Jednego Pasa i Jednego Szlaku". (2015). Retrieved from http://www.prezydent.pl/aktualnosci/wizyty-zagraniczne/art,35,prezydent-o-partnerstwie-z-chinami-ws-jednego-pasa-i-jednego-szlaku. html. Last accessed on 7 May 2016.

Prezydent podsumował wizytę w Chinach. (2011). Retrieved from http://www. prezydent.pl/archiwum-bronislawa-komorowskiego/aktualnosci/wypowiedzi-prezydenta/wywiady/art,79,prezydent-podsumowal-wizyte-w-chinach. html. Last accessed on 5 May 2016.

Priorytety Polskiej Polityki Zagranicznej 2012–2016. (2012). Retrieved from https://www.msz.gov.pl/pl/polityka_zagraniczna/priorytety_polityki_ zagr_2012_2016/. Last accessed on 6 May 2016.

Rozmowa ministra Witolda Waszczykowskiego z Prezesem Azjatyckiego Banku Inwestycji Infrastrukturalnych. (2016). Retrieved from http://www.msz.gov.pl/ pl/aktualnosci/wiadomosci/prezes_azjatyckiego_banku_inwestycji_infrastrukturalnych__aiib__z_wizyta_w_warszawie. Last accessed on 7 May 2016.

Rząd za współpracą z Chinami w programie "Pas i Szlak". (2015). Retrieved from http://biznes.gazetaprawna.pl/artykuly/907376,rzad-za-wspolpraca-z-chinami-w-programie-pas-i-szlak.html. Last accessed on 7 May 2016.

Stosunki dwustronne: Chiny. (2015). data from 22 October 2015 provided by the Main Statistical Office, quoted after the Polish Ministry of Foreign Affairs: *Stosunki dwustronne: Chiny.* Retrieved from https://www.msz.gov.pl/pl/ polityka_zagraniczna/inne_kontynenty/azja_i_pacyfik/stosunki_dwustronne_ azja_pacyfik/chiny;jsessionid=5F8AD1E3AD733B9601139FFE63496F61. cmsap1p. Last accessed on 6 May 2016.

Szczudlik-Tatar, J. (2014, December 12). *Chiny i Europa Środkowo-Wschodnia: w poszukiwaniu nowych możliwości rozwoju*, Biuletyn PISM, No. 122 (1234).

Szczudlik-Tatar, J. (2015a, September 28). *Chińska gospodarka: W poszukiwaniu nowej normalności.* Biuletyn PISM, Nr 84 (1321).

Szczudlik-Tatar, J. (2015b, July 2). *Jedwabny Szlak: czym jest nowa priorytetowa chińska strategia*, Biuletyn PISM, Nr 65 (1302).

Szczudlik-Tatar, J. (2015c, November 19). *Polsko-chińskie „strategiczne partnerstwo": w oczekiwaniu na wymierne rezultaty*, Biuletyn PISM, No. 101 (1338).

Szczudlik-Tatar, J., & Wnukowski D. (2015, May 27). *Azjatycki Bank Inwestycji Infrastrukturalnych: szanse dla polskiego biznesu*, Biuletyn PISM, No. 52 (1289).

Szef MSZ: możliwości współpracy z Chinami są nieograniczone. (2016). Retrieved from https://www.msz.gov.pl/pl/aktualnosci/msz_w_mediach/szef_msz__mozliwosci_wspolpracy_z_chinami_sa_nieograniczone. Last accessed on 7 May 2016.

Tao, X. (2015). *Is China's 'Belt and Road' a Strategy? When is a strategy not a strategy?* Retrieved from http://thediplomat.com/2015/12/is-chinas-belt-and-road-a-strategy/. Last accessed on 7 May 2016.

Wiceminister spraw zagranicznych Chin z wizytą w Warszawie. (2016). Retrieved from http://www.msz.gov.pl/pl/p/msz_pl/aktualnosci/wiadomosci/wiceminister_spraw_zagranicznych_chin_z_wizyta_w_warszawie. Last accessed on 5 May 2016.

Winter, T., *One Belt, One Road, One Heritage: Cultural Diplomacy and the Silk Road*. (2016). Retrieved from http://thediplomat.com/2016/03/one-belt-one-road-one-heritage-cultural-diplomacy-and-the-silk-road/?utm_content=bufferbdeff&utm_medium=social&utm_source=facebook.com&utm_campaign=buffer. Last accessed on 6 May 2016.

Wizyta prezydenta w Chinach. (2011). Retrieved from http://www.prezydent.pl/archiwum-bronislawa-komorowskiego/aktualnosci/wizyty-zagraniczne/art,141,wizyta-prezydenta-w-chinach.html. Last accessed on 5 May 2016.

Wspólne Oświadczenie Rzeczypospolitej Polskiej i Chińskiej Republiki Ludowej w sprawie ustanowienia partnerskich stosunków strategicznych, (2011) [in:] *Wizyta Prezydenta Rzeczypospolitej Polskiej Bronisława Komorowskiego w Chińskiej Republice Ludowej 18-22 grudnia 2011 roku. Wymiar gospodarczy*, p. 4–7, Retrieved from http://www.prezydent.pl/archiwum-bronislawa-komorowskiego/aktualnosci/wizyty-zagraniczne/art,141,wizyta-prezydenta-w-chinach.html. Last accessed on 5 May 2016.

Współpraca handlowa i inwestycyjna. (2015). Retrieved from http://www.pekin.msz.gov.pl/pl/wspolpraca_dwustronna/wspolpracagospodarcza/wymianahandlowa/. Last accessed on 6 May 2016.

Wymiana handlowa i aktywność inwestycyjna. (2016). Retrieved from http://www.pekin.msz.gov.pl/pl/wspolpraca_dwustronna/wspolpracagospodarcza/wymianahandlowa/. Last accessed on 6 May 2016.

CHAPTER 7

One Belt, One Road: A Comparative Regionalism Approach

Ikboljon Qoraboyev

President Xi Jinping proposed revival of the traditional Silk Road in the form of the Silk Road Economic Belt and the twenty first-Century Maritime Silk Road during his visits to Kazakhstan and Indonesia in September 2013 and October 2013, respectively (Xi 2013a, b). Systemic links between these two projects were further consolidated in an official document published jointly by three Chinese institutions in March 2015. "Vision and Actions on Jointly Building Silk Road Economic Belt and twenty first-Century Maritime Silk Road," issued by the National Development and Reform Commission (NDRC), the Ministry of Foreign Affairs, and the Ministry of Commerce of the People's Republic of China outlined in detail the principles, priorities, and mechanisms of the OneRoad, One Belt initiative (NDRC 2015). Since then, these twin proposals came to be known as the One Belt, One Road (OBOR) initiative.

OBOR is thus a relatively recent topic, but has already attracted huge interest from the media, policy-makers, and scholars. However, most of these studies are of exploratory nature. Scholars and journalists

I. Qoraboyev (✉)
Higher School of Economics, KAZGUU University, Astana, Kazakhstan

© The Author(s) 2018
Y. Cheng et al. (eds.), *The Belt & Road Initiative in the Global Arena*,
https://doi.org/10.1007/978-981-10-5921-6_7

alike are trying to explore the nature of the OBOR initiative, which is still an open question. It is an important task to conceptualize OBOR and undertake projections about future research projects concerning it.[1] Choosing the right concepts and analytical prisms for elaborating on policy initiatives is not something to be ignored as merely a scholarly exercise. OBOR is clearly an outwardly directed project and, as such, needs approval and acceptance from target countries to succeed. Framing and conceptualizing particular policy initiatives by external participants are important in determining their success. This is especially true for successful realization of OBOR, which is planned to materialize across different geographical and political spaces.

Initial scholarship regarding OBOR seems to concentrate on policy analysis and geopolitical evaluation.[2] The prevalent image of OBOR as a geopolitical tool is partly a result of the lack of clear definition of OBOR as a concept. This lack of precision on the content and scope of OBOR has been pointed out by many observers of Chinese foreign policy. For Theresa Fallon, "the precise contours of the Belt and Road initiative have not been completely defined. At the moment, the Belt and Road appears to be a versatile label for China's foreign policy in Eurasia" (Fallon 2015, p. 142). For Nadine Godehart, accounts of OBOR proposed by Chinese officials remain diffuse and vague because they have not yet proposed "a language—that works in Chinese as well as in Western languages" to tell the world what OBOR is really about (Godehart 2016, p. 23).

Even if geopolitical thinking is essential in reading international politics, restricting analysis of OBOR-related projects to geopolitical approaches alone could lead to skepticism about the initiative. It is important to ensure that OBOR avoids repeating the experience of recent Eurasian regional initiatives such as the Shanghai Cooperation Organization (SCO) or Eurasian Economic Union. These institutional

---

[1] For the scope and nature of explanatory studies, see Mouton and Marais (1996). Mouton and Marais define the goal of exploratory studies as "the exploration of a relatively unknown research area. The aims of such studies may vary quite considerably. They may be: - to gain new insights into the phenomenon; - to undertake a preliminary investigation before a more structured study of the phenomenon;—to explicate the central concepts and constructs; - to determine priorities for future research; - to develop new hypotheses about an existing phenomenon."

[2] I thank Maximilian Mayer (Tongji University) for pointing to this feature of emerging scholarship on OBOR.

initiatives were perceived as foreign policy tools of China and Russia to be used in geopolitical confrontation with the West. This perception slowed down emergence of comprehensive scholarship around these Eurasian regional organizations. Most scholarship on the SCO and Eurasian Economic Union produced during the last decade includes a heavy dose of geopolitical analysis (Qoraboyev 2010b). Another feature of recent scholarship is prevalent skepticism about the successful outcome of regional institutions in Eurasia and Central Asia (Hancock and Libman 2016; Laruelle and Peyrouse 2012). It is important that the work of conceptualizing OBOR using alternatives to geopolitical analytical tools is carried out from the beginning, without delay.

7.1 OBOR: The Need to Go Beyond Geopolitical Analysis

Relying exclusively on geopolitical thinking may hinder emergence of sound analyses of different international phenomena. The SCO case is a good example to illustrate this point. Created in 2000, SCO is a regional organization with broad perspectives. It aspires to be part of a multilateral international order. However, it was conceptualized either as a regional organization defending authoritarian norms or a Chinese geopolitical tool to counter US and Russian advances in Central Asia (Ambrosio 2008; Collins 2009; Bailes et al. 2007; Allison 2008; European Parliament Directorate-General for External Policies 2012; Flikke and Wilhelmsen 2008). For Emilian Kavalski, the SCO seemed "to confirm the re-enactment of the normative power of *Pax Sinica*" (Kavalski 2007). In the West, the SCO came to be known as "a political and military block led by anti-Western Russia and China against US and Western interests in the region" (Dadabaev 2014).

The same trend seems to be emerging with respect to OBOR. Initial reactions present OBOR as another tool in the Chinese foreign policy inventory. Two points are made with respect to OBOR from this perspective. First, OBOR is seen as China's instrument for strengthening its negotiating position in different forums of global governance. China uses OBOR to push the West to bend to Chinese requests for increasing its say in global governance. Otherwise, China threatens to restrict its engagement with global institutions and instead to rely on China-led frameworks such as OBOR or SCO to increase its global leverage. Shaun

Breslin's analysis of China-led global initiatives illustrates this approach well. He notes, "if reforms of existing structures are not possible, or slow in emerging, then China is prepared to introduce new structures of governance to coexist alongside existing ones. The creation of BRICS and the SCO are both examples of groupings that aim to provide at least some governance functions in arenas where China can exert considerable influence" (Breslin 2016).

The second approach depicts OBOR as a reactionary move by China to counter advances that are being realized by the USA in the Asia-Pacific region. From this perspective, China was obliged to come up with its own interpretation of the modern Silk Road only after initial US declarations on the same matter. Theresa Fallon's genealogy of OBOR is representative of this trend. Here is her account of how China came up with the OBOR initiative:

> Hillary Clinton first referred publicly to her vision of a "New Silk Road," in a speech in Chennai, India on July 20, 2011 [...] Chinese officials were flummoxed to find that she used the term Silk Road to describe a US policy. According to one Chinese diplomat, "When the US initiated this we were devastated. We had long sleepless nights. And after two years, President Xi proposed a strategic vision of our new concept of Silk Road. (Fallon 2015, p. 141)

An initial reaction by the West to launching of the Asian Infrastructure Investment Bank (AIIB), considered one of the main pillars of OBOR, in 2015 is also helpful in seeing the prevalence of these geopolitical arguments. China-skeptics Mike Callaghan and Paul Hubbard explain how the West approached the AIIB with suspicion:

> China is frustrated with the US reluctance to cede it power at the IMF and the World Bank, and so is attempting to usurp the US economic leadership by creating its own institutions to rival the Bretton Woods institutions, starting with the AIIB. The AIIB [...] will not be a true multilateral institution committed to common objectives. Instead, it will be a vehicle for China to advance its own unilateral strategic objectives in Asia at the expense of the US. (Callaghan and Hubbard 2016, p. 116)

One way or another, the above-mentioned factors are leading to establishment of primarily a geopolitical viewpoint of OBOR. Although acknowledging the necessary presence and usefulness of geopolitical logic in international affairs, it would be unfortunate to limit analysis of a comprehensive and complex initiative such as OBOR to geopolitical aspects alone. Association of OBOR with zero-sum thinking may lead to increased skepticism and resistance, a real risk for the success of OBOR, as underlined by some Chinese scholars (ECFR 2015, p. 4). Furthermore, conception of OBOR as a Chinese tool against the interests of US or other great power's foreign policy will also cause reluctance on the part of target countries. Professor Zhan Yungling, a member of the Chinese People's Political Consultative Conference, writing about external threats to OBOR, says that "the most serious one [threat] is the suspicion with which other countries view China's aims and strategic purposes. Many fear that the OBOR is a veiled attempt by China to dominate its neighboring regions. These doubts mean that many countries are reluctant to cooperate in the initiative" (ECFR 2015, p. 11). This is even more delicate because China needs willing participation of countries situated along Belt and Road, The OBOR is presented as a "systematic project," which depends on engagement of countries other than China to succeed (NDRC 2015). As Tommy Koh rightly points out, "the best outcome is for the proposal to evolve from being seen as a Chinese project to being the region's project. It is desirable for China to obtain the region's ownership of the proposal" (Koh 2015). Focusing exclusively on exogenous readings of OBOR will also undermine endogenous dynamics and the normative value that it carries for going beyond Western-centered approaches to international relations. The prospect of geopolitics claiming exclusivity over OBOR analytics is not desired by either China or other interested countries. Understandably, in March 2015, Chinese Foreign Minister Wang Yi felt obliged to reject geopolitical stipulations by stating that the OBOR is "the product of inclusive cooperation, not a tool of geopolitics, and must not be viewed with an outdated Cold War mentality" (IISS 2015).

This void in conceptualizing OBOR and the prevalence of zero-sum thinking in OBOR-related analyses pushes scholars to look for alternative frameworks for discussing OBOR. This chapter argues that comparative regionalism studies could be an apt alternative to geopolitical readings of OBOR. The discipline of comparative regionalism is one of the main frameworks that endeavors to go beyond zero-sum thinking to come up with the long-term prospects of sociopolitical and economic processes in different parts of the world. This paper does not aim to give a detailed account of the discipline. Instead, it discusses OBOR, relying on premises and concepts drawn from comparative regionalism studies.[3]

7.2   REGIONAL FEATURES OF OBOR

Note that Chinese thinking on OBOR relies heavily on regionalist premises. Regional basis is evident in official speeches and documents that introduced the initiative to the international community. For President Xi Jinping, who is usually presented as the leader whose vision was essential in launching OBOR,[4] building an economic belt along the Silk Road will "deepen cooperation and extend development space in the Eurasian region," while the twenty first-Century Maritime Silk Road "will take China–ASEAN cooperation to new levels" (Xi 2013a, b). Official clarification regarding OBOR in 2015 further accentuated the regional focus of the initiative. According to the official position of the Chinese government, OBOR's objective is "to promote the connectivity" of different regions in Asia, Europea, and Africa and their adjacent seas (NDRC 2015). Michael Swain underlines this focus on particular regions by quoting Chinese sources:

> "Central Asia, Russia, South Asia, and Southeast Asian countries will be given priority consideration . . . while Middle Eastern and East African countries are in the junction" linking the Asian with European countries. The author adds that over the long term, "Europe, the Commonwealth of Independent States, and some African countries may also participate in cooperation". (Swaine 2015, p. 6)

As for the objectives, Chinese government documents outlining actions and visions for realizing OBOR illustrate these objectives:

> The initiative [...] is aimed at promoting orderly and free flow of economic factors, highly efficient allocation of resources and deep integration of markets; [...] and, jointly creating an open, inclusive and balanced regional economic cooperation that benefits all. (NDRC 2015)

---

[3] For a comprehensive account of comparative regionalism in world politics, see Börzel and Risse (2016).

[4] For presentation of OBOR as closely linked to the foreign policy thinking of Xi Jinping, see Fallon (2015), IISS (2015), and Godbole (2015).

The same document lists several regional cooperation instruments among mechanisms for realization of OBOR: SCO, ASEAN, APEC, ASEM, and CAREC. On a more substantial level, harmony of OBOR is maintained through "five links": unhampered trade, road links, currency circulation, linked-up policy, and links between people's hearts.[5] These announced objectives of OBOR and methods of realization fit well with traditional goals sought by regionalism projects in the modern world. Luk van Langenhove and Marchesi elaborated on three main objectives that are sought by different generations of contemporary regionalism: economic integration, regional governance of public goods, and regional actorness in international arena (Van Langenhove and Marchesi 2008). Although the first two objectives are more evident in the OBOR list of goals, successful realization of OBOR will surely lead to increasing importance of several Eurasian and Asian regional organizations as regional actors in world politics.

From these developments, it is evident that OBOR can be appropriately described as a regionalism project. Recent works by Chinese scholars tend to underline the regionalism aspects of the OBOR initiative. Wang Yiwei states that OBOR has three main objectives: (1) finding a way for global economic growth, (2) realizing global rebalancing, and (3) creating a new model for regional cooperation (Yiwei 2016). For Zeng Lingliang, the OBOR initiative relies on the two main instruments of regional integration and interstate partnership in order to realize a new model of regional community based on shared interests, shared destiny, and shared responsibilities (Lingliang 2016). Thus, theories and concepts forged by comparative regionalism scholars could be useful in furthering analysis of OBOR as a regionalism project.

7.3   OBOR AS A "FUNCTIONAL REGION" OF PROSPERITY AND PEACE: EMERGENCE OF NEW REGIONAL IDENTITIES IN EURASIA

Raimo Vayrynen distinguishes between two different types of regions, physical and functional. For him, "physical regions refer to territorial, military, and economic spaces controlled primarily by states. Functional

---

[5]This is description given by Michael Swaine. In the official document, these links are presented with slightly different wording: policy coordination, interconnectivity, unimpeded trade, financial integration, and people-to-people bond (Swaine 2015).

regions are defined by non-territorial factors such as culture and the market that are often the purview of non-state actors" (Väyrynen 2003). If we use these categories to ponder upon OBOR, how can it be conceptualized as a region? First, it is based on a physical notion of region. This is because it aims to link together several physical regions, such as Central Asia, Southeast Asia, and Europe. Its objective is to increase connectivity across Eurasia. OBOR depends also on willing cooperation of the states that control these spaces. The relevance of physical regions for OBOR is thus evident. However, it is not merely about linking several physical regions. The long-term aim of OBOR is to consolidate these linkages further and create a functional region, or even a megaregion. OBOR will "connect countries that represent 55% of world GNP, 70% of global population, and 75% of known energy reserves" (ECFR 2015). In another account, Beijing has estimated that the Belt and Road will eventually reach 4.4 billion people in more than 65 countries.[6]

At the same time, OBOR fits more with the description of a functional region. It aims to form an extended space of interconnectivity, unimpeded trade and financial integration, and a common space where people-to-people bonds are consolidated. It will be apt for realization of large-scale investment projects across countries along OBOR. Most importantly, the aim is for OBOR to become the main vehicle for integrating the development strategies of involved countries. In the long term, the aim is to achieve a "region of harmony, peace, and prosperity." In Zeng Lingliang's words, the OBOR initiative will realize a new model of regional community based on shared interests, shared destiny, and shared responsibilities. Use of the term of "regional community" implies not only creation of new trade and economic opportunities, but also a focus on values and distribution of responsibilities among participating countries.

If OBOR succeeds its launch on these premises, many target countries may be willing to join. One compelling reason could be that OBOR projects will help to forge new regional identities along the Road and Belt. The question of regional identity appears prominently in regionalism studies. An important contribution from this perspective is the work of Annsi Paasi. For him, regional identity is a key element in the making of regions as social and political spaces. We have to distinguish between a region's identity and regional identity. For Paasi, a region's identity is linked to external features of the region (for example, features of nature, culture, or

---

[6] Verlare and Van der Putten (2015).

people) by which other actors try to identify and distinguish one region from others. Regional identity is a "process consisting of the production of territorial boundaries, symbolism, and institutions" (Paasi 2003).

In the case of several regions that are today linked through OBOR, their regional identities were mainly forged through outside-in processes. Central Asia, a regional concept that is a historically imported concept, is an example of an outside-in regional identity where external actors identify it with such factors as authoritarianism, terrorism, and political instability. Central Asia is a clear example of an outside-in approach to regions, whereby powerful states name and shape regions according to their own purposes and interests.[7] Images of Africa and its subregions as lacking the capacity for collective action and failing to achieve economic development are corroborated by the realities of the region. Local governments must not only to tackle problems of socio-economic development, but must also address the necessity of correcting regional images in order to be attractive for foreign investments and international trade. From this perspective, the target countries and regions of OBOR will engage with the Chinese initiative with enthusiasm if they are convinced of successful launch and completion of the initiative. They would prefer to be perceived, from the outside, as parts of OBOR's dynamic space and thus acquire new "clean" regional identities. Positioning OBOR as an advocate of a "new type of international relations" based on the principle of wide consultation, joint contribution, and shared benefits may sound attractive for countries across Eurasia and Africa from several perspectives. Principles of consultation and joint contribution imply actorness of these states, which are traditionally viewed as passive actors in international politics. Principles of mutual respect and shared benefits could facilitate participation of these countries in the initiative, because they would perceive that their sovereignty concerns will be better addressed. Addressing issues of infrastructure, transportation, and logistics implies a comprehensive approach to economic development, which will be appreciated by these countries. The large number and diversity of participating countries is another attractive point of the initiative, because it will foster an image of OBOR as an inclusive project integrating both north–south and south–south relationships, promoting economic cooperation and cultural exchanges between different sets of countries.

---

[7] Qoraboyev (2010a). For outside-in construction of regions, see Neumann (1994) and Katzenstein (2005).

7.4   Conclusions

Approaching the OBOR initiative from the perspective of comparative regionalism studies helps to address several issues faced by OBOR in its early stages. First, comparative regionalism enables smooth communication between major regions covered by OBOR. Comparative regionalism studies were mainly inspired by successful experience of European integration. In recent years, scholarship on regionalism has been integrating the experiences of other regions of the world. From this perspective, the main premises of comparative regionalism and its theoretical and conceptual frameworks are shared and understood across different regions today. This is an important opportunity for OBOR because it is in need of a common language that will be understood in both the West and East. Comparative regionalism may well serve as such a common language. A shift to comparative regionalism, which includes discourse on both regional integration and regional cooperation, seems to be consolidating. Two recent works by Wang Yiwei and Zheng Lingliang rely on discussion of regionalism. Wang Yiwei focuses on the potential of OBOR for developing regional cooperation and regional integration in Eurasia. Zheng Lingliang emphasizes that OBOR may even carry regional integration further and achieve a coherent regional community. From these perspectives, comparative regionalism may be very relevant. "Functional regions" and "regional identity" are some examples from the vocabulary of comparative regionalism that may help develop discussion of OBOR as regional community. Focus on OBOR as a functional region may facilitate participation of a large number of countries located across different physical regions. It will also shape OBOR as an inclusive and dynamic space. Focus on comprehensive approaches to economic development could enable reshaping of regional identities across Asia, Europe, and Africa to enable inclusive mechanisms of intercontinental cooperation and integration.

References

Allison, R. (2008). Virtual regionalism, regional structures and regime security in Central Asia. *Central Asian Survey, 27*(2), 185–202.

Ambrosio, T. (2008). Catching the 'Shanghai Spirit': How the Shanghai cooperation organization promotes authoritarian norms in Central Asia. *Europe-Asia Studies, 60*(8), 1321–1344.

Bailes, A., Dunay, P., Guang, P., & Troitskiy, M. (2007). The Shanghai Cooperation Organization. *SIPRI Policy Paper* N° 17, Stockholm International Peace Research Institute.

Börzel, T., & Risse, T. (2016). *The Oxford handbook of comparative regionalism*. Oxford: Oxford University Press.

Breslin, S. (2016). China's global goals and roles: Changing the world from second place? *Asian Affairs, 47*(1), 59–70.

Callaghan, M., & Hubbard, P. (2016). The Asian infrastructure investment bank: Multilateralism on the Silk Road. *China Economic Journal, 9*(2), 116–139.

Collins, K. (2009). Economic and security regionalism among patrimonial authoritarian regimes: The case of Central Asia. *Europe-Asia Studies, 61*(2): 249–281.

Dadabaev, T. (2014). Shanghai Cooperation Organization (SCO) regional identity formation from the perspective of the Central Asia States. *Journal of Contemporary China, 23*(85), 102–118.

ECFR. (2015). One belt, one road: China's great leap outward. *China Analysis.*

European Parliament Directorate-General for External Policies. (2012). Old games, new players: Russia, China and the struggle for mastery in Central Asia. *Policy briefing.*

Fallon, T. (2015). The new Silk Road Xi Jinping's grand strategy for Eurasia. *American Foreign Policy Interests, 37*(3), 140–147.

Flikke, G., & Wilhelmsen, J. (2008). Central Asia: A testing ground for new great-power relations. *NUPI Report.* Norwegian Institute of International Affairs.

Godbole, A. (2015). China's Asia strategy under president Xi Jinping. *Strategic Analysis, 39*(3): 298–302.

Godehart, N. (2016). No end history: A Chinese alternative concept of international order? *SWP Research Paper.*

Hancock, K., & Libman, A. (2016). Eurasia. *The Oxford Handbook of Comparative Regionalism,* 202–224.

IISS. (2015). China's ambitious Silk Road vision. *Strategic Comments, 21*(6): iv–v.

Katzenstein, P. (2005). *A world of regions: Asia and Europe in the American imperium.* Ithaca: Cornell University Press.

Kavalski, E. (2007). Partnership or rivalry between the EU, China and India in Central Asia: The normative power of regional actors with global aspirations. *European Law Journal, 13*(6), 839–856.

Koh, T. (2015, August 4). 21st century maritime Silk Road. *The Strait Times.*

Laruelle, M., & Peyrouse, S. (2012). Regional organizations in Central Asia: Patterns of interaction, dilemmas of efficiency. *Institute of Public Policy and Administration Working paper.*

Mouton, J., & Marais, C. H. (1996). *Basic concepts in the methodology of the social sciences.* Pretoria: HSRC Press.

National Development and Reform Commission. (2015). Vision and Actions on Jointly Building Silk Road Economic Belt and 21st-Century Maritime Silk Road. Document issued by National Development and Reform Commission,

Ministry of Foreign Affairs, and Ministry of Commerce of the People's Republic of China, with State Council authorisation.

Neumann, I. (1994). A region-building approach to Northern Europe. *Review of International Studies, 20*(1), 53–74.

Paasi, A. (2003). Region and place: Regional identity in question. *Progress in Human Geography, 27*(4), 475–485.

Qoraboyev, I. (2010a). Around the names of regions: The case of Central Asia. *UNU-CRIS Working Papers.*

Qoraboyev, I. (2010b). From Central Asian regional integration to eurasian integration space? Changing dynamics of post-soviet regionalism. *Eurasian Integration Yearbook*, 210–211.

Swaine, M. (2015). Chinese views and commentary on the "One Belt, One Road" initiative. *China Leadership Monitor, 47.*

Van Langenhove, L., & Marchesi, D. (2008). The Lisbon Treaty and the emergence of third generation regional integration. *European Journal of Law Reform, 10*(4), 477–496.

Väyrynen, R. (2003). Regionalism: Old and new. *International Studies Review, 5*(1), 25–51.

Verlare, J., & Van der Putten, F. P. (2015). One belt, one road: An opportunity for the EU's security strategy. *The Clingendael Policy Brief.*

Xi, J. (2013, September 7). Promote friendship between our peoples and work together to build a bright future. Speech at Nazarbayev University, Astana.

Xi, J. (2013, October 3). Speech to Indonesian Parliament, Jakarta.

Yiwei, W. (2016). *The belt and road initiative. What will China offer the world in its rise?* New World Press.

Lingliang, Z. (2016). Conceptual analysis of China's belt and road initiative: A road towards a regional community of common destiny. *Chinese Journal of International Law, 15*(3), 517–541.

PART III

Economic Cooperation in the "Belt and Road" Initiative

CHAPTER 8

Political Economics of the New Silk Road

Balázs Sárvári and Anna Szeidovitz

8.1 ONE BELT, ONE ROAD AS ONE WORLD, ONE ORDER

The Silk Road project is a key element of a "new round of opening to the world" as the Chinese strategy, defined by Xi Jinping, reveals the goals and barriers of the country's global responsibility.

Our age is the transition period during which China is being included in the globalization process. Although the global networks will have more and more Chinese characteristics as a result of China's intensifying presence, the concrete process is how China joins globalization and not how China modifies the current workflow or how China spreads its own global narrative around the world. In other words, "China is seeking to 'supplement' the existing international order rather than to revise it" (Godement 2015, p. 2). This restructuring does not mean weakening of the USA, but a turn to global partnership, which empowers developing countries.

B. Sárvári (✉) · A. Szeidovitz
Corvinus University of Budapest, Budapest, Hungary

B. Sárvári
Rector, Saint Ignatius Jesuit College, Budapest, Hungary

© The Author(s) 2018
Y. Cheng et al. (eds.), *The Belt & Road Initiative in the Global Arena*,
https://doi.org/10.1007/978-981-10-5921-6_8

117

It is essential to differentiate China's One Belt, One Road initiative (*yidai yilu*, hereafter OBOR) from any alliances because there are no direct political strings attached (Brugier 2014; Hansen 2012). On one side, this refers to national concerns, and on the other side to global geopolitical challenges. The rhythm of the Chinese economy means a continuously increasing need for resources and markets, and hence a need for a progressive policy that ensures this broad meaning of national security. It already includes maintaining the infrastructure and the institutions needed for China's sustainable development (Geeraerts 2011, p. 58).

Because "Foreign Minister Wang Yi said that 'economic imbalances' are the root causes of conflict and that China should provide more 'public goods' to mitigate them" (Godement 2015, p. 7), it is possible to make a comparison of the OBOR initiative with the Marshall Plan, which used similar rhetoric (Xie 2014). In his speech at Harvard University (5 June 1947), George C. Marshall stated, "Our policy is directed not against any country or doctrine but against hunger, poverty, desperation, and chaos." Next to the above-mentioned similarity, there are also basic differences between the initiatives. The goal of the American project was to prevent the escalation of a new World War by consolidating the poverty in Europe and containing the Soviet Union. The Chinese initiative aims to build a strong partnership with the EU that fits the new global order, use market rules to pacify the (potential) conflict zones that routes will cross, and develop its poor western regions by linking them into the world economy.

In European countries, there was a lack of investment and a need to alter their relations after the economic downturn of 2007. This motivated them to intensify relations with China (Inotai 2010, 2011b, 2014; Txabarriaga 2010; Zheng 2015). China's economic presence in the region is highly connected to the modern Silk Road concept, which will be fully realized in about 35 years. A recent report (Li 2014) describes how this could coincide with the centenary of the foundation of the People's Republic of China (2049). The historical timing has special meaning because it is understood as one of the first steps of China's high-profile diplomacy (Huang 2015). China–EU relations are an essential milestone on the road that China is pursuing within the global framework.

All these factors indicate a complete geopolitical plan (Gervai et al. 2015). Its economic side is motivated by disillusionment with the effectiveness of Western institutions. Until the beginning of the economic crisis, Western economies, and mainly the USA, were accepted as the powers responsible for the balance of the global economy. The downturn served as a wake-up call for China to take its part in rebalancing these imbalances through initiatives such as OBOR. China decided to accept the law of globalization and to fill the given void. China is adapting to the change in global governance, which turns the OBOR concept into a contribution to the stability of the new world order.

It is necessary to build a supply-based commercial system that differs from the historical Silk Road, which was an organically developed infrastructure to meet foreign demand for Chinese silk. The idea of the OBOR comes from China, more concretely from its understanding of the distribution of global power in the twenty-first century. This time, unlike ancient or medieval times when cultural exchange was subsidiary, the production process will follow geopolitical planning and a global vision (China Institute in America 2015; Felföldi 2009; Juhász 2015; Karluk and Karaman 2014; Liu 2010; Trautmann 1999; Waugh 2015; Wood 2002). This normative convergence is the primary goal and forms the political side of the OBOR intitiative.

It is a much deeper strategy than a simple cost–benefit analysis and shows that China did not simply import the laws of classic capitalism. China's cultural heritage is the source of this development, and the OBORproject is a pragmatic tool in that regard. This proves that common global interests are the sources of competitiveness. Hence, it is a misunderstanding to explain this or any other Chinese project as a regime-changing tool, as expressed by Zhang Jun:

> Clearly, China has faced major challenges within the existing global system as it tries to carve out a role befitting its economic might. That may explain why, with its "One Belt, One Road" initiative and its establishment of the Asian Infrastructure Investment Bank (AIIB), China's government is increasingly attempting to recast the world order – in particular, the monetary and trading systems – on its own terms (Zhang 2015).

The Sino-European partnership has vast strategic potential. China is increasingly suspected of being a Trojan horse in the European Union because its growing activity could weaken the continent's political economic power. However, that is far from Chinese interests. Consideration of the complexity of the phenomenon needs to take into account (1) China is not a leading power in Europe and (2) it does not have the capacity to serve as a dividing force. The suspicious rhetoric does not harmonize with Chinese foreign policy guidelines that promote a strong and united Europe, because only this can maintain the international environment for sustainable development of the Chinese economy and society. From a European point of view, the normative convergence of a global vision at a European level is difficult, not to mention the strain of merging it with the Chinese vision. It is false to think of Europe as a single entity. In reality, various national interests compete against each other and many cultural restraints hinder the creation of a single common European standpoint.

China currently has interests in a multipolar world instead of an America-dominated unipolar one. This view highlights the role of a prosperous and strong EU because "it is the most likely candidate to become another pole" (Turcsányi 2014). As Geeraerts expresses it, "The unipolar moment is definitely fading and slowly giving way to an international system characterized by multilayered and culturally diversified polarity" (Geeraerts 2011, p. 57).

To further the OBOR, the Chinese government has set up two institutions, the Asian Infrastructure and Investment Bank (AIIB) and the Silk Road Fund. The AIIB was set up with 50 members, including countries outside Asia. Like many other aspects of the OBOR, the AIIB will become fully operational in the future, intended for use by the end of 2015. Its authorized capital is US$100 billion (by comparison, shareholders of the World Bank own over US$250 billion) (The World Bank Treasury). The Silk Road Fund Co Ltd. is a US$40 billion fund dedicated exclusively to developing the transport and trade links in countries and regions along the Silk Road (Fung Business Intelligence Centre 2015, p. 8). Other regional funds have also been set up, such as the China–ASEAN Investment Cooperation Fund (for Southeast Asia) and the China–CEE Investment Cooperation Fund (for Central and Eastern Europe), which assist China's large international infrastructure construction policies (van der Putten and Meijnders 2015, p. 31). The latter is endowed with US$3 billion and was announced in December 2014 with the aim of enhancing cooperation, including plans to construct "a new corridor of interconnectivity" (Rolland 2015, p. 2).

Even if these concepts seem to be well founded, we should acknowledge both aspects of China's benefit from its presence in the region: the short-term goal of economic self-enrichment and the long-term (geo) political goals. Only the future will show how China will use its influence to push its interests.

8.2   THE SILK ROAD ECONOMIC BELT

Xi Jinping delivered a speech at Nazarbayev University in Kazakhstan entitled "Promote People-to-People Friendship and Create a Better Future," which outlined China's foreign policy toward its (foremost) immediate neighbors (Ministry of Foreign Affairs of the People's Republic of China 2013). He revealed a regional cooperation plan with the Central Asian nations revolving around a pentagram of collective issues: communication, connectivity, trade facilitation, enhancement of monetary circulation, and strengthened people-to-people exchanges. In essence, the five complementary elements create a tighter economic bond between the region's economies to the extent where China cannot become an estranged member. Two methods to achieve this bond were disclosed, the Silk Road Economic Belt and the 21st-Century Maritime Silk Road.

The Belt and the Road together "create an economic cooperation area that stretches from the Western Pacific to the Baltic Sea" (Fung Business Intelligence Centre 2015, p. 3). The Belt railroad has various proposed routes (outlined in the following section) but, in general, it is directed from the Chinese coast toward the West, through China's Xinjiang province and the Central Asian countries into Eastern Europe, the destination being the Baltic Sea. The Maritime Silk Road is a sea-trade route to Europe, which complements the Belt but incorporates China's Southeast Asian neighbors and the Indian Ocean's coastal states. The two together not only tie China unconditionally into the trade circuit of Europe and Asia, but also promote it into a country that acts unambiguously on its global responsibility.

Before discussing details of the Silk Road Economic Belt, several elements of the current state of affairs must be highlighted. First, this proposal was initially intended to reinforce relationships between China and its neighbors; thus, the global initiative that has evolved from this plan is subordinate to it. Second, the proposal in its current form is not definite, "rather it is an umbrella concept under which many inter-related projects will be converging" (Vangeli 2015, p. 21). Explicitly speaking, there is no blueprint of the intended trade routes and hubs, nor is there a comprehensive collection of international agreements backing the initiative. At the time of writing, what we have is a fluid concept encompassing many countries and multiple potential routes, all converging under the label of OBOR. Third, and stemming from the above, the proposal is not solely economic and trade-related; in the future, this initiative also aims to enclose other social, cultural, and security areas. Last, at present, the first stage of the Chinese proposal focuses on building an infrastructure network that will later flourish to become a ferry for ideas and goods. For this reason, Chinese investment and infrastructure development is currently the priority.

8.3   INFRASTRUCTURAL PERSPECTIVES

Trade via railroads between East Asia and Europe only accounts for 3.0–3.5% of the total trade between the continents. This is a trifling percentage in comparison with the 95–96% of the trade conducted by sea (Erdősi 2015, p. 109). Furthermore, transport by land is significantly more expensive than transportation by sea. This is primarily due to the long delays at the borders caused by bureaucracy, tariffs, and logistical ineptitude. Yet, what brings so much potential to the Silk Road Economic Belt is the shorter journey that could be achieved by high-speed railway (van der Putten and Meijnders 2015, p. 28). Maritime transportation takes roughly 2.5–3 weeks, but the duration is only 13–15 days by land. This, coupled with China's need to diversify its overdependence on sea transportation in foreign trade, indicates the initiative's importance (Liu 2014, p. 3). Analyzing the advantages and disadvantages of various forms of transport, transportation by land is more expensive; thus, this route is reserved for more expensive and valuable commodities that are immune to colder weathers but sensitive to sea travel. In terms of Chinese aims, the purpose of rejuvenating the Silk Road through the OBOR initiative is not first and foremost intended to improve cost-efficiency. Rather, it proposes to incorporate China's western region into the global economy, thereby geopolitically partaking in the establishment of a multipolar world order.

There are currently two main routes connecting China to Europe, the Trans-Siberian Railroad and the Second/New Eurasian Continental Bridge. The Trans-Siberian Railroad runs almost exclusively through Russia, between Vladivostok and Rotterdam, and is not considered part of the Chinese proposal. The New Eurasian Continental Bridge runs from Lianyungang to Rotterdam and is the main target of the Silk Road Economic Belt initiative. Some also raise the possibility of a third (southern) Eurasian land bridge, but this is merely hypothetical because of the brutal physical difficulties and high cost of its establishment, especially

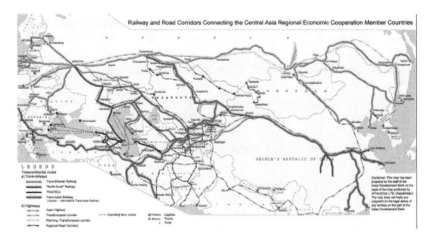

Fig. 8.1 Railway and road corridors connecting China and Europe. *Source* Central Asia Regional Economic Cooperation (edited by author)

as the maritime route is nearby (Erdősi 2015). From the Chinese viewpoint, the Eurasian Continental Bridge is the main route connecting East to West, which is to be supplemented by several smaller north–south corridors along the route to connect more areas into the initiative and to international trade (van der Putten and Meijnders 2015, p. 25).

Currently, there are various routes in use connecting China to Europe: the YuXinOu railway between Chongqing, China through Duisburg, Germany to Antwerp, Belgium; the fast (12-day journey) Rongou railway between Chengdu and Lodz, Poland; the Zhengzhou railway between Hamburg and Zhengzhou (Railway Gazette 2015); the HanXinOu railway connecting Wuhan, Hubei province with Lodz, Poland; and the YuXinOu railway, which starts at Yiwu, Zhejiang Province and ends in Madrid, Spain (Fig. 8.1) (Dawber 2015). "All of these railways are designed for cargo trains transporting goods between China and Europe, and are said to effectively help save costs and time" (Men 2015, p. 13).

The Chinese aim is to build a single, uniform railroad perhaps toward Iran or Turkey, which would be completely independent (Erdősi 2015, p. 120). The main aim of the Chinese efforts to develop the New Eurasian Continental Bridge is to bypass Russia and counter the monopoly it has on trade (Erdősi 2015, p. 116). The proposal, also known as the TRACECA Silk Wind train route, aims to connect Central Asia with

Turkey through Azerbaijan and Georgia, which (according to the plans) would significantly decrease the cost and time of transportation between China and Europe. It "aims to construct new high-speed multimodal container transit routes with advanced technologies such as electronic information exchange, simplification of border crossing procedures, and reduction of transportation time" (Fedorenko 2013, p. 17).

The Silk Wind would cross Kazakhstan, use a ferry across the Caspian Sea between Aktau and Baku, diverge toward the Black Sea, and cross northern Turkey through Istanbul into Europe. This would amount to an estimated 11–12 day journey and cost about half the Chongqing–Duisburg journey (National Secretariat of IGC TRACECA in the Republic of Kazakhstan 2012). However, the route's development depends on various hurdles, such as switching between gauges at border crossings, a ferry across the Caspian Sea, the Kars–Edirne railway traversing Turkey, and the rail tunnel under the Bosporus. In terms of China's geopolitical strategy in the region, the hurdles are peripheral.

Chinese interests in joining the new world order include the growth of developing neighboring regions and the problems involved in its venture. The long-term goal for China is construction of a new high-speed railway from China to the UK through Kazakhstan, Uzbekistan, Turkmenistan, Iran, Turkey, Bulgaria, Romania, Hungary, Austria, Germany, Belgium, and France. The project is estimated to cost around US$150 billion and should be finished between 2020 and 2025 (van der Putten and Meijnders 2015, p. 27).

Nonetheless, at the moment, the path of Chinese efforts remains ambivalent; the Eastern half of the route is roughly fixed, but the Western half (especially the entry to the EU) remains undecided. There are two possible routes that the initiative can take: (1) China–Central Asia–Russia–Europe or (2) China–Central Asia–West Asia/Persian Gulf–Mediterranean.

The European railway infrastructure is relatively well endowed, but large infrastructure development projects are needed in the Central Eastern European countries because they "lack unified standards." Furthermore, the technical elements of the railways (double track rate and electrification of railway lines) are not in sync with Chinese railways, which impedes the uninterrupted transport, storage, and handling of goods (Liu 2014, p. 11).

The establishment of good Sino-European relations is an element of the new multipolar world order currently under construction in China's regional geopolitical strategy. By this reasoning, cooperation in multiple elements, as outlined by Xi Jinping, and the establishment of uniformity in relations are symbolized by building of the OBOR. The flow of ideas and goods, which promotes "people-to-people friendship and creates a better future" begins with the creation of unimpeded traffic, as symbolized by the construction of a single, uniform, synchronized railway line. These developments serve as a possibility for Chinese investment in the region, which in some instances has already begun.

China's infrastructure development policy has long incorporated the element of connecting ports and railways (van der Putten and Meijnders 2015, p. 28). Because the Maritime Silk Road and the Economic Belt are complementary, there are efforts to connect the two in the Greek Piraeus hub (van der Putten and Meijnders 2015, p. 14). Chinese investment in the Greek port started in 2009, when the Chinese state-owned enterprise China Ocean Shipping Company (COSCO) obtained a 35-year concession to operate piers II and III of the port.[1] The large investments resulted in a fivefold increase in container throughput and substantially higher efficiency (van der Putten and Meijnders 2015, pp. 10–11). This, coupled with the improved transit capacity of the port and its connection to the national railway lines, has resulted in the port's development into a major hub of the eastern Mediterranean. It now functions as the "world's fastest growing container port" and is pivotal to China's policy for the eastern Mediterranean (Vangeli 2015, p. 24). To further this development, the Chinese government has announced the intended construction of a high-speed railway from Piraeus to Budapest[2] via Skopje and Belgrade (van der Putten and Meijnders 2015, p. 28).

Another line is also being proposed, which would connect the port of Constanta on the Black Sea to Vienna through Bucharest and Budapest (van der Putten and Meijnders 2015, p. 28). Development of Sino-European relations through the construction of railway lines in southeastern Europe is an example of China's geopolitical strategy in the region. The partnership it tries to establish fits the new global political order, which converges on common global interests.

---

[1] Pier I remained in the ownership of the Greek state-owned Piraeus Port Authority.

[2] The Chinese, Hungarian, and Serbian Prime Ministers decided in November 2013 to reconstruct the Budapest–Belgrade railway from Chinese capital. In September 2015, the Hungarian Prime Minister Viktor Orbán empowered his ministers to finalize the construction plan with the People's Republic of China.

The first phase of the OBOR initiative is establishment of the infrastructure necessary for development, including rail, highway, aviation, and maritime infrastructure (Liu 2014, p. 6). Under the OBOR initiative, these construction projects are primarily financed, constructed, supplied, and operated by Chinese state-owned firms, or firms close to the Chinese government.[3] Southern Europe boasts especially amiable ties with China. Countries such as Greece, Portugal, Cyprus, and Malta are home to large- and mid-scale Chinese investments.[4] Once finished, these firms would have a high degree of influence over the transportation network. From a Chinese perspective, this would maintain the stability of the flow of trade and further enable the government to allow alternative routes by which trade could take place. What would essentially manifest is a strong Chinese influence and the dependence of others on these trade routes (van der Putten and Meijnders 2015, p. 32).

Most of the goods traded between the EU and China are manufactured goods. Currently, the YuXinOu railway connects Asia's largest laptop production base in Chongqing with Europe. The main goods it transports to Europe are IT products. However, a common feature of all railway lines is the lack of return trips from Europe to China. There are numerous reasons for this discrepancy. First, the Chinese destinations are not distribution hubs; in comparison with maritime trade, which localizes around ports that are simultaneously distribution hubs, it costs too much to transport the imported goods to other cities via international railways (Maxxelli Consulting 2015). Second, due to its infancy, publicity is not yet wide enough and many Chinese firms do not want to relinquish alternatives already in use. What many already understand is that unless the value of Chinese exports increases, the proposed railroad investment would be deficient (Erdősi 2015, p. 120).

What spikes up the cost of transportation by railway is the lack of goods on the return journeys from Europe and the inefficient modes of transport of various goods. Furthermore, government subsidies for hubs in various Chinese provinces have led to distorted prices and unbalanced competition in the market (Liu 2014, p. 8). However, in spite of the current state of affairs, the Chinese foreign policy's geopolitical strategy of connecting into the new world order and endowing it with

---

[3] van der Putten and Meijnders (2015), p. 8.
[4] Vangeli (2015), p. 24.

both Western and Chinese characteristics dominates the short-term cost inefficiency.

8.4   China–Eastern European Relations: Trade, Investment, and Politics

EU–Chinese relations were established in 1975 and since then the two partners have developed cooperation in various fields. The EU is especially important to China as its largest trade partner and host of the maritime corridor to the USA (van der Putten and Meijnders 2015, p. 29). Within this framework, Central Eastern Europe has the theoretical possibility to enjoy amicable relations with China that are not plagued by historical conflicts or outstanding issues (Liu 2014, p. 2).

The importance of Central Eastern Europe for China lies in its possibility to become a threefold gateway to Europe, geographically, cooperatively, and brand-wise (Liu 2014, p. 7). The physical placement of Central Europe makes it unavoidable in the path of the Economic Belt. Furthermore, its mentality and capabilities bridge the two potential partners, making it easier for Chinese companies to enter the EU market. This, however, must not be mistaken for overall Chinese dependence on the EU. The Chinese government at present has "an increased ability to influence which routes the trade between China and the EU flows," and is simultaneously developing routes toward Africa and the Middle East that bypass Europe (van der Putten and Meijnders 2015, p. 6).

The Chinese OBOR program provides a structure that allows Chinese diplomatic, commercial, and foreign infrastructure policies around the world to expand Chinese exports and access to raw materials, and obtain new markets for Chinese trade and investment (van der Putten and Meijnders 2015, p. 29). In effect, China can concurrently contribute to Eastern Europe's rise and to a new, more balanced Europe.

8.4.1   Trade

Trade between the EU and China is on the rise and exceeded US$615 billion in 2014, an increase of 9.9% over the previous year (Yang 2015, p. 6). At present, the trade balance of the EU10 with China remains significantly negative. There is a threefold difference between EU imports from and exports to China, a proportion that is slightly improved by the fact that many of the imports contribute to higher value-added re-exports to Western Europe (Matura 2012, p. 108). German exports to China make up 47% of the EU total, a ratio in which its Eastern European counterparts remain strikingly at a disadvantage. The EU10's share of trade to China was only slightly more than 3.5% (Matura 2012, p. 108). There is great potential for Eastern European trade with China, but it is hindered by the inability of Eastern European enterprises to meet Chinese quantity demands.

The Ukraine and Belarus, two countries whose geographical position bridges the Silk Road Economic Belt with Russia and Central Asia, have the potential to offer China agricultural produce, and military and advanced technology in return for investment (Vangeli 2015, p. 24). China has already invested several billion dollars in multiple Ukrainian projects, of which an industrial and technology park is of salient importance (Vangeli 2015, p. 24). The Western Balkan countries are of great potential for Chinese investment. The countries are not yet members of the EU and therefore relatively poor and "more flexible" regarding eligibility for Chinese developmental aid (Vangeli 2015, p. 23). Alternatively, they might be considered a disadvantageous investment in the eyes of Chinese investors because of their lack of EU membership (Matura 2012, p. 107).

8.4.2   Investment

In terms of investment, the Chinese became net capital exporters in 2014 when Chinese outward direct investment (ODI) overtook inward foreign direct investment(FDI) (KPMG 2015, p. 10).

Policies of the European countries toward China in the era before the financial crisis can be categorized into four groups: ideological free-traders, assertive industrialists, accommodating mercantilists, and European followers (Matura 2012, p. 106). The first group stressed the importance of politics, without diminishing trade relations. The assertive industrialists were willing to confront both political and economic issues. The third group aimed to create good economic relations with China in the hope of that spilling over to other areas of cooperation. Finally, the last group deferred their relations with China to the EU. The financial crisis significantly opened the state of minds of the region's leaders, and their policies became increasingly more economically liberal toward China (Matura 2012, p. 106). As the region's traditional partners (the USA and Western Europe) had rescinded, the region was in desperate need of FDI (Vangeli 2015, p. 23). This is visible in recent statistics, such as "Chinese investment in the EU reached US$9.41 billion in the first 11 months of 2014, a nearly threefold increase" (Yang 2015, p. 6).

The recent trend in Chinese ODI is that, as the Chinese economy develops and becomes more innovative, investment destinations are also beginning to change from resource-rich developing countries to developed countries. At present, the top ten countries receiving Chinese ODI are USA, Peru, UK, Australia, France, Italy, Singapore, Portugal, Canada, and the Netherlands (KPMG 2015, p. 12). This trend is especially convenient for Europe and, to some extent, Central Eastern Europe as well.

On the other hand, although Chinese FDI to the EU is a real phenomenon, it remains comparatively insignificant. In 2010, Chinese investments in the EU exceeded US$12 billion, but the total level of FDI to the EU in that year was US$6,890 billion; Chinese investment equaled less than 1% (Matura 2012, p. 106). In the EU10 countries, Chinese investments only amounted to US$828 million, which equaled 0.12% of the total FDI in that region (Matura 2012, p. 106). As the transition of Central Eastern European states ensued from their accession to the EU, most of the flow of Chinese capital has tended to seep to the subregion of the Commonwealth of Independent States (Matura 2012, p. 107). The potential of Central Eastern Europe is in its advantageous geographic location and infrastructure, which have value for Chinese investors who plan to export to the EU (Matura 2012, p. 108).

The above phenomenon is only slightly outbalanced by the Bilateral Investment Agreement with the EU, which the Chinese chose as replacement for the plethora of investment treaties (Stahl 2015, p. 18). This new and ambitious initiative is currently under negotiation and will serve as a two-way investment opportunity that would greatly serve China's economy and, in the event of slower Chinese economic growth, would help bring stability (Schweisgut 2015, p. 9).

8.4.3   Politics

China and the EU are celebrating the 40th anniversary of their relationship this year. The two entities have dealt with both positive and negative elements during their relationship, including the Iranian nuclear issue, climate change, and international trade negotiations (Yang 2015,

p. 6). The main constituents of the countries' relationship are outlined in the *China-EU 2020 Strategic Agenda for Cooperation*. The Agenda was agreed upon in 2013 and serves as the basis and the main document of the future EU–China Summit (Schweisgut 2015, p. 8). It comprises four pillars: peace and security, prosperity, sustainable development, and people-to-people exchanges. These include various areas of cooperation such as trade and investment, agriculture, industry and information, transport and infrastructure, and urbanization.

Chinese and European leaders share common interests related to foreign policy, namely "the necessity to invest in infrastructures in regions that still need to create the enabling framework to raise their income and access international markets" (Schweisgut 2015, p. 9). Within this context, the EU welcomes the OBOR Chinese initiative, although it places inherently large emphasis on reinforcing competitiveness and a requisite for transparent bidding processes (Schweisgut 2015, p. 9). This, however, can also become a source of political friction, because European companies will receive heightened foreign competition and there is the possibility that Chinese state-owned enterprises will be unable to comply with EU norms (Vangeli 2015, p. 26).

Regarding the Silk Road, cooperation between China and Europe has the possibility to run on three platforms: Central Eastern European countries, the EU, and the Asia–Europe Meeting (ASEM). The cooperative mechanism between China and CEE countries is the primary mode of communication between China and the EU (Liu 2014, p. 4). This is primarily a result of the Eastern European countries' foreign policies of "opening East." However, there is a lack of common EU policy toward China in EU Member States.

Bilateral relations, such as the "16+1" summits, have the possibility of fracturing unanimous EU positions. These summits between the heads of government of 16 CEE countries and China have quasi-institutionalized the cooperation and are relatively important within the Chinese Foreign Affairs Ministry (Stahl 2015, p. 18). Chinese scholars believe that the 16+1 is "crucial" in enhancing the connectivity between Asia and Europe, thereby facilitating the Silk Road (Vangeli 2015, p. 23). Yet, CEEcountries are in competition for Chinese investment (Matura 2012, p. 105). Furthermore, because the region does not have a cooperative China policy, the Chinese have the ability to cherry-pick the best offers (Matura 2012, p. 105).

8.5   GLOBAL POLITICAL CONTEXT

8.5.1   Chinese Interests

China has numerous interests in promoting the Silk Road Economic Belt. Most importantly, the Belt serves to develop the western regions; China sees the Silk Road and the establishment of transportation infrastructure as the answer to developing its western region and the neighboring Central Asian nations. In the future, trade liberalization and monetary cooperation will serve as the basis of a new regional economic community, with new regional hubs and large industrial parks (Rolland 2015, p. 1). The basis of the initiative is that transcontinental connectivity could "boost trade, stimulate technological development, and transform the strategic landscape" (Rolland 2015, p. 2). At present, the western autonomous Ujghur region of the country is lagging in growth compared with the coast. Historically, this area had not enjoyed positive relations with the Chinese leadership, spurring social tensions that amounted to security threats. The government is trying to resolve these issues through embracing the region in the Chinese economy. The market on the other hand is still irresponsive to developing that region and there is a large discrepancy between the amount of FDI that the eastern and western regions receive. Although Central China is becoming a more popular investment destination (7.5% registered FDI growth in 2014), the western provinces are behind with a registered 1.6% growth in 2014 (KPMG 2015, p. 27).

Another reason why this initiative is important to China is the questionable future of the Chinese economy (Wang 2015; Yanchun 2015). The main concerns are about economic growth and to what extent domestic consumption could be a pillar of that, especially as China did not achieve its trade objectives in the last three years. However, although it is popular to state that China is giving up its export-oriented model, this is far from reality. Following the global economic crisis and the emergence of its middle class, the government urged a shift to a consumption-led economy, but this does not mean that China has given up its export targets.

From 1979 onwards, China—as a developing country—chose export-oriented development as a sustainable development model. In comparison, many other developing countries focused on increasing their domestic demand. The Chinese model proved to be successful; yet, from

2006, the financial crisis coupled with pressure from the EU and USA, along with Chinese priorities, prompted China to focus its growth on increasing domestic demand.

However, the shift from an export-oriented growth model to one relying on domestic demand is not instantaneous. Currently, the Chinese economy still has abundant resources in terms of an educated labor force, infrastructure, small and medium-sized enterprises (SMEs), and a strong domestic propensity to save, which foreshadow a dual growth path of both increasing domestic demand and exports (Freedholm 2011; Jia 2015). Not only does switching to domestic demand rely heavily on households to reduce savings and focus on consumption, but also collides with the goals of Chinese SMEs that were able to enter the international market. The Chinese strategy of the twenty-first century to establish a strong institutional background and quick decision-making go hand-in-hand with development of the export-oriented model. As Inotai argues, China will shift its economic policy from being simply export-driven (that China had chosen as a single country among the big developing states) to a more balanced structure (Inotai 2011a). Chinese exports will not decrease while the government motivates increased consumption, hand-in-hand with increased imports.

Growth of the tertiary sector has become the driver of the economy, accounting for 48.2% of Chinese economic output in 2014, whereas the manufacturing sector displayed a negative trend (KPMG 2015, p. 26): "China's economic restructuring [focuses on the following segments of the economy: infrastructure investment, SMEs, real estate, service sector, agriculture, financing cost, exports] is creating more development potential for private capital, especially small and medium enterprises" (KPMG 2015, p. 5).

A further positive element for China is the possibility of securing energy resources from its western neighbors, which could minimize the state's reliance on the Strait of Malacca (Rolland 2015, p. 2). Although the OBOR policy indicates that China does not solely view Central Asia as the provider of energy resources, China is willing to provide generous loans to Central Asian countries to develop their gas fields. It has already provided US$4 billion to Turkmenistan and US$5 billion to Kazakhstan (Fedorenko 2013, p. 13). In return for the financial aid provided by Beijing to its neighbors and the development of their transport and communications infrastructures through contracts and subsidies for China's national railcar manufacturer, Kazakhstan will strengthen its position in foreign competition and advance in overseas markets (Rolland 2015, p. 2). Transparent bidding processes are a prerequisite within the EU, which would increase Chinese companies' competitiveness in that region (Schweisgut 2015, p. 9).

However, following a micro- and macroeconomic approach, there are significant criticisms of Chinese planning. Many scholars (e.g., Anbound, Xu Gao) point out that the new concept of three commercial directions (east, west, and south) is beyond Chinese capacity. They warn that the western route is logical but further diversification will disperse Chinese resources; meanwhile, China does not have an advantage in competitiveness compared with ASEAN countries. As Xu (Xu 2014) argues, this project is a "micro-hazard" because it makes huge investments in infrastructure, which already represent a quarter of China's total investment, and offers low returns and thus a potential debt crisis.

8.5.2   Central Asian Interests

Central Asian economies are beginning to rely heavily on China. From a Chinese viewpoint, the basis of their relationship is to secure and diversify its supply of energy. In this regard, the "proximity and abundant resources of Central Asia makes the region a perfect business partner" (Fedorenko 2013, p. 14). As a form of repayment, China provides investment. For Kazakhstan, entry to the world market is possible via China, which has become the country's primary recipient of its minerals and other raw materials (Erdősi 2015, p. 122). China's dominance in the region has become apparent. The "infrastructure for oil" barter exchange has led many Chinese companies to battle with the high altitude and build railroads, paying for oil and other raw materials with preferential loans (Erdősi 2015, p. 119). China is also planning to convert the Kyrgyz railway from Russian track gauge sizes to the international standard (Fedorenko 2013, p. 14).

On the one hand, the Central Asian states are delighted by Chinese investment; on the other hand, they do not want to rely exclusively on China (Fedorenko 2013, p. 14). In this regard, the Silk Road project, if it runs toward Iran and Turkey, would help secure a market for the grain produce of the Central Asian states (Erdősi 2015, p. 122). This is just one example of the possibilities that the Silk Road Economic Belt could bring to the region, which at present has only limited links to international trade (Laruelle 2015; Tao 2014).

8.5.3   Russian Interests

Russia's main interest in the Silk Road project is to continue securing its interests (a legacy of the Soviet Union) in Central Asia. To that end, following the collapse of the USSR, the region received ample aid from Russia, which means to prolong those investments and maintain ties with the region (Fedorenko 2013, p. 15).

Because of the inherently different trade practices of Russia and China, the Second Eurasian Continental Bridge has little direct impact on Russian interests. Russia relies on the Trans-Siberian railroad to transport raw materials eastward to satisfy China's demand. This relationship is unlikely to be changed (Erdősi 2015, p. 121). Instead, Russia is focusing on the Eurasian Union. Through this initiative, it aims to continue holding the Central Asian states within its sphere of influence (Fedorenko 2013, p. 16).

8.5.4   US Interests

The USA also has a New Silk Road strategy in the region, which was revealed in 2011. Its primary focus is the political stability of Afghanistan and its neighbors. Afghanistan needs integration into the world economy, which is to be done in much the way as China is doing in Central Asia—by building infrastructure to enable that (Fedorenko 2013, p. 5). Such projects include the TAPI (Turkmenistan–Afghanistan–Pakistan–India) gas pipeline and exporting hydropower from Kyrgyzstan and Tajikistan to Pakistan and Afghanistan (Fedorenko 2013, p. 6).

8.5.5   European Interests

Uniquely, Europe's aim in cooperation with rising China is to achieve its normative convergence. It would like to mobilize the private sector for infrastructure investment and promote regional cooperation (Schweisgut 2015, p. 10). For that purpose, Europe is prepared to invest in the development of China, but in turn expects China to meet European standards. This is the European scheme to maintain global peace and to qualify itself fully as a first tier, leading global actor: "Europe sees itself as the model China should aspire to. EU policy is based on the belief that 'human rights tend to be better understood and better protected in societies open to the free flow of trade, investment, people, and ideas'" (Geereaerts 2011, p. 63).

The EU aims to build international collaboration with China to promote peace, prosperity, and sustainable development within Eastern Europe and Central Asia (Schweisgut 2015, p. 10). Its main purpose is diversification and the potential to gain investment (especially for Central Eastern Europe). In that regard, CEE countries would like to become the gateway to the EU for Chinese investors. Hence, the OBOR vision provokes dynamic competition in the CEE region because all countries are intent on becoming the bridge between China and EU through this commercial project. Hungary was the first European country to join China's new Silk Road project officially.

The New Silk Road policy of China has the possibility of providing a great opportunity for Europe, especially if the EU and China can harmonize their policies and "explore common initiatives" (Vangeli 2015, p. 25). At the same time, its complexity means that the EU's relations with its neighbors will include another player. In addition, the distance between Europe and Asia will significantly decrease and incorporate numerous other players that enhance the new global order, the so-called global partnership.

China is obviously ready to learn from Europe as it extracts common interests, but finds it culturally impossible to respect the EU as a political model because the power of Chinese unity has a historical precedent that Europe cannot aspire to achieve. The challenge is that, in the event that a fractured Europe remains without a single common policy regarding China, the possibility of Chinese ventures contributing to a two-track Europe will be threatened (Vangeli 2015, p. 25).

8.6   Conclusion

The Silk Road Economic Belt is not purely a trade route, but neither was the historical Silk Road because it was also a corridor by which at least seven religions and several influential Western thinkers arrived in China (Heilmann et al. 2014; Kaczmarski 2015; Lawton 2008; Szczudlik-Tatar 2013; Wang 2012). Although the concept remains the same as that of the historical Silk Road, the new initiative means to consciously develop regions along the route primarily through trade. China's interest is to participate in the establishment of an international environment, as opposed to being an adherent of rules set up by other nations. Consequently, the current trends of globalization will hold not just Western characteristics, but also Chinese characteristics. Developing its neighboring regions and building the Silk Road Economic Belt symbolize the strategy China will follow in establishing itself and Europe in the multipolar world. Historically, cities along trade routes flourished and China's incentive is to flourish and develop its western regions and neighbors.

Europe is China's major trade partner. In that regard, it is impossible to exclude it from any of the China's plans related to trade. The route (or routes) that the trade currently takes is prevalently by sea and only marginally by land. Most of the goods currently traded between China and Europe travel by cargo ship from east to west. If this trend inverts in the future, the Silk Road route will have a decisive economic impact on the future of Central and Eastern Europe. At present, the Chinese initiative has greater importance in terms of geopolitical strategy than economic benefit (Jun 2015). In comparison to maritime trade, the amount of goods crossing Asia is minimal. The current initiative is important because it can improve not only trade but also connectivity between the two continents. It raises both political entities—China and Europe—simultaneously, offers more opportunities for cooperation, and creates a foundation of common principles to ascertain a new world order: an international environment with both Western and Chinese characteristics dominated by amity. These are the long-term goals of the OBOR initiative. However, first and foremost, Chinese efforts lie in the development of its western neighbors; thereby, the routes and the shape of the European end of the Economic Belt remain a secondary issue (Liu 2014, p. 5).

REFERENCES

Anbound. (2015). 'One Belt, One Road' is facing increasing challenges, Caijing Wang (Opinion).

Brugier, C. (2014). *China's way: The new Silk Road*. Retrieved from: http://www.iss.europa.eu/publications/detail/article/chinas-way-the-new-silk-road. Accessed in October 2015.

China Institute in America. (2015). *Exchange of goods and ideas along the Silk Roads*. Retrieved from http://www.chinainstitute.cieducationportal.org/cimain/wp-content/themes/chinainstitute/pdfs/education/fromsilktooil_pdf5.pdf. Accessed in October 2015.

Dawber, A. (2015). *China to Spain cargo train: Successful first 16,156-mile round trip on world's longest railway brings promise of increased trade*. Retrieved from http://www.independent.co.uk/news/world/europe/china-to-spain-cargo-train-successful-first-16156-mile-round-trip-on-worlds-longest-railway-brings-10067895.html. Accessed in July 2015.

Erdősi, F. (2015). Trans-Eurasian transport links in great and medium-size spaces of power. *Tér és Társadalom, 29*(2), 106–126.

Fedorenko, V. (2013). The new Silk Road initiatives in Central Asia. *Rethink Paper 10.* Retrieved from http://www.rethinkinstitute.org/wp-content/uploads/2013/11/Fedorenko-The-New-Silk-Road.pdf. Accessed in October 2015.

Felföldi, Sz. (2009). *Egy új szemléletű Selyemút történet alapvonalaihoz.* Retrieved from http://okorportal.hu/wpcontent/uploads/2013/06/2009_2_felfoldi.pdf. Accessed in October 2015.

Freedholm, J. (2011). *The dynamics of trade along the Silk Road.* Retrieved from http://www.globalcultures.net/shepard/worldblog/wp-content/uploads/2011/01/Dynamics-of-Trade.pdf. Accessed in October 2015.

Fung Business Intelligence Centre. (2015). The Silk Road economic belt and the 21st-Century Maritime Silk Road.

Geeraerts, G. (2011). China, the EU and the new multipolarity. *European Review, 19*(1), 57–67.

Gervai, P., Sárvári, B., Trautmann, L. (2015). A globalizáció politikai gazdaság-tanáról. *Typotex Kiadó.* Budapest

Godement, F. (2015). "One belt, one road": China's great leap outward. European Council on Foreign Relations.

Hansen, V. (2012). *The Silk Road: A new history.* Retrieved from https://books.google.hu/books?hl=hu&lr=&id=nPg4UVV_JTYC&oi=fnd&pg=PP2&dq=silk+road+history&ots=bkCFgDf5Ai&sig=M9Uxs-_ypPWtzjxyA4MCsuB6dOQ#v=onepage&q=silk%20road%20history&f=false. Accessed in October 2015.

Heilmann, S., Rudolf, M., & Buckow, J. (2014). *China's shadow foreign policy: parallel structures challenge the established international order.* Retrieved from http://www.merics.org/fileadmin/templates/download/china-monitor/China_Monitor_No_18_en.pdf. Accessed in October 2015.

Huang, Y. (2015). Don't Let 'One Belt, One Road' Fall into the trap of Japan's overseas investments. *ZhongguoGaige Wang.*

Inotai, A. (2010). Impact of the global crisis on trade relations between the European Union and China. *Hungarian Statistical Review, 14,* 46–67.

Inotai, A. (2011a). Kína világgazdasági szerepének erősödése, az exportorientált "modell" jövője. *Köz-gazdaság, 6*(1), 215–218.

Inotai, A. (2011b). Impact of the global crises on EU-China relations: Facts, chances and potential risks. In T. Matura (Ed.), *Asian studies* (pp. 80–102). Budapest: Hungarian Institute of International Affairs.

Inotai, A. (2014). Economic relations between the European Union and China. *L'Europe en Formation* 2013/4, 47–84.

Jia, Q. (2015). A number of issues that the OBOR urgently needs to clarify and prove. *Aisixiang.*

Juhász, O. (2015). A Selyemúton oda-vissza. *Remény.* 2015/2. Retrieved from http://www.remeny.org/remeny/2015-2-szam/juhaszotto-aselyemuton-oda-vissza/. Accessed in December 2015.

Jun, Z. (2015). *China's pursuit of a new economic order.* Retrieved from http://www.project-syndicate.org/commentary/china-new-world-order-by-jun-zhang-2015-06. Accessed in October 2015.

Kaczmarski, M. (2015). *The new Silk Road: A versatile instrument in China's policy.* Retrieved from http://www.osw.waw.pl/en/publikacje/osw-commentary/2015-02-10/new-silk-road-a-versatile-instrument-chinas-policy. Accessed in October 2015.

Karluk, S. R., & Karaman, S. C. (2014). *Bridging civilizations from Asia to Europe: The Silk Road.* http://www.davidpublisher.org/Public/uploads/Contribute/55346f0d88c7a.pdf. Accessed in October 2015.

KPMG. (2015). *China Outlook 2015.* KPMG Global China Practice.

Lai, S., & Zhang, L. (2013). Challenging the EU's economic roles? The impact of the Eurozone crisis on EU Images in China. *Baltic Journal of European Studies. 3*(3), 13–36.

Lawton, J. (ed.). (2008). *Integral study of the Silk Roads roads of dialogue.* Retrieved from http://unesdoc.unesco.org/images/0015/001592/159291eo.pdf. Accessed in October 2015.

Laruelle, M. (2015). *The Chinese Silk Road and their reception in Central Asia.* Retrieved from http://www.uscc.gov/sites/default/files/Laruelle%20Testimony_3.18.15.pdf. Accessed in October 2015.

Li, J. (2014). Report: Silk Road Economic Belt may be divided into three phases; initial completion predicted in 2049, *Zhong-guoXinwen Wang.*

Liu, X. (2010). *The Silk Road in world history.* Oxford: Oxford University Press.

Liu, Z. (2014). Central and Eastern Europe in building the Silk Road economic belt. *Working Paper Series on European Studies, Institute of European Studies, Chinese Academy of Social Sciences 8*(3).

Matura, T. (2012). The pattern of Chinese investments in Central Europe. *International Journal of Business Insights & Transformation., 5*(3), 104–109.

Maxxelli Consulting. (2015). *West China's international railway development.* Retrieved from http://www.maxxelli-consulting.com/west-chinas-international-railway-development/. Accessed in October 2015.

Men, J. (2015): China's new Silk Road and EU-China relations. *EU-China Observer* 1.15, 12–15.

Ministry of Foreign Affairs of the People's Republic of China. (2013). *President Xi Jinping delivers important speech and proposes to build a Silk Road Economic Belt with Central Asian countries.* http://www.fmprc.gov.cn/mfa_eng/topics_665678/xjpfwzysiesgjtfhshzzfh_665686/t1076334.shtml.

National Secretariat of IGC TRACECA in the Republic of Kazakhstan. (2012). *Silk Wind: The Route of multimodal block train* (Project Progress Presentation). Retrieved from http://www.traceca-org.org/uploads/media/14_Presentation_Silk_Wind_07-11-12_eng.pdf Accessed in October 2015.

Railway Gazette. (2015). *DB Schenker launches Hamburg – Zhengzhou train.* http://www.railwaygazette.com/news/freight/single-view/view/db-schenker-launches-hamburg-zhengzhou-train.html. Accessed in October 2015.

Rolland, N. (2015). China's New Silk Road. *The National Bureau of Asian Research.*

Schweisgut, H. D. (2015). EU-China 40th Anniversary: Expectations for Expanding Connections. *EU-China Observer 1.15*, 7–10.

Stahl, A. K. (2015). China's New Silk Road diplomacy: Implications for China's relations with Europe and Africa. *EU-China Observer 1.15*, 16–19.

Szczudlik-Tatar, J. (2013). *China's New Silk Road diplomacy.* https://www.pism.pl/files/?id_plik=15818. Accessed in October 2015.

Tao, X. (2014). *Back on the Silk Road: China's version of a rebalance to Asia.* http://www.globalasia.org/wp-content/uploads/2014/03/548.pdf. Accessed in October 2015.

The World Bank Treasury. (2015). *The World Bank Investor Brief.* http://treasury.worldbank.org/cmd/pdf/WorldBankInvestorBrief.pdf. Accessed in October 2015.

Trautmann, L. (1999). Ázsiai kultúra és információs társadalom, *Fordulat* 1999/ősz, 53–76.

Turcsányi, R. (2014). *Central and Eastern Europe's courtship with China: Trojan horse within the EU?* Retrieved from http://www.eias.org/sites/default/files/EU-Asia-at-a-glance-Richard-Turcsanyi-China-CEE.pdf. Accessed in June 2015.

Txabarriaga, R. (2010). *Implications of increasing Europe's trade with China.* http://www.tcworld.info/emagazine/outsourcing/article/implicationsof-increasing-europes-trade-with-china/. Accessed in October 2015.

van der Putten, F., & Meijnders, M. (2015). China, Europe and the Maritime Silk Road. *Clingendael.* Retrieved from http://www.clingendael.nl/sites/default/files/China%20Europe%20and%20the%20Maritime%20Silk%20Road.pdf. Accessed in October 2015.

Vangeli, A. (2015). China's New Silk Road and its impact on Sino-European relations. *EU-China Observer 1.15*, 20–26.

Wang, J. (2012). Marching towards the West, China's geopolitical strategy of rebalancing. *Huanqiu Shibao.*

Wang, Y. (2015). Reconstructing China's trade, *Caijing.*

Waugh, D.C. (2015). *The Silk Roads in history.* http://faculty.washington.edu/dwaugh/publications/waughexpeditionfinal.pdf. Accessed in October 2015.

Wood, F. (2002). *The Silk Road: Two thousand years in the heart of Asia.* Berkeley: University of California Press.

Xie, Z. (2014). One Belt, One Road' is not 'China's Marshall Plan. *Huanqiu Wang.*

Xu, G. (2014). Looking at the 'One Belt, One Road' strategy from a return on investment point of view. *Financial Times (Chinese version).*

Yanchun, W. (2015). Reconstructing China's trade. *Caijing.*

Yang, Y. (2015). China-EU Relations: Broader, Higher and Stronger. *EU-China Observer,* 1.15, 6–7.

Zhang, J. (2015). China's Pursuit of a New Economic Order. *Project Syndicate.*

Zheng, Y. (2015). The 'One Belt, One Road' strategy helps the world economy rebalance. *LianheZaobao – Oriental Morning Post.*

Primary Souces

Ministry of Foreign Affairs of the People's Republic of China. (2013). "President Xi Jinping Delivers Important Speech and Proposes to Build a Silk Road Economic Belt with Central Asian Countries". Retrieved from http://www.fmprc.gov.cn/mfa_eng/topics_665678/xjpfwzysiesgjtfhshzzfh_665686/t1076334.shtml. Accessed in October 2015.

National Secretariat of IGC TRACECA in the Republic of Kazakhstan. (2012). Silk Wind: The Route of Multimodal Block Train (Project Progress Presentation). Retrieved from http://www.traceca-org.org/uploads/media/14_Presentation_Silk_Wind_07-11-12_eng.pdf. Accessed in October 2015.

Railway and Road Corridors Connecting the Central Asia Regional Economic Cooperation Member Countries. *Central Asia Regional Economic Cooperation.* Retrieved from http://www.carecprogram.org/uploads/events/2005/4th-MC/001_101_213_Railway-Road-Connections-Map.pdf. Accessed in October 2015.

The World Bank Treasury. (2015). *"The World Bank Investor Brief". World Bank (International Bank for Reconstruction and Development, IBRD).* http://treasury.worldbank.org/cmd/pdf/WorldBankInvestorBrief.pdf. Accessed in October 2015.

CHAPTER 9

Subnational Development Policy as the Area of Common Interest Under the One Belt, One Road Initiative? The Case of Regional Policy-Making in Poland

Ida Musiałkowska

9.1 Introduction

In the contemporary world, there are still disparities among regions, understood as subnational administrative units, societies, or economies. In the European Union (EU), one of the policies aimed at cohesion is its cohesion/regional policy. The effects and policy-making in the area are subject of interests of international organizations and third countries because the EU has accumulated knowledge and know-how in the field. Despite criticism, the policy seems to bring positive results and is one of the most important development policies for particular Member States, their regions, and the whole EU. Policy aims to deepen the integration process through partial removal of structural barriers to economic, social, and territorial development. It is now treated as a policy of more developmental character.

I. Musiałkowska (✉)
Poznań University of Economics and Business, Poznań, Poland

© The Author(s) 2018
Y. Cheng et al. (eds.), *The Belt & Road Initiative in the Global Arena*,
https://doi.org/10.1007/978-981-10-5921-6_9

Regional development and policy-making is put in the wider context of the debate between the Organisation for Economic Co-operation and Development (OECD) (Sanchez-Reaza 2009) and the World Bank (2009), which present different proposals in the sphere of regional development models that can be used in many world areas.

Currently, scientists and policy makers refer to two basic models of regional policy:

1. Distributive model, where the aim of regional policy is to concentrate on the development of marginalized country areas.
2. Diffusion-polarization model, where one may observe barriers to development in either marginalized or developed (growth centers) regions. The regional policy in that model concentrates on overcoming existing barriers in all regions. Thus, spillover effects appear and the level of existing differences decreases.

While analyzing policy recommendations, one must take into consideration that the World Bank (2009) presents a different model from that of the OECD (and EU) and uses different and instruments of intervention to develop a region, regardless of its territorial size. The types of instruments proposed by both organizations are similar but the difference is in the mode of using them. In the case of the World Bank, the instruments and interventions do not always need to be used together (one instrument serves to solve one problem, a "dimension"). For example, if the main problems of a particular country region are the result of large distances, only the development of infrastructure will be a solution. If there are two or three problems, then two or three instruments should be used. At the same time, the OECD considers that regional development depends on the three pillars of investment in infrastructure, human capital, and business environment (OECD 2009) and therefore proposes a multidimensional and integrated approach. The latter approach has been implemented in the majority of states (for example, EU Member States) with some difficulties; however, over many years it has brought positive effects because of visible activation of endogenous potentials and the involvement of regional and local authorities. The OECD model, as more influential and efficient, has also started to be used in South American countries such as Brazil, Chile, and Mexico (CEPAL 2015[1]).

---

[1] www.eclac.org last accessed on 21 November 2015.

Most recent changes show that EU policy for the years 2014–2020 is now twofold ("hybrid"), aiming at obtaining convergence via its redistributive function, and at development and bigger mobilization of endogenous potential of the regions via its allocation function (Bachtler and Reines 2008; Kawecka-Wyrzykowska 2015).

In recent years, the growing interest of third countries and organizations in introducing their own structural reforms has prompted the European Commission to start dialogue in the area of regional policy with China, Brazil, Argentina, Chile, Mexico, and other partners. As a consequence, the EU Cohesion Policy[2] and its programming method, strategic planning, and instruments have been promoted worldwide.

The aim of this chapter (based partly on the research made for the Polish Parliament, see Musiałkowska 2017) is to present the evolution and evaluation of regional policy-making in Poland, one of the EU countries recognized as a potential partner in the One Belt, One Road initiative. The following research questions were asked:

- What are the main achievements, failures, and barriers of regional policy-making in Poland?
- What are the drivers/determinants of regional policy-making in Poland and to what extent are regional authorities involved in the process of programming the development of their regions (is the decentralization process continuing)?

A brief discussion of potential areas of common interest for cooperation at regional and local level is also given. The methods comprise analyses of legal acts, strategic documents, evaluation reports, and our own research in the field.

9.2   Administrative Reform and Strategic Management at Subnational Level in Poland

Contemporary Polish regional policy[3] is the result of the reform of territorial division of the country, introduced after the transition from a centrally planned economy to a market economy, which started in 1989.

---

[2] The notions of "cohesion" or "regional" policy are very often used interchangeably. They address either the aim of the policy or its subject.

[3] Regional development policy, as it is officially named in the act on the principles of the regional policy of 2006.

Two legal acts are the basis of current territorial/administrative division of the country:

- Act on territorial self-government of 1990 (Dz.U. 1990 No. 16 item 95)
- Act on regional self-government of 1998 (Dz.U. 1998 No. 91 item 576)

The reform prepared Poland for accession to the EU with regard to pursuing regional policy with the use of EU budgetary support (EU structural funds). One of the pre-requirements was to create administrative units according to the standards used for statistical reasons and for comparative analyses made across the whole EU (NUTS, *Nomenclature des Unités Territoriales Statistique*), which goes in line with the classification of so-called economic regions. This standardization and division into statistical administrative units is one of the tools that enables monitoring of the results achieved under EU Cohesion Policy. The division is made with respect to two criteria, the population inhabiting a certain territory and the size of the territory.[4] In Poland, three levels of subnational NUTS regions were introduced: NUTS 1—macroregions, NUTS 2—regions/voivodships, and NUTS 3—groupings of local units (counties/poviats) and big cities that have rights of a county. Only NUTS 2 level regions have their own regional authorities, self-government, and administration, whereas the remaining units were created only for statistical purposes. The remaining territorial units are classified as Local Administrative Units (LAU), which were previously classified as NUTS 4 and NUTS 5 regions according to the EU classification. Therefore, in Poland there are LAU 1 (counties or poviats) and LAU 2 (municipalities or communes) areas, both of which have their own local authorities and territorial self-government. Taking into consideration only those units with their own self-governments in Poland, there is the following division (Ministry of Regional Development 2011, Główny Urząd Statystyczny 2017)[5]:

---

[4]NUTS 1 regions may be inhabited by 3–7 million people, NUTS 2 by 800,000 to 3 million, and NUTS 3 by 150,000 to 800, inhabitants. Regulation (EC) No 1059/2003 of the European Parliament and of the Council of 26 May 2003, on the establishment of a common classification of territorial units for statistics (NUTS), *Official Journal* L 154, 21.6.2003.

[5]Available at http://espanontheroad.eu/dane/web_espon_library_files/671/pl_regional_policy.pdf last accessed on 21 March.2016.

- 16 NUTS 2—voivodeships
- 6 NUTS 3[6]—the biggest Polish cities
- 379 LAU 1—counties/poviats
- 2479 LAU 2—municipalities

After introducing this division, Poland was classified as a unitary but decentralized state (Nyikos and Talaga 2014, p. 120).

According to the OECD model, regional growth, development, and creation of innovation should be based on three parallel types of interventions in the areas of business environment, human capital, and infrastructure (Sanchez-Reaza 2009). Because democratization is favorable to decentralization (Zalewski 2007), new tasks were delegated to the established Polish regions and local administrative units. At the same time as introduction of the administrative reform, regional and local authorities (RLA) have gradually been given broader competence in order to pursue regional and local policy, along with new concepts of management (New Public Management; NPM) and governance (multilevel governance; MLG), followed by network cooperation and project design (Ministry of Regional Development 2011).[7]

The NPM concept was imposed on the bureaucratic Weberian model at each level of administration. Therefore, the adopted model is mixed and combines elements from both bureaucratic and NPM concepts. Some crucial aspects have evolved significantly in recent years (strategic management, management accounting, financial strategic planning, project task delegation, services marketization) (Kożuch 2004; OECD 1993).

Moreover, for the first time, the following elements attributed to NPM were introduced in Poland (Hood 1991; Zalewski 2007):

- Disaggregating public sector entities
- Monitoring and controlling the results of activities
- Setting down the indicators of achievements; achievement of better efficiency of public activities
- Implementing sustainable development

---

[6]The remaining 66 NUTS 3 are groupings of counties without local self-government (GUS 2017).

[7]http://espronontheroad.eu/dane/web_espron_library_files/671/pl_regional_policy.pdf accessed on 21 November 2012.

Evidence shows that not all market-oriented goals of NPM can be easily achieved in the public sphere (Hausner 2003). However, introducing many of the goals facilitates the planning and design of strategies of regional development that are required in order to participate in the EU Cohesion Policy. Membership of the EU forced Polish public administration at different levels to more efficient and effective spending of public money, and made the officials more aware of the meaning of statistical indicators, results measuring, and so on. Changes in the quality of governance and management have been visible in the entities of public administration that are involved in the process of programming, implementation, and surveillance of the Cohesion Policy (namely, the Ministry of Development[8] and boards of the regions and regional offices—marshal offices).

Multilevel governance has brought other challenges for the Polish public administration (Bachtler and Yuill 2001; Marks and Hooghe 2004; Faludi 2011; Dąbrowski 2012; Davies and Imbroscio 2009; Hausner 2003; Kożuch 2004): especially with regard to the following:

- Division of tasks and competences with regard to public policy-making (including regional policy-making)
- Cooperation and coordination of activities, where the latter is the most difficult to achieve (Gruchman 2012; Talaga 2013)

In general, the main objective for all regional and local authorities is to create optimal conditions of living for citizens through achieving the following goals (Ziółkowski 2000):

- Economic (development of conditions for operating of enterprises)
- Social (provision of good quality social services: education, healthcare, social protection, culture and art, sport and recreation, housing, and public safety/security)
- Spatial (rational design and use of space/territory)
- Ecological (protection and conservation of natural environmental resources)
- Cultural (protection and conservation of cultural values and heritage)

---

[8]Previously named the Ministry of Regional Development, Ministry of Infrastructure and Development.

The role of territorial self-governments and authorities is to manage all activities in a certain territory in order to achieve the objective and goals. The functions of the self-governments are to regulate, initiate, stimulate, and be responsible for achieving the overall objective (Ziółkowski 2000).

9.3 Changes in Strategic Management at the Regional Level in the Light of Implementation of the Cohesion Policy in Poland 2004–2020

When joining the EU in 2004, Poland was one of the poorest countries in terms of many indicators, including the most often used, GDP per capita (see Sect. 9.4). Polish regions were classified as "less developed regions."[9] Thus, according to the principles of the EU Cohesion Policy, all regions became eligible for funding under specific policy aims. The EU Cohesion Policy has been implemented in the multiannual financial frameworks (or previously financial perspectives), which are certain periods of time during which, according to their level of wealth and other indicators and formulas used for calculation of aid, countries and their regions may obtain additional support from the EU budget in order to eliminate structural barriers to functioning of their economies, re-design social policies that have clear impact on labor market, and exchange experiences with other European partners in transnational and international cooperation. The main objective of the policy is economic, social, and territorial convergence among the regions and countries, which should be beneficial to the whole internal market of the EU (Treaty on Functioning of the EU, 2012; article 174). Polish regional policy-making can be analyzed together with implementation of the Cohesion Policy in the country, because the latter has a large impact on the whole process of policy designing.

---

[9] Classification to the category of less or more developed region is based mainly on the level of regional GDP per capita. If the regional GDP per capita is lower than 75% of the average GDP per capita for all EU regions, the region is classified as less developed and may obtain structural funds, mainly for convergence/cohesion objectives. The more developed regions are also given the possibility to benefit from the Cohesion Policy but the allocations are earmarked to more innovative enterprises and the share of public aid in the investment is lower than in the case of the poorer regions.

So far, Poland has participated in three cycles of EU Cohesion Policy: 2004–2006,[10] 2007–2013, and 2014–2020. To spend the funds, each region (and the whole country) is required to elaborate its development strategy for the years and clearly state the objectives and priorities of the national (sectoral) and regional development. Then, the strategies are the basis for formulation of the content of the operational programmes (OPs) and the documents that show how, through the chosen activities and projects, the regions and country wish to achieve the objectives of both the EU Cohesion Policy and their own specific development objectives. Each programme has its own authorities responsible for its programming, implementation, and evaluation (managing authorities, intermediary bodies). Coordination of the whole cohesion policy cycle lies in the hands of the Polish Ministry of Development.

Analysis of all the strategies and OPs in the three periods[11] allows detection of the changes, levels of decentralization/centralization, and determining factors in the subsequent periods (see Table 9.1).

In 2004–2006, when Poland joined the EU, the country factor was dominant when the strategies were formulated. Most of the strategies were prepared in 2000+; therefore, only some of the priorities fully reflected EU objectives. Furthermore, strategic techniques were not very strong (for example, there was a lack of indicators in many of the strategies, which made the measurement of results difficult).

In terms of OPs, only one programme was prepared for all 16 Polish regions, and the regions were allowed to differentiate the amount of money for each part (priority axis) of the programme. The reason for only one OP was that it was the beginning of the learning process for regions on how to deal with EU funds and the national authorities preferred to have control over the process. Thus, centralization dominated regional policy-making regarding spending of EU money.

In 2007–2013, the shift toward the EU factor is strongly visible in preparation of both national (sectoral) and regional development strategies. Sometimes, even the same formulation of the objectives (taken from EU documents) is found in the documents.

---

[10]The whole cycle in the EU comprised the years 2000–2006 but as a Member State that joined the EU in 2004 Poland was participating only in one third of this perspective.

[11]From the author's expertise and consultion with public and private sector with regard to the Cohesion Policy.

Table 9.1 Impact of EU Cohesion Policy on strategic documents regarding regional development in Poland in the years 2004–2020

2004–2006	2007–2013	2014–2020
Prospect of EU membership for Poland	Move toward EU factor	Move toward EU factor
Country factor dominates in the strategies	Growth of decentralization (EU factor) in implementation and at the same time, a slight increase in inter-institutional coordination in programming (through national guidelines for regions, driven by the country factor)	National authorities gain significance in the EU (through promotion of territorial approach to development)
EU factor is—partially present (OP, regional development strategies)		Further increase in inter-institutional coordination (through national guidelines for regions and institutions of all levels)
National strategies (country and regionally-oriented factor)		Regional factor and further decentralization very much visible (regional OPs, smart specialization strategies) but caused by the EU factor (so-called ex-ante conditionality)
Operational programmes: OPs adopted as generally applicable law—regulation:	Operational programmes: OPs adopted as non-generally applicable law—resolution of the Council of Ministers:	Operational programmes: OPs adopted as non-generally applicable law—resolution of the Council of Ministers:
- Five sectoral OPs + technical assistance OPs—national level	- Five sectoral OPs—national level	- Six sectoral OPs—national level
- One integrated regional OP implemented in 16 regions (the same content)—regional level	- 16 regional operational programmes (different contents)—regional level	- 16 dual-funded regional OPs (different contents, more decentralization in the European Social Fund part)

Elaborated and adapted by the author on the basis of Idczak et al. (2012) and Musiałkowska and Talaga (2013)

In the same period, regions were given more competence with regard to the OPs and these documents followed the priorities established in their strategies of development. This confirmed bigger decentralization with regard to regional policy-making in Poland. The national authorities tried to coordinate and standardize the procedural aspects of the implementation of the programmes through issuing national guidelines to the institutions responsible for the programmes, which was partially successful.

In the current period, 2014–2020, there is strong EU influence over regional policy-making in Poland. Nevertheless, Polish authorities play an important role in promoting new trends and paradigms of regional development (territorial approach, underlining that all public policies should be territorially oriented) for the whole EU during negotiations at the EU level. Both national and regional strategies go beyond the EU priorities underlying aspects crucial for Poland, which confirms the appearance of regional and country factors. Regions were given competence to elaborate "smart specialization"[12] strategies and OPs that respond to the strategies. Elaboration of smart specialization strategies was one of the ex-ante conditions written down in EU law. Therefore, one may observe the desire for bigger coordination of the implementation of the policy at the EU level. Also, the national authorities in Poland issued a legal act and a set of guidelines aimed at greater inter-institutional procedural coordination. It seems that a better legal solution has been chosen for this process (generally binding legal act instead of non-generally applicable law of guidelines).

The changes observed in recent years confirm that regional authorities are learning over time.

---

[12] As Inger Midtkandal and Jens Sörvik (2012) explain, smart specialization is "a strategic approach to economic development through targeted support for research and innovation. It involves a process of developing a vision, identifying the place-based areas of greatest strategic potential, developing multi-stakeholder governance mechanisms, setting strategic priorities and using smart policies to maximize the knowledge-based development potential of a region, regardless of whether it is strong or weak, high-tech or low-tech" http://www.nordregio.se/en/Metameny/Nordregio-News/2012/Smart-Specialisation/Context/ last accessed on 5 May 2016.

9.4   EFFECTS OF THE COHESION POLICY AND POLICY IMPACT ON REGIONAL CHARACTERISTICS IN POLAND

Poland is the sixth biggest EU Member State and, at the same time, the biggest beneficiary of the EU Cohesion Policy among all the Member States.[13]

The positive effects of the Cohesion Policy may be obtained if the remaining policies pursued in the country are coherent and the general economic situation is not deteriorating. With the use of macroeconomic models like that of Hermin or the EUImpactModIV, it is possible to isolate the impact of the Cohesion Policy on national and regional economy from other factors.

In the first years of experience with the use of EU funds, the demand effects prevailed, but supply effects have also appeared in recent years (accumulation of public and private capital). The Cohesion Policy has contributed to improvement in the macroeconomic situation in Poland, especially in the years when the effects of the global financial and economic crisis were visible. The impact on investment, construction, labor market, and public finance was positive. In 2004–2012, the impact on the growth of GDP was bigger than if this policy had not been implemented (non-EU scenario). It oscillated between 0.2 percentage points (2004) to 1.6 percentage points (2009) of policy contribution to GDP growth. In 2009, the Cohesion Policy was the only source of growth. Due to the relatively high growth of GDP in Poland in the analyzed period, the distance from the average GDP of EU27 (27 Member States) dropped by 17 percentage points. The level of GDP per capita for 2013 was 66% of the EU average. There are still inter-regional disparities and the process of convergence has been slow; however, according to estimations made by the Ministry of Development, EU funds should help stop excessive differentiation between Polish regions in the years to come.

In the regions, the lowest impact of the Cohesion Policy on development was noticed in relatively well-developed regions (see Table 9.2) such

---

[13]Between 2004 and 2012 the net flow to and from EU budget was 54 billion euros (Ministerstwo Infrastruktury i Rozwoju 2014, pp. 17–20). All Member States are obliged to pay contributions to the EU budget and then the money is redistributed to Member States along EU policies and according to regulations. For the years 2007–2013 and 2014–2020, Poland was allocated the biggest amount of EU funds for the Cohesion Policy (more than 67 billion euros and 82 billion euros, respectively). The allocation is supplemented by national contribution at an agreed level that increases the amount of all available resources for interested beneficiaries.

Table 9.2   Development of Poland and Polish regions compared with the European Union in 2004–2012

	GDP growth 2004-2012	PKB per capita in PPS* UE-27=100		Productivity (PKB per worker) UE-27=100		Employment rate 20-64		Unemployment rate (BAEL)		R&D spending (% GDP)		Investment rate	
	(constant prices)	2012	change 2004-2012	2012	change 2004-2012	2012	change 2004-2012	2012	change 2004-2012	2012	change 2004-2012	2012	change 2004-2012
	%	%	p.p.**	%	p.p.	%	p.p.	%	p.p.	%	p.p.	%	p.p.
EU	10.7	100	x	100	x	68.5	1.5	10.5	1.4	2.1	0.2	17.9	-1.6
Poland	**46.3**	**66.0**	**17.0**	**73.5**	**13.2**	**64.7**	**7.6**	**10.1**	**-9.7**	**0.9**	**0.4**	**19.1**	**0.9**
regions	2004-2011	2010	change 2004-2010	PL=100 2011	change 2004-2011	2012	change 2004-2012	2012	change 2004-2012	2010	change 2004-2010	2011	change 2004-2011
dolnośląskie	**110.3**	**70.0**	**20.0**	**116.0**	7.5	62.2	**10.2**	11.1	**-14.5**	0.5	0.1	19.0	-3.3
kujawsko-pomorskie	73.5	52.0	8.0	89.7	-4.9	**63.4**	6.2	11.9	-9.4	0.3	0.1	21.2	4.2
lubelskie	77.8	42.0	7.0	69.9	-1.7	65.8	3.8	10.5	-4.9	0.7	**0.3**	23.0	5.9
lubuskie	81.6	53.0	11.0	93.2	-8.7	62.1	**10.9**	**9.0**	-14.9	0.1	0.0	**29.5**	**9.6**
łódzkie	82.5	58.0	13.0	89.4	-0.1	65.7	7.2	11.1	-7.8	0.6	0.1	22.2	2.3
małopolskie	91.3	53.0	11.0	85.4	-1.1	64.7	4.7	10.4	-7.3	**1.1**	0.2	20.3	-1.5
mazowieckie	**100.6**	**102.0**	**26.0**	**135.3**	6.8	**71.1**	9.2	**8.0**	-8.7	**1.4**	0.2	17.2	-2.3
opolskie	80.0	50.0	11.0	93.9	**0.3**	64.0	**10.1**	9.5	-10.6	0.1	0.0	19.3	1.9
podkarpackie	78.1	42.0	7.0	70.3	-2.6	63.2	3.9	13.2	-4.8	**1.0**	**0.6**	**29.3**	**9.6**
podlaskie	74.5	45.0	8.0	78.4	-0.5	**67.2**	6.1	9.2	-8.2	0.3	0.1	**25.5**	3.9
pomorskie	90.6	60.0	11.0	103.1	-4.7	64.0	8.8	9.5	-11.3	0.6	0.2	20.6	0.7
śląskie	78.3	**67.0**	**14.0**	108.8	-0.9	62.0	9.1	9.4	-9.9	0.5	0.1	18.7	0.6
świętokrzyskie	74.5	47.0	9.0	75.6	-0.9	64.2	7.5	13.1	-4.9	0.5	**0.4**	22.3	**6.5**
warmińsko-mazurskie	74.1	46.0	8.0	88.0	-8.5	58.5	7.0	11.0	**-14.0**	0.5	0.2	23.9	1.4
wielkopolskie	**93.2**	65.0	**14.0**	95.3	-2.2	65.9	4.7	**8.5**	-7.6	0.6	0.1	19.0	-0.7
zachodniopomorskie	72.0	54.0	8.0	100.1	-7.0	60.4	8.5	10.9	**-15.8**	0.3	0.2	19.4	-1.4

Poland and three best performing regions in each category are highlighted with bold text
PPS purchasing power standard, *p.p.* percentage points
Source Elaborated by the author on the basis of Eurostat and BDL GUS (Ministerstwo Infrastruktury i Rozwoju 2014, pp. 99–100)

as wielkopolskie,[14] dolnośląskie, and małopolskie. The biggest impact was seen in the poorest regions of świętokrzyskie, podkarpackie, and warmińsko-mazurskie. High impact was also seen in the capital region of mazowieckie because of the high absorption capacity and location of central offices that implement big projects (Ministerstwo Infrastruktury i Rozwoju 2014, pp. 17–20). However, the biggest amounts of EU funds went to the following regions: mazowieckie (54 billion PLN, ca. 13 billion euros), śląskie (34 billion PLN, ca. 8 billion euros), dolnośląskie (26 billion PLN, ca. 6.5 billion euros), małopolskie (24 billion PLN, ca 6 billion euros), and łódzkie and wielkopolskie (23 billion PLN each, ca. 5.7 billion euros). The smallest amounts went to opolskie (7 billion PLN, ca. 1.75 billion euros), lubuskie (8.5 billion PLN, ca. 2.1 billion euros) and podlaskie (9.6 billion PLN, ca 2.4 billion euros) (Ministerstwo Infrastruktury i Rozwoju 2014, pp. 14–16).

Analyses of the projects implemented between 2004 and 2013 in the various sectors showed that the majority of funds were spent in the following areas (Ministerstwo Infrastruktury i Rozwoju 2014, pp. 14–16):

• Transport and energy (25–46% of the total amount)
• Human resources (ca. 20%)
• Research and development (R&D) and entrepreneurship (ca. 20%)

Despite the big improvement in the development of road infrastructure in many regions and an increase in value-added and network effects at the country level, at the local level construction of roads is not a sufficient condition of development (which is compliant with the OECD model). In many cases, the demand effect of investment was lower than expected (Ministerstwo Infrastruktury i Rozwoju 2014, p. 42). The most dynamic development was noticed in airport infrastructure, but railway infrastructure is still the area of the most desirable potential development.

Projects in the area of human resources showed an impact on the labor market. Employment rate increased to 64.7% in 2012. More than 1.7 million people were covered by the training schemes and about 240,000 new enterprises were opened by the previously unemployed. There was slight increase in discrepancies between regions with regard to labor market statistics (see Table 9.2).

Many investments in R&D co-financed from EU funds did not bring satisfactory results in terms of innovativeness of the Polish enterprises

---

[14]Polish names of the regions are used.

and economy. Poland is still classed as a "moderate" innovator (together with Latvia, Bulgaria and Romania). The biggest regional spending was noticed in the richest regions; however, the impact of EU funds on R&D in enterprises was very low and there is a room for change in the years 2014–2020 (Ministerstwo Infrastruktury i Rozwoju 2014, p. 57).

The general investment rate is expected to grow and Polish enterprises are prone to invest. Projects co-financed from EU funds showed a growth in competitiveness. New technologies were bought and many new products and services of good quality entered the markets, contributing to the increase in companies' turnover and number of clients. New cooperation alliances and business environment institutions were also supported by programmes designed under the Cohesion Policy (Ministerstwo Infrastruktury i Rozwoju 2014, p. 57).

9.5   Overall Assessment of Regional Policy-Making in Poland and Recommendations for Further Decentralized Cooperation

In summary, the most important achievements and problems/barriers in the implementation of regional policy in Poland in 2004–2015 can be divided into two categories of strategic and procedural character[15] (see Table 9.3). These categories may serve as a source of potential learning for further cooperation at local and regional levels.

9.6   Further Directions of Decentralized Cooperation Between China and the EU and Poland

The EU has already launched cooperation on regional policy with China (initiated by the Memorandum of Understanding on regional policy cooperation between the EU and China, signed on 15 May 2006[16]).

---

[15]On the basis of author research (interviews with the stakeholders), participation in consultation processes with public authorities, personal experience, and participatory observation.

[16]Memorandum of Understanding on Regional Policy Cooperation between the European Commission and the National Development and Reform Commission of the People's Republic of China, 15 May 2006. Available at: http://ec.europa.eu/regional_policy/international/pdf/mou_china_en.pdf, last accessed on 25 April 2016.

Table 9.3 Achievements and barriers in the implementation of the Cohesion Policy and regional development policy in Poland

Achievements	Problems
Strategic achievements	*Strategic problems*
• Design of regional development policy based on multiannual planning (strategic approach) • Creation of 16 regional self-governments (subsidiarity principle accomplished) • Decentralization in the implementation of regional policy • Dissemination of best practices in the area of regional policy-making • Introduction of monitoring, evaluation, audit, and certification of expenditure as common elements of public policies • Attempts to increase capacities for better use of the endogenous potential of regions • Development of production factors such as road infrastructure, human capital, R&D, and business environment • Significant impact of the policy on economy (GDP, GDP per capita.) • Significant contribution of Poland in shaping the EU Cohesion Policy 2014–2020 • Creation of structures of civil society • "Learning by doing," which brings results through regional development policy investing in areas or territories with bigger development potential (not disparities but potentials are the subject of the policy in the current perspective) • Regional policy determines spatial development in Poland and is coherent with other strategic documents (e.g., National Spatial Development Concept 2030) • In 2014–2020 focus is on territories and institutions (MLG, network cooperation) • Increased coherence of the policy with the OECD model	• Bigger focus on spending funds than on achieving the results • Elimination of risky and complicated, but potentially more beneficial, projects • Lack of strategic choices with regard to areas of support in 2007–2013 • Dispersion of interventions and in the result—weaker impact on economy • Low value added for many small projects—inconsistent with the assumptions of regional development policy • Too small an effect of synergy of the projects • Too much attention on direct results of the projects (output) than on the medium/long-term effects (outcome), for example, number of people who attended training programmes instead of new jobs created • Imposing additional national procedures on EU requirements

(continued)

Table 9.3   (continued)

Achievements	Problems
Strategic achievements	Strategic problems
Procedural achievements	Procedural problems
• Attempts to unify/standardize and coordinate procedures through generally applicable and horizontal guidelines	• Excessive bureaucracy
	• Problems with public procurement procedures (reports of the European Court of Auditors for the years 2007–2013)[a]

Elaborated on the basis of Idczak and Musiałkowska (2014)
[a]European Court of Auditors (2008–2015). Reports on annual budgets of the EU (years 2007–2013). Available at http://www.eca.europa.eu/Pages/Splash.aspx, last accessed on 10 November 2015

It was implemented through the EU–China Policy Dialogues Support Facility (PDSF), established in 2007, and served as a source of inspiration for re-design of its regional policy in the context of preparation of the 12th Five-Year Plan. For example, the notion of "block areas" was based on the concept of lagging regions and the convergence objective of the Cohesion Policy of the EU. Many officials and civil servants from both China and the EU have cooperated during seminars, workshops, joint research studies, study visits, and the bilateral cooperation agreements of particular regions or cities. Therefore, there are general and solid foundations for cooperation at the decentralized level (Musiałkowska and Dąbrowski 2013). Many policy-makers from both China and the EU have been learning from past experience, both successes and failures, especially during recent analysis of the results of initiatives in the western regions of China (Cohen 2015; Runde et al. 2016).

In 2004–2013, the dynamic of Chinese–Polish relations was concentrated on trade. Polish exports to China grew by 200%, from 2 billion PLN to 7.1 billion PLN in 2013, which represents about 1% of total exports. The value of Chinese imports to Poland was ten times higher and grew from 15 billion PLN to 60.9 billion PLN in the same years, corresponding to 9.4% of the total value of Polish imports (Ministerstwo Skarbu Państwa 2016[17]). So far, the main imported goods are machinery, electronics, computers, textile, clothes, shoes, metal and metal products,

---

[17] https://www.msp.gov.pl/pl/przeksztalcenia/serwis-gospodarczy/wiadomosci-gospodarcze/28624,Polsko-chinska-wspolpraca-gospodarcza-miarowy-rozwoj-wzajem-nych-stosunkow.html last accessed on 6 May 2016.

chemicals, and transport machines. Exported goods include metal products, copper, electronics, automotive products, chemicals, rubber, and plastics.

There are also examples of on-going cooperation between Polish and Chinese regions and cities. Some examples are the cooperation between the Polish city of Łódź and Chengdu on the issues of trade and investment of enterprises under cross-border cooperation, between the cities of Kraków and Nanjing, or the between the self-governments of the wielkopolskie region and its four Chinese counterparts (Skorupska 2015). In general, Polish regions consider cooperation in the area of trade, investment, and development as the most important in international cooperation, followed by education and culture (Skorupska 2015).

The new Chinese international strategy, the One Belt, One Road initiative, opens new potential horizons of bilateral cooperation; however, one must take into consideration the following differences and potential areas of common interest:

1. Two different development models and different models of regional policy-making are followed by Poland (OECD and EU models of development) and China. This can lead to concentration on chosen policy areas of cooperation, including those aimed at providing "public goods" (Cohen 2015; Runde et al. 2016).

2. There are some commonalities such as a general need to develop quality infrastructure (Runde et al. 2016), but at different scales and presumably of different types of infrastructure (see Sect. 3).

3. There is a crucial level for developing cooperation in education (including higher education) that is essential for overcoming cultural barriers and facilitating further business cooperation (through exchanges, participation in language school programmes, and so on).

4. There is a strong interest in business cooperation in areas such as smart specializations elaborated at national and regional levels.

5. It is necessary to identify and analyze diverse institutional arrangements, together with coordination issues and the possibilities of establishing international cooperation agreements.

6. There are opportunities with regard to financing joint projects. Recently, new agreements on cooperation between development banks have been signed that may help to evaluate the cost and benefits of joint/separate enterprises, exchange experiences, and co-finance particular undertakings. Many European countries,

including Poland,[18] joined the newly created Asian Infrastructure Investment Bank(AIIB), which is assessed as a success of public diplomacy (Kranz 2015, pp. 14–16). Cooperation with other Polish development banks (for example, Bank Gospodarstwa Krajowego) is being considered.

7. Many instruments and business environment institutions (for example, forums of regional cooperation between Chinese and Polish regions, the "Go China" programme, centers of support for importers and exporters, financial assistance for participation in fairs and missions, and so on) are already in place for development and strengthening of already established relations, the "business capacities" of companies of both countries (Kranz 2015, pp. 14–16), and regional development in China and Poland.

REFERENCES

Bachtler, J., & Reines, P. (2008). *A new paradigm of regional policy? Reviewing recent trends in Europe. Executive Summary,* European Policies Research Centre University of Strathclyde, Glasgow.

Bachtler, J., & Yuill, D. (2001). Policies and strategies for regional development: A shift in paradigm? 'Regional and Industrial Policy Research Paper' 46, 7–12, available at http://www.eprc.strath.ac.uk/eprc/documents/PDF_files/R46PoliciesandStrategiesforRegionalDevelopment.pdf last accessed on 16.11.2012.

CEPAL. (2015). http://www.cepal.org/es last accessed on 21 November 2015.

Cohen, D. (2015, June). *China's "second opening": Grand ambitions but a long road ahead,* China Analysis "One Belt, One Road": China's Great Leap Outward, European Council on Foreign Relations, pp. 3–5.

Dąbrowski, M. (2012). Towards strategic regional development planning in Central and Eastern Europe? *Regional Insights, 3*(2), 6–8.

Davies, J. S., & Imbroscio, D. (2009). *Theories of Urban politics* (2nd ed.). Thousand Oaks: Sage Publications.

---

[18]Polish contribution in the AIIB is estimated at ca. US$830 million. *Gazeta Wyborcza* (2016) available at: http://wyborcza.biz/Gieldy/1,132329,20029736,aiib-liczy-na-udzial-polskich-firm-w-projektach-infrastrukturalnych.html last accessed on 8 May 2016; Dz. U. 2016 poz. 559 Ustawa o ratyfikacji Umowy o utworzeniu Azjatyckiego Banku Inwestycji Infrastrukturalnych, sporządzonej w Pekinie dnia 29 czerwca, 2015.

Dz. U. 2016, item 559. Ustawa o ratyfikacji Umowy o utworzeniu Azjatyckiego Banku Inwestycji Infrastrukturalnych, sporządzonej w Pekinie dnia 29 czerwca 2015 r.

Dz.U. 1990 No. 16 item 95. Ustawa z dnia 8 marca 1990 r. o samorządzie terytorialnym.

Dz.U. 1998 No. 91 item 576. Ustawa z dnia 5 czerwca 1998 o samorządzie województwa.

European Court of Auditors. (2008–2015). Reports on annual budgets of the EU (years 2007–2013) available at http://www.eca.europa.eu/Pages/Splash.aspx last accessed on 10 November 2015.

Faludi, A. (2011). *Multi-level (Territorial) Governance: Three Criticisms*, RSA Workshop, Vienna, November 29–30, 1–23.

Gazeta Wyborcza. (2016). Available at: http://wyborcza.biz/Gieldy/1,132329,20029736,aiib-liczy-na-udzial-polskich-firm-w-projektach-infrastrukturalnych.html last Accessed on 8 May 2016.

Główny Urząd Statystyczny. (2017). Klasyfikacja NUTS w Polsce. Available at http://stat.gov.pl/statystyka-regionalna/jednostki-terytorialne/klasyfikacja-nuts/klasyfikacja-nuts-w-polsce/ last accessed on 8 August 2017.

Gruchman, B. (2012). *Braki koordynacji w teorii i praktyce rozwoju regionalnego*. In E. Molendowski (Ed.). *Globalizacja i regionalizacja we współczesnym świecie: księga jubileuszowa dedykowana Profesor Irenie Pietrzyk* (pp. 34–38). Kraków: Wydawnictwo Uniwersytetu Ekonomicznego w Krakowie.

Hausner, J. (2003). *Administracja publiczna*. Warszawa: PWN.

Hood, C. (1991). A public management for all season? *Public Administration*, 69(1), 3–19.

Idczak, P., Musiałkowska, I., & Sapała, M. (2012). Performance turn in the Cohesion Policy in Poland in the years 2014–2020? Analysis of the strategy of development of Łódź region. Conference paper—*Regional Studies Association Research Network on EU Cohesion Policy workshop*, Glasgow.

Idczak, P., & Musiałkowska, I. (2014). Changes in regional policy-making in Poland—10 years of Polish experiences with EU Cohesion Policy, *Political Studies Association Conference*, Manchester, April 14–16.

Kożuch, B. (2004). *Zarządzanie publiczne w teorii i praktyce polskich organizacji*. Warszawa: Placet.

Kranz, A. (2015, June). China's AIIB: A triumph in public diplomacy, In *China Analysis "One belt, one road": China's great leap outward*, European council on foreign relations, 14–16.

Kawecka-Wyrzykowska, E. (2015). In A. Ambroziak (Ed.). *Alignment of the cohesion policy in Poland to objectives and principles of the EU economic strategies (the Lisbon and Europe 2020 strategies)* (pp. 49–74). Warsaw: Warsaw School of Economics Press.

Marks, G., & Hooghe, L. (2004). Contrasting visions of multi-level govern-ance. In I. Bache & M. Flinders (Eds.), *Multi-level governance* (pp. 15–30). Oxford: Oxford University Press.

Memorandum of Understanding on Regional Policy Cooperation between the European Commission and the National Development and Reform Commission of the People's Republic of China, 15 May 2006 available at: http://ec.europa.eu/regional_policy/international/pdf/mou_china_en.pdf last accessed on 25 April 2016.

Midtkandal, I., & Sörvik, J. (2012). *What is smart specialisation? Nordregio News, 5 available at:* http://www.nordregio.se/en/Metameny/Nordregio-News/2012/Smart-Specialisation/Context/ last accessed on 5 May 2016.

Ministerstwo Infrastruktury i Rozwoju. (2014). *Wpływ członkostwa Polski w Unii Europejskiej i realizowanej polityki spójności na rozwój kraju,* Warszawa.

Ministry of Regional Development. (2011). *Regional Policy in Poland.* Warsaw, available at: http://espanontheroad.eu/dane/web_espon_library_files/671/pl_regional_policy.pdf last accessed on 21 March 2016.

Ministerstwo Skarbu Państwa. (2016). Available at: https://www.msp.gov.pl/pl/przeksztalcenia/serwis-gospodarczy/wiadomosci-gospodarcze/28624,Polsko-chinska-wspolpraca-gospodarcza-miarowy-rozwoj-wzajemnych-stosunkow.html last accessed on 6 May 2016.

Musiałkowska, I. (2017). Polityka rozwoju regionalnego jako płaszczyzna oddziaływania UE w sferach prawa i ekonomii. Teraźniejszość i perspek-tywy in Z. Czachór & A. Dudzic (Eds.). Wyzwania dla Unii Europejskiej i Polski. W poszukiwaniu nowych ujęć i sposobów myślenia. (pp. 180–203). Warszawa: Wydawnictwo Sejmowe

Musiałkowska, I., & Dąbrowski, M. (2013). EU-China regional policy dialogue: Unpacking the mechanisms of an unlikely policy transfer, Conference paper presented at the *"EU-China Soft Diplomacy"* Brussels April 18–19.

Musiałkowska, I., & Talaga, R. (2013). *Legal aspects of the implementation of EU Funds 2007–2013 in Poland—Practice and challenges.* Conference materials of 21th NISPAcee Annual Conference "Regionalisation and Inter-regional Co-operation", Belgrade, May 16–19, 1–10.

Nyikos, G., & Talaga, R. (2014). Cohesion policy in transition comparative aspects of the Polish and Hungarian systems of implementation. *Comparative Law Review, 18,* 111–130.

OECD. (1993). *Public Management Studies, Private Pay for Public Work Official Journal C 326, 26/10/2012 P. 0001—0390,* Treaty on Functioning of the European Union.

Regulation (EC) No 1059/2003 of the European Parliament and of the Council of 26 May 2003, on the establishment of a common classification of territorial units for statistics (NUTS), OJ L 154, 21.6.2003.

Runde, D. F., Savoy, C. M., & Rice, C. F. (2016). *Global infrastructure development. A strategic approach to U.S. leadership* (pp. 1–30). Washington: Centre for Strategic and International Studies.

Sanchez-Reaza, J. (2009). *Some preliminary results in the background report (TDPC Ministerial)*. Warsaw: Ministry for Regional Development and OECD conference.

Skorupska, A. (2015). *Dyplomacja samorządowa. Przykład Wielkopolski*. Polski Instytut Spraw Międzynarodowych, Warszawa, available at: http://www. umww.pl/attachments/article/45532/Dyplomacja%20samorzadowa%20 przyklad%20Wielkopolski.pdf last accessed on 20 April 2016.

Talaga, R. (2013). Need for stronger coordination in the system of EU Cohesion policy. *Journal of European Court of Auditors, 6*, 23–32.

World Bank. (2009). *Reshaping economic geography*. Washington.

Zalewski, A. (2007). *Reformy sektora publicznego w duchu nowego zarządzania publicznego*. In *Nowe zarządzanie publiczne w polskim samorządzie terytorialnym* (pp. 11–74). Warszawa: SGH.

Ziółkowski, M. (2000). Proces formułowania strategii rozwoju gminy. In M. Majchrzak & A. Zalewski (Eds.). *Samorząd terytorialny i rozwój lokalny. Monografie i Opracowania 483*. Warszawa: SGH.

CHAPTER 10

Comparative Study of the Labor Markets for Distant High-Profile Specialists in China and Russia

Dmitry Doronin

10.1 INTRODUCTION

In the modern world, creative industries are playing a crucial role in countries' development through their high margins and correlated support of other sectors of economy. Just as technology and innovation drove economies in the twentieth century, creativity now plays this role. In the 1990s, the service sector overtook others segments of the economy in developed countries, and companies and businesses faced the dilemma of whether to continuously innovate and create new offers (or even markets) or withdraw. Thus, the importance of creative thinking was determined. Basically speaking, in the creative economy, mass production is less important than the ability to create new ideas, concepts, products, and processes (Florida 2003).

One of the main characteristics of creative industries is their accessibility to any point on the Earth, connected by contemporary telecommunications such as the internet (Bilton 2007). On the one hand, it brings

D. Doronin (✉)
Donghua University, Shanghai, People's Republic of China

© The Author(s) 2018
Y. Cheng et al. (eds.), *The Belt & Road Initiative in the Global Arena*,
https://doi.org/10.1007/978-981-10-5921-6_10

difficulties in development because a company or individual working in this sector is competing with the rest of the world. On the other hand, this characteristic brings enormous opportunities, such as distant cooperation on one product or service. Companies are able to operate without having a physical presence anywhere or by having non-administrative or non-client-related departments outsourced in other cities or countries. However, governments often do not recognize these tendencies or recognize them too late to introduce a legal base for smooth transformation of businesses. This can mean that international regulations and cross-governmental projects appear slowly and opportunities to give an additional boost to the economy are often missed.

I would like to propose a Sino-Russian cooperation project aimed at developing a cross-national platform for distant outsourcing of high-profile specialists working in creative industries. The proposal covers economic, political, educational, and cultural issues and discusses the benefits of the initiative for both countries, as well as obstacles and problems that need to be overcome in order to implement the idea. The initiative is considered as a possible outcome of declared intentions of cooperation and mutual support between China and the Eurasian Economic Union regarding the Silk Road project, which was signed in May 2015 by Xi Jinping and Vladimir Putin.

Section 10.2 starts with a brief description of creative industries in China and Russia, their state, and forecasts for development. It continues with discussion of the differences between the countries and opportunities for potential cooperation between China and Russia with regard to creative industries. Section 10.3 describes the theoretical framework for an open labor market for high-profile specialists, outlining the legal and fiscal specifications of the initiative. Information is provided regarding technical gaps to overcome and their possible solutions. Section 10.4 explains the benefits that cooperation can bring to China and Russia and points out areas that require more clarification in future research.

10.2   Economic and Political Conditions in China and Russia

10.2.1   Creative Industries in China

Industrialization of China and transformation of it from a traditional agricultural economy into the "world's factory" was performed in a relatively short space of time as a result of the country's lag behind and overwhelming penetration of technologies and capital from other countries after the path of reformation and opening was adopted by the Communist Party of China. We are now observing China's even faster transition from secondary to tertiary economic sectors. According to the National Bureau of Statistics, for the past seven years from 2008 to 2015 primary industries have shrunk from 40 to 30%, secondary industries grew from 25 to 30%, and tertiary industries increased from 33 to 40%. It is worth mentioning that the primary sector of the economy contributed to 10% of the GDP in 2013, while secondary and tertiary sectors accounted for 43 and 46%, respectively. Thus, the service sector is the biggest driver of growth and the biggest provider of employment. About 38% of Chinese labor works in the service sector, whereas 31 and 30% are occupied in primary and secondary sectors, respectively.

As the Chinese economy is moving from export-lead to consumption-based, and the service sector is becoming more and more important, creative industries are receiving increased attention from government officials, scholars, and businesses. In the UK, the term "creative industries" refers to advertising, architecture, arts and antique markets, crafts, design, fashion, film, video and photography, software, electronic publishing, and television and radio. From another point of view, the UN has adopted classification of creative industries into four sectors: cultural heritage (traditional cultural expressions and cultural sites), art (visual arts and performing arts), media (publishing and print media, audio-visuals), and functional creation (design, new media, and creative services). In China, the term differs from national level to municipal level and there is no exact definition. In this paper, I take a broad definition, covering all areas where knowledge-intensive labor is presented. It would be limiting to adopt the UK classification because high-profile specialists might be employed in other sectors, for example, a graphic designer in a car manufacturing company (Zhang 2007).

China is developing unevenly, meaning that eastern regions are ahead of their western counterparts. The same thing can be said about the creative economy of China. Only major eastern cities such as Beijing, Tianjin, Shanghai, and Guangzhou possess enough assets to transform into next level of development and compete internationally (Hong et al. 2014). It is worth mentioning that the Chinese government has made several efforts to boost this process. Special zones have been opened where internet and knowledge-based companies can obtain tax relief or other means of subsidies. The educational model has been reformed to allow students to feel less stressed and have some time for analysis and critical thinking, instead of constant learning by rote. Intellectual property legislation has been improved so that companies feel safe about their investment in research and intangible assets. Furthermore, China is doing a lot to attract talents from abroad, understanding that only talents are the main drivers of a creative economy (Florida 2005).

Taking into account the current situation and observable tendencies, it is possible to say that China is on the way to smooth development of a creative economy; however, there are a few obstacles that should be mentioned. First, in spite of the overwhelming number of new graduates that China is acquiring each year, their quality is still considered insufficient by many company owners and managers. Unfortunately, possession of a university degree and the amount of time spent studying have pushed salary expectations too high. This, in turn, is an additional factor for the second issue—the rapid increase in salaries in the industry (Bodycott 2009). A creative economy requires a highly skilled and talented labor force; therefore, a lot of funds are being spent on attracting the best people. This implies that salaries in this segment of economy are rising faster than average, creating misbalance. This misbalance leads to a situation in which smaller companies cannot afford qualified employees and must withdraw from the market because they cannot compete locally or internationally.

Another view on the topic is given by the Toronto-based Martin Prosperity Institute, a world-leading think-tank on the role of creative economy in regional development. This institute publishes annual reports on the level of advancement of countries and regions based on three main preconditions of creative economy: technology, talent, and tolerance. Technology here refers to the concentration and national share of high-technology employment within a region and the number of patents produced. The talent mark is the percentage of the population over the age of 25 having a bachelors degree or above multiplied by share of the population occupied in creative industries. Tolerance describes the share of the population that belongs to ethnic, religious, or sexual minorities multiplied by the percentage of artistically creative people employed within a region's workforce, which includes authors, designers, musicians, composers, actors, and directors (Martin Prosperity Institute 2011).

The Global Creativity Index published by Martin Prosperity Institute in 2015 revealed that China is far behind developed countries in the rating, and behind its partners in BRICS (Brazil, Russia, India, and South Africa), being placed at number 62 (out of 139 countries observed).

China is in 87th place in the talent index and 96th in the tolerance index. The good news is that China is in 14th position for technology, overtaking developed nations such as the Netherlands and Italy. However, these numbers cannot fully describe the real situation because each nation has its own way of development. We will take this index as supporting information to compare countries, complementing other statistical observations.

10.2.2   Creative Economy in Russia

There have always been always ups and downs in Russian history. After collapse of the Soviet Union, the country is now taking back its position on the world stage as a supplier of technological products. Industrialization of Russia took place nearly simultaneously with other developed nations. However, intensive involvement in international affairs was very resource-consuming, meaning that the country could not maintain the same speed of development and, thus, transformation into a service-oriented economy occurred late and unevenly. Overreliance of modern government on income from export of national resources, instead of investment in developing a knowledge-based economy, is also creating additional obstacles for further development and successful international competition.

However, Russia still has a leading position in several knowledge-based industries, such as nuclear energy, aerospace, and defense. In addition, government-led segments also require massive investment. Russia is taking steps in the IT industry and there are several remarkable examples of Russian startups that have conquered international IT markets, such as Kaspersky (world-leading antivirus), VK (Europe's largest social network), Yandex (leading Cyrillic search engine), and many others, besides those established abroad by Russian immigrants such as Google, Oracle, United Technologies, and others (Immigration and Nationality Lawyers 2014). Unfortunately, government-led IT projects have not been successful enough to survive without financial support, in spite of the fact that the Kremlin, from time to time, makes announcements about government foundations and programs for development of knowledge-based industries (Surviving in the City 2013).

Research and development (R&D) centers owned by foreign multinationals first began to appear in Russia in the 1990s. Debis (now T-Systems) was the first, opening in 1995, followed by Intel and

Deutsche Bank in 2001, and Oracle (which now incorporates Sun Microsystems) in 2004. The trend continues, with recent R&D centers being opened by Nokia and Microsoft. Russia is regarded as a key destination for development units by major US and European companies because of the high quality of Russian programmers and the lower costs of doing business. Companies that maintain captive R&D centers in Russia and continue to see the country as a strategic source of talent include Intel, IBM, Huawei, HP, Google, and many others (Software Russia 2013).

All this implies that Russia is rich in skilled and qualified labor, which is also indicated by Global Creativity Index 2015 report created by Martin Prosperity Institute that puts the country in 38th position. As mentioned, the rating has three components—technology, talent, and tolerance—and the position of Russia in those indexes is 22nd, 15th, and 123rd respectively. The report shows that Russia has its strength in talents. Breakdown of this component into the two dimensions of creative class (occupational share and educational attainment) reveals a solid base because both measures are high, 19 and 15, respectively (Martin Prosperity Institute 2015).

As in China, salaries in Russia in creative industries are above average; however, because of economic slowdown related to international sanctions imposed by Western powers, wage growth has stopped. Furthermore, because the Russian ruble has devaluated by more than 100% against the US dollar and euro for the past two years, the labor force has become substantially cheaper than in the West or East, taking into account the productivity level of talents.

10.2.3   Outline of Differences and Potential Cooperation

At the beginning of the new millennia, Russia and China were considered to be in the same pattern of development, along with India and Brazil. These countries were combined into the economic club BRIC, first nominally and then operationally. However, after the global crisis of 2008 only China was able to maintain a substantial rate of economic growth so BRIC can no longer be considered homogeneous. Moreover, economic sanctions imposed on Russia are pushing the country backwards and forcing it to look for cooperation in the East, so that the Russian economy is now in a state of turbulence and semiblind transition. Thus, political and economic partnership with China is vital, but the Russian government is advancing carefully, making simultaneous steps in India and ASEAN countries (and even Japan, in spite of the high US presence there) so that it does not fall too much under Beijing's influence.

In May 2015, the leaders of Russia and China signed a declaration of joint cooperation in terms of the Silk Road program promoted by China and the Eurasian Economic Union led by Russia. In addition to paragraphs devoted to mutual development of infrastructure and trade between the countries, there are also clauses regarding support of small and medium enterprises and introduction of new schemes, regulations, and standards to enhance the volume of mutually beneficial cooperation. The declaration was signed and announced in the time of global tectonic changes in economic and political areas, which were also indicated by declining mutual trust between Russia and Western powers.

Sino-Russian economic cooperation also changed with the dramatic drop in the value of the Russian ruble. Chinese goods are not that cheap anymore for customers in Russia and the volume of trade fell by 27% in 2015. Volume of the main Russian export to China, hydrocarbons, is also shrinking because of the shift in energy sources and slowdown of manufacturing in the PRC. This is happening in spite of the huge drop in oil and gas prices in the past two years. However, reliable political relations between two countries are opening doors for other types of cooperation, such as banking, tourism, e-commerce, and bilateral venture investments complementing traditional partnerships in the defense industry (TASS Russian New Agency 2016).

Service trade between the countries has a relatively small share of the overall trade balance, less than 5%, and its structure is uneven and undeveloped. For an instance, in 2011, more than 76% of Russian service exports to China were in the areas of travel and transportation. In comparison, the share of the above mentioned sectors in overall Russian service exports (worldwide) was less than 50%, the rest being made up of construction, consulting, IT, and R&D. The same situation occurs with Chinese service exports to Russia. The share of travel and transportation sectors in exports to Russia is 79%, whereas these sectors occupy little more than 53% in the overall balance (Ponkratova 2013).

As mentioned above, creative industries are emerging in China and Russia although within different patterns of development, so that obstacles to overcome are different in the two countries. In the case of China, the main constraints to expansion are related to the productivity–cost ratio of the labor force. In Russia, issues are related to market entry, such as high bureaucratic barriers and tax pressures, in spite of the fact that the Russian government has announced its desire to develop a knowledge-based economy. China lacks a talented and skilled labor force to fuel its creative economy and Russia has an excess and is even experiencing brain-drain, which endangers further development of the country. Thus, China and Russia have something to offer each other and could bring their partnership to a new level (Nagibina and Mylnikova 2013).

This idea would not be so important if the labor market conditions did not align with the positive political relations between Moscow and Beijing. Analysis of the present situation and medium-term trends indicates that the salaries of knowledge-intensive and creative professionals such as designers, software developers, media editors, and web programmers are substantially lower in Russia than in the PRC.

Table 10.1 presents average wages in the creative sector in China and Russia. The data were taken from Chinese job portal jobui.com and its Russian analog mojazarplata.ru. The salaries are presented in Chinese Yuan (salaries in Russia were calculated by applying the average 2015 exchange rate) and were obtained by taking the mean value from job offers deployed on the portals.

The statistics presented in Table 10.1 show that Russian specialists earn half as much as their colleagues in China, and that 56% of those specialists work in Moscow, where salaries are much higher than in other regions (Tagline 2016). Thus, hiring a professional from somewhere another than Moscow would be even cheaper.

Table 10.1 Average salaries in the creative sector in China and Russia (in Yuan)

Profession	Salary in China	Statistical population	Salary in Russia	Statistical population
Graphic designer	5490	>60,000	2872	>7000
Software developer	7800	>200,000	4532	>8000
Video editor	5120	>2000	2875	>3000
Website editor	4220	>2600	3440	>6000

10.3   Theoretical Framework for an Open Labor Market

10.3.1   Technical Issues

An open labor market for distant high-profile specialists between Russia and China would be a novel type of cooperation, without any historical precedents, that will require extensive and complete work on legal, fiscal, and technical sides of the proposal. This chapter gives a brief description of the items that should be developed before the idea can be turned into reality.

Although the PRC copied governmental arrangements, and particularly labor law, from the Soviet Union, the situation is completely different now and direct distant hiring would require adjustments. At the moment, services between the countries are traded only by legal entities, which that implies that a huge share of the market is unexploited or hidden and uncontrolled, because establishment of a company with an international trade license requires additional expenditure. Lessening of the barriers and introducing distant employee and freelancer legal protection schemes would definitely enhance Sino-Russian partnership. Luckily, there are good examples of open labor markets in the EU and the North American Free Trade Agreement (NAFTA) so that a pragmatic first step is partial localization and adjustment of these experiences to the particular need, namely, for employing distant high-profile specialists and contracting freelancers.

Apart from direct hiring, it is important to analyze other ways of cooperation. For an instance, clients and specialists could be connected by an intermediate entity that could take legal and fiscal responsibilities, so that all the payments are controlled and taxed, contracts ensured, and statistical information gathered. Such an approach could also enhance cooperation reliability because the named entity might take market and business risks.

The fiscal side of the question is also difficult. How would retirement payments be calculated? What is the best approach for income tax deduction? Which government should ensure social support for retired, disabled, or pregnant employees? These are basic questions regarding fiscal policy that should be resolved in order to implement the idea of an open labor market for distant high-profile specialists. It is possible to assume that the tax burden should be divided between employees and employers, so that employees pay for their own retirement and potential social support and companies are obliged to pay for education and unemployment benefits.

10.3.2   Gaps to Overcome

Because political and economic conditions are favorable for the project, the legal and fiscal framework can be developed but there are still many questions regarding technical implementation of the idea. At first glance, it seems almost impossible to imagine that Chinese companies would benefit from hiring Russian professionals. The purpose of this chapter is to dispel the fog of doubt.

The first problem is the geographical distance between the countries. Although China and Russia are neighbors, the population of Russia is concentrated in the western part of the country, and in China it is eastern part, thus the time difference between the main cities is up to 5 hours. Therefore, it is understandable that simultaneous work is only possible to some extent; however, piecework does not require much instant communication. The creative industries require highly specialized personnel so that often a project is divided into several subprojects, which are performed by individuals rather than teams. Teamwork is necessary for planning and integration, but that can be done distantly so the time difference between Russia and China is not a big obstacle for smooth cooperation.

Probably the biggest technical issue is arranging flawless communication between counterparts. English is not widely spoken in Russia or China and few Russians can understand Chinese, and vice versa. Hiring a translator for each project would probably overshadow the economic benefits of the cooperation. However, it is possible to share this cost by utilizing the services of an intermediate entity who could batch-translate communication flows. Apart from human translation, there are also much cheaper or even free translation machines that are improving daily. It is still not possible to replace a human translator by a machine completely; however, an approach involving use of translation software for general and common conversations, supplemented with a human interpreter where necessary, seems to be vital.

Another issue is the difference between business cultures in China and Russia. There are differences in perceptions of deadlines, problem-solving approaches, expense calculations, evaluation of results, and other working details that might affect cross-national cooperation. Obviously, all these obstacles have more influence when communication is direct and much less when an intermediate entity is involved to deal with those issues.

Internet-based partnership implies that there is higher possibility for cheating and fraud due to geographical distance and differences in legal systems. Therefore, policy-makers and other responsible people should ensure safe cooperation by measures such as creation of a database that collects evaluations and opinions about clients and performers, or building a safe payment system using letters of credit (or similar method). Such simple steps can substantially decrease the amount of inappropriate business activity.

10.4   BENEFITS OF THE PROPOSAL

This section underlines the benefits that an open labor market for distant high-profile specialists between China and Russia can bring. In general, all the benefits mentioned are of a medium- and long-term nature and differ from country to country; however, it is difficult not to admit their value.

The most obvious advantages are related to material gains. In the case of China, savings can be made by hiring distant employees and outsourcing piecework to freelancers in Russia. In the case of Russia, additional input to the country's economy is made through an increase in service export.

Apart from savings in human resources, Chinese companies could gain extra competitive advantage by acquiring Western-style expertise from Russian partners. However, such a diversification of workflow definitely requires proper management solutions to obtain synergetic outcomes. This cooperation might help Chinese companies have a better outlook abroad, particularly in Russia, because small and medium-sized enterprises (SMEs) (and sometimes even market giants) do not generally care about their image in foreign markets, but push their products through lower prices. Furthermore, diversification, if managed accordingly, gives impulse to team creativity, which is a core element in the current economy.

Another macroeconomic benefit the countries could obtain once the cooperation is established is development of a labor force. In the case of Russia, more professionals will be attracted to serve the market because the amount of work to be done will increase with the demand from China. This distant cooperation will diminish brain-drain, which is a substantial problem for Russia at the moment. However, how could Chinese labor develop if Russian specialists take their place? The Chinese economy is much bigger than that of Russia and developing faster, so it is impossible to substitute all Chinese high-profile professionals. Inclusion of a share of the labor force from Russia allows Chinese employees to gain overseas expertise and know-how.

The proposed project will also enhance Sino-Russian integration politically and culturally. Established legal and fiscal frameworks can allow bigger cross-national projects without direct involvement of government officials. Also, the gained experience of joint cooperation can dissolve existing cultural obstacles, particularly those within the business environment, so that smoother and more fruitful working processes between Russian and Chinese counterparts can be launched.

Thus, the proposal of a Sino-Russian open labor market for distant high-profile employees suggests a real and pragmatic supplementation of existing friendly political ties between the two nations. This solidification can enhance the partnership with connections that serve as a base for multinational cooperation in a more concrete way than announcements by government officials and less practical memorandums.

10.5   Conclusion

The possible benefits from implementing the above-mentioned proposal are clear; however, it is still not certain whether they can cover all related expenses. It is only possible to say that success of the venture depends on establishing easy-to-operate-in conditions and introduction of an intermediate entity that will support connections between clients and developers to diminish risks and other business-related obstacles.

This chapter has given a brief description of an opportunity available to China and Russia. To fully understand the potential and cost of the project, further deep research is necessary in the areas of labor legislation in China and Russia, fiscal policy in both countries, and similar national and multinational ventures.

REFERENCES

Bilton, C. (2007). *Management and creativity: From creative industries to creative management*. Malden: Blackwell Publishing.

Bodycott, P. (2009). Choosing a higher education study abroad destination what mainland Chinese parents and students rate as important. *Journal of Research in International Education, 8*(3), 349–373.

Florida, R. (2003). Entrepreneurship, creativity, and regional economic growth. *The emergence of entrepreneurship policy*, 39–58.

Florida, R. L. (2005). *The flight of the creative class* (p. 326). New York: Harper Business.

Hong, J., Yu, W., Guo, X., & Zhao, D. (2014). Creative industries agglomeration, regional innovation and productivity growth in China. *Chinese Geographical Science, 24*(2), 258–268.

Immigration and Nationality Lawyers. (2014). *Top 10 US companies started by immigrants*. Available at http://greencard-us.com/top-ten-fortune-500-companies-owned-by-immigrants/. Last accessed on March 18 2016.

Martin Prosperity Institute. (2011, February). *Understanding the creative economy in China* [Press release].

Martin Prosperity Institute. (2015). *Creative economy report 2015* [Press release].

Nagibina, N. P., & Mylnikova, E. M. (2013). Problems of forming innovative economy in Russia. *Journal of Creative Economy, 75*, 81–85.

Ponkratova, L. A. (2013). Assessment of the main trends and structural changes in trade of services between Russia and China. *Vesntik TSU*.

Software Russia. (2013). *Captive R&D centers*. Available at http://www.software-russia.com/why_russia/captive. Last accessed on March 19 2016.

Surviving in the City. (2013). *The Russian IT giants, overview of Russian IT companies*. Available at http://survincity.com/2013/08/the-russian-it-giants/. Last accessed on March 18 2016.

Tagline. (2016). *Все о кадрах в Российском Digital*. Available at http://tagline.ru/staff-salaries-rates-education-hiring/. Last Accessed on January 11 2016.

TASS Russian News Agency. (2016). *Russia-China trade turnover falls by almost 30% in 2015*. Available at http://tass.ru/en/economy/849074. Last accessed on March 21 2016.

Zhang, J. (2007). *Development of creative Industries in China*. Beijing: China's Economy Publishing.

CHAPTER 11

China–Europe Investment Cooperation: A Digital Silk Road

Mireia Paulo

11.1   THE DIGITAL ERA: A COMMON GROUND FOR SINO-EUROPEAN COOPERATION

The year 2015 was the 40th anniversary of the establishment of diplomatic relations between the European Union (EU) and the People's Republic of China (PRC). Related events celebrating the partnership—intoxicated with positive official signals, warm tributes to each other, and an evident economic need to survive in an increasingly volatile international context—provided an appropriate institutional environment for looking at domestic economic initiatives and outlining new areas for cooperation.

The proliferation and enhanced integration of the internet of things (IoT) in daily life and increased opportunities involving information and communication technologies (ICTs) have pushed governments to look at the digital industry, develop a regulation framework, and promote research and innovation. The internet provides new ways of communicating, doing business, and providing services, but also opens new risks

M. Paulo (✉)
Ruhr University Bochum, Bochum, Germany

© The Author(s) 2018   177
Y. Cheng et al. (eds.), *The Belt & Road Initiative in the Global Arena*,
https://doi.org/10.1007/978-981-10-5921-6_11

of cybercrime. Internet and the digitalization of citizens' habits bring potential avenues for cooperation between China and the EU, and even more for private industry because neither country holds a top ranking with regard to digital industries.

There is a lack of scholarly literature on the Sino-European Investment Cooperation, and particularly in the 5G field due to its novelty. Therefore, this research is based on an in-depth review of official documents and material from business, finance, industry, and politics. In addition to interviews with 6 European officials, 4 Chinese officials, and 5 scholars, this explorative research was informed by direct participation of the author in various working groups and debates. This chapter argues that both partners must boost resources to enhance their digital strategies through the EU–China Investment Cooperation. This will, at the same time, support two significant domestic economic initiatives, the European Fund for Strategic Investments (EFSI) and the Belt and Road (B&R) initiative.[1]

The starting point of this chapter is a brief overview of the B&R and EFSI initiatives as the background for launching the EU–China Investment Cooperation. It will trace the origins of this investment cooperation and attempt to outline the institutional cooperation and possible avenues. This chapter then looks at the cooperation regarding digital industries, with particular reference to the plan to establish a 5G market.

11.2   The Belt and Road Initiative

Coined in 2013, the B&R initiative refers to a direct translation from the Chinese *yī dài yī lù* (一带一路). This slogan refers to the traditional Silk Road, understood by Chinese politicians (with Chinese scholars following) as an impressive route that has historically connected the West and East through economic, trade, and cultural exchanges. When President Xi spoke for the first time about the modern Silk Road in September 2013, at a Kazakhstan university, he referred to it as the "Silk Road Economic Belt" (丝绸之路经济带) (Wen 2015). Later, in

---

[1] This chapter will apply to the official concept and acronym used by the national Chinese government that officially states how to translate the Chinese concepts into English. For more information visit: http://language.chinadaily.com.cn/2015-09/24/content_21970378.htm.

October, during a meeting of the ASEAN countries, he also mentioned the proposed "21st-Century Maritime Silk Road" (21世纪海上丝绸之路), highlighting the initiative as a new model for the geoeconomy (世界地缘经济) (Wen 2015).

The B&R is not an entirely new initiative; it has built upon previous initiatives based on projects in various regions of China, such as Yunnan, Chongqing, and Xinjiang. These regions were developed in terms of infrastructure and economic networks in the past decade ("EU, China sign key partnership on 5G 2015; Zhou 2015; Lu 2015). The initiative is also perceived as an opportunity to improve and develop Chinese products, to adapt to new competition, and to market and internationalize companies (Summers 2015; Guancha 2015a). However, the B&R boundaries and limits, plans, and concrete actions for implementation still are unclear for many (Zhou 2015; Lu 2015; Guancha 2015b).

National and local governments urge the business sector to "Go Global," learn from international best market practices, expand business, develop brands, and apply for high technology and overseas talents (Summers 2015; Lu 2015). At the same time, the initiative is developing mechanisms for funding through co-sponsoring of the New Development Bank, but has also has sought to raise the profile of its global financial diplomacy with other funds; for instance, the China Development Bank expressed the intention to finance 900 projects with around US$890 billion, while the Bank of China committed US$100 billion (Donnan 2015; Wildau 2015).

As with any ambitious initiative, challenges appear everywhere. Among these, three difficulties stand out. The first concerns the security of infrastructure, especially when persuing the ambitious project of building 81,000 km of high-speed railway through 65 countries. Many of these projects are planned in countries with unstable political and economic environments, or even suffering from armed conflicts, where providing security for the workers will be difficult. The second challenge regards territoriality. On the land side, the belt crosses much of the former Soviet Union, and on the maritime side, several territorial disputes remain unsolved. Third, the issue of funding and returns on investment needs to be addressed. Infrastructure projects have long funding cycles, low interest rates, and provide ample room for corruption when investing in low-income countries with unstable politics and emerging economies. All these challenges pose a severe risk to the initiative (Jing 2015; Zhu 2015).

Thus, the B&R is an initiative, but also a rhetoric discourse, that is linked to the fact that the Chinese economy is suffering a slowdown and needs to find a more stable growth path.

11.3   THE EUROPEAN FUND FOR STRATEGIC INVESTMENTS

Geopolitics is less ambitious in the European Commission's Investment Plan for Europe, known as the "Juncker Plan," initiated by the current President of the European Commission, Jean-Claude Juncker. On 24 June 2015, the plan entered its proceeding phase, with the European Parliament voting in favor of establishing the European Fund for Strategic Investments (EFSI). On 22 July, the Commission agreed on a package of measures that allowed the EFSI to be up and running by the end of 2015.

The EFSI aims to address the situation where the EU has sufficient liquidity, but private investors are not investing at the levels needed to reignite economic growth in the EU. It has three main objectives: removing obstacles to investment by deepening the single market, providing visibility and technical assistance to investment projects, and making smarter use of new and existing financial resources. The European Investment Group and the European Commission signaled support of the Juncker Plan by injecting around €315 billion over three years into four key areas in Europe: infrastructure, education, energy, and SMEs (European Commission 2016a; European Investment Bank 2016).

The investment plan has obtained funding support from Germany and France, who will contributing €8 billion each. Other European countries such as Bulgaria are set to fund around €100 million (Delegation to China, 2015). Investment is also open to non-European countries such as China, who have already pledged to invest over €10 billion (Gray 2015). China could become the largest external investor in the EFSI, according to Vice-Premier Ma Kai during the High-Level Economic and Trade Dialogue (HED) on 28 September 2015. At this meeting, Ma Kai informed Jyrki Katainen, Vice-President of the European Commission, that China will contribute to the EFSI with over €315 billion in investment projects (Cao 2015; European Commission 2015a).

The Investment Plan for Europe has already begun to show positive results and the EC has recently published the workings of the EFSI on its online portal. As of January 2016, the EFSI implemented its initial steps by approving the investment of €5.7 billion to 42 infrastructure projects across 16 European countries, including Germany, the UK, Slovenia, and Croatia (Steinbock 2015).

11.4   EU–China Investment Cooperation: Aligning Economic Initiatives

Sino-European official discussions have gradually included new areas of cooperation contributing to the development of the present institutional framework. During the latest EU–China HED that took place in Beijing on 28 September 2015, officials from both regions explored possible areas of collaboration open to the EU and China in the light of both B&R and EFSI initiatives (European Commission 2015b). Hans-Dietmar Schweisgut, the EU Ambassador to China, quoted the European Commission President Jean-Claude Junker by declaring, "the benefits of B&R are not just for China itself; Europe, too, stands to benefit from better connections with Asia's dynamic economies" (Pavlićević 2015). Officials from both parties stated that they would look at areas and projects of common benefit.

A number of similarities between both economic initiatives have been identified, given the fact that they will be investing heavily in infrastructure in different European countries. The overlap of investment areas allows both the B&R and the EFSI to benefit from inward investment into the recipient countries, improved connectivity and advanced technology, and improved infrastructure in these countries (Jing 2015; Pavlićević 2015).

The EU–China Investment Cooperation was established less than one year ago, but has already taken some steps forward. The first step was to set up a joint working group comprising experts from both EFSI and B&R initiatives, which is charged with the responsibility of establishing cooperation mechanisms on the Investment Plan for Europe, EFSI, and other European Investment Bank group activities. At the HED, the European Commission and the Chinese government signed a Memorandum of Understanding to enhance synergy between B&R and the EFSI, launching the EU–China Connectivity Platform and the Trans-European Transport Network policy.

The EU–China Connectivity Platform was the second opportunity identified. It aims to facilitate discussions on cooperation strategies, plans, policies, and projects to provide visibility on investment opportunities along the Silk Road. Additionally, the Trans-European Transport Network policy endorses projects related to infrastructure, equipment, technology, and standards. The third step was creation of a European Investment Project Portal, which is used to attract future domestic and international investment into projects in the EU. It is a public and user-friendly database that lists investment projects. (European Commission 2015b; Jing 2015).

Official meetings and conferences on the EU–China Investment Cooperation have been held in Brussels and Beijing. Their aim was to discuss the achievements of the EU–China Investment Cooperation in 2015 and to exchange views between European and Chinese official institutions, and business and investment experts working on the EU–China Investment Cooperation. On 16 February 2016, a workshop on the topic was held at the European Parliament in Brussels.[2]

During the workshop, Madame Yang Yanyi, Chinese Ambassador to the EU, emphasized the many converging interests that exist between Europe and China's economic agendas, such as China's Internet Plus (互联网 +)[3] and Europe's Digital Agenda. She also elaborated on the advancement of EU–China cooperation in the digital economy, including the development of 5G wireless networks. At the same time, Miguel Gil-Tertre[4] and Laurent Bardon[5] highlighted four strategic areas for the EU–China Investment Cooperation to focus on for the present year:

1. Encourage Chinese investments to advance European digital infrastructure and services in accordance with the Juncker Plan
2. Create a high-level task force to identify specific opportunities for European businesses in China. Also, expand Chinese business in Europe in fields such as high-technology innovation, green and renewable energy, and agricultural equipment

---

[2] The author of this chapter, Mireia Paulo, participated in the workshop as a speaker.

[3] A plan that focuses on the internet of things, mobile internet, big data, and cloud computing.

[4] Member of the cabinet of Commissioner/Vice-President Jyrki Katainen for jobs, growth, investment, and competitiveness.

[5] Policy Coordinator, China, Hong Kong, Macao, Taiwan, and Mongolia at DG TRADE.

3. Establish major investment funding and incentives focused on incubating high-technology startups and collaborative innovation in both Europe and China

4. Enhance cooperation on "smart cities"

The EU is currently considering ways in which Chinese funds can be aligned with the EFSI in a way that works in conjunction with the B&R. The European Investment Bank has set up a team to explore how best to facilitate the investment, which will include experts from China's Silk Road Fund, the European Investment Bank, and the European Commission.[6]

The EFSI aims to focus on non-EU and private sector companies, which could be a natural gateway for European countries to invest and participate in the B&R through the EFSI. The other gateway will be first through the B&R, which could promote investment or manufacturing opportunities for European companies, as well as opportunities in R&D, clean energy, and education (Pavlićević 2015; Valero 2015). Chinese officials hope that by China investing in EFSI, Europe will be more likely to invest in the Asian Infrastructure Investment Bank (AIIB) and B&R initiatives (Emmot and Taylor 2015).[7]

It appears that, at the top-level, both the EU and China have confirmed their interest in each other's initiative with their respective investment pledges. The current Investment Plan for Europe's budget stands at US$358 billion, while the B&R currently commits about US$1.4 trillion (Pavlićević 2015; Jing 2015). The investment from China is of great value for the EFSI because it grants the EFSI increased monetary capability to inject into significantly more projects.[8] The main Sino-European common voice at the institutional level is that China's contribution to the new investment fund represents a "win–win situation" for both partners. Beijing seeks to bolster its soft power in Europe, looks for large-scale projects to invest in, and brings some solutions to the economic slowdown in both areas (Casarini 2015a; Gray 2015; Valero 2015). The

---

[6]Based on interviews conducted with European officials in Brussels during February 2016.

[7]Based on interviews conducted with Chinese officials in Shanghai during April–May 2016.

[8]Based on interviews conducted with Chinese officials in Shanghai during April–May 2016.

EU can benefit from the injection of capital in a diversified portfolio that can provide the acceleration required by European SMEs struggling from a liquidity shortage. These businesses have an enormous potential for expansion in the Chinese market thanks to their added value in terms of know-how and high technology. The EFSI alone is of considerable interest to many European countries and companies; however, the collaboration of the EFSI and the AIIB is of worldwide interest and many investors across the globe will be keeping a watchful eye on it.[9]

The combination of both European and non-European countries, namely China, investing in the initiative has been met with both appraisal and doubt. The primary criticism that such outside investment has attracted is from European companies that are seeking to implement projects, such as construction companies looking to secure infrastructure deals (Steel industry calls for EU action on Chinese imports 2015; Protests show strength of German attachment to steel 2016). These companies view Chinese investment in a negative light because outside investments may require non-EU companies with cheaper products to complete certain projects.

It remains to be seen how the cooperation will develop once both initiatives are fully functional. At the moment, it seems that the collaborative functioning of both initiatives could be fruitful for both Europe and China. This institutional cooperation is perceived as a further cooperative step for the organizations involved.

11.5   The Locked Doors of Opportunity

Sino-European investment cooperation could be what is needed to stimulate growth in both Europe and Asia. However, its primary focus on infrastructure projects is extremely narrow for achieving optimal results.

The EFSI and B&R initiatives share a common interest in that both projects seek to funnel investment into infrastructure. There have been talks of a China–EU joint investment fund for contracting and financing. The co-financing will primarily begin with Sino-European infrastructure projects in Eastern Europe and the Balkans. The Investment Plan for Europe plans to spend 20% of its €315 billion fund on infrastructure

---

[9]Based on interviews conducted with European officials in Brussels during February 2016.

projects across Europe through the EFSI, whereas China's US$1.4 trillion funding focuses solely on investment projects from China (Jing 2015). The link between infrastructure projects in Asia and Europe can be seen as complementary: an incentive for China to invest in Europe's infrastructure initiative as well as an essential boost for European infrastructure projects, given that only 20% of EFSI funds will be dedicated to infrastructure.

Looking past these initial positive plans, the complex nature of intercontinental investment projects increases the likelihood of conflicting interests in the early stages of the projects. A common problem is the allocation of construction contracts to companies seeking to secure the infrastructure deals. An example is evident in the negative perception that—by financing European infrastructure projects—the Chinese government will impose on Chinese companies (including state-owned enterprises) to carry on those projects harming European companies, as the European steel industry indicated throughout the first semester of 2016 (Protests show strength of German attachment to steel 2016). This gives China a gateway into Europe, whereas European companies have a lesser chance of winning contracts to build infrastructure projects in China (Casarini 2015b). As with many intercontinental initiatives, teething issues such as the one highlighted above are both common and expected.

Furthermore, clashes of interests also exist. China hopes that European markets will absorb its goods and industrial overcapacity, meanwhile Europe is more interested in the increased exporting opportunities that B&R may provide. The competition between companies from both regions is also evident. Chinese products compete with 35% of European goods. It can never really be a win–win situation because one country is likely to end up losing a market share to the other (Pavlićević 2015).

There is also European skepticism regarding Chinese-backed platforms and their compliance with technical and environmental requirements (Pavlićević 2015). The Chinese government and companies are commonly criticized for breaking transparency rules, limited implementation of international standards, and partial compliance with environmental, technical, and safety requirements (Casarini 2015b). An example that illustrates this fact is the case of the construction of a prototype nuclear reactor in Bradwell, Essex near London, by a Chinese company (Graham-Harrison 2015; Sykes 2015). The plans for the nuclear plant have stirred controversy among the British population because of the subsidies the British Government has agreed to pay, but also for security reasons. British public opinion depicts a fear pertaining to the Chinese design, technology, and expertise in building a safe nuclear plant near their homes (Chinese reactor plan fuels British security fears 2015).

Despite these frictions, it is possible to identify key common sectors in the new smart manufacturing technologies that are of equal interest to both European and Chinese companies, such as big data, cloud computing, mobility, and the internet of things (IoT). Furthermore, possible avenues for business opportunities have been identified in the following sectors: pharmaceutical and healthcare, automotive, research and innovation, high-technology innovation (robotics, low carbon technologies, and green energy), and transportation (railway equipment, aerospace and aviation equipment, maritime engineering equipment, and high-technology vessel manufacturing).

For instance, Miao Wei, China's Minister of Industry and Information Technology, encouraged local internet companies to develop electric vehicles, which can reduce reliance on imported oil and reduce carbon footprints (Tate 2015). A McKinsey Global Institute report shows that China's chemical industry is exploring new ways to employ big data on inventory levels. Big data also has the potential to provide better support to farmers, enabling them to monitor crop conditions in real time, which will cut production costs, increase farm yields, and allow product customization. The IoT also entails new business opportunities for the healthcare sector, such as the implementation of remote patient monitoring. This is a growing field that offers advantages to home healthcare, elderly care sectors, and anyone residing in an isolated area (Woetzel 2014).

The success of the EU–China investment cooperation relies on the ability of the EU and China to cooperate through regular communication at all levels, not simply at the institutional level. Both potential avenues and profound frictions exist. This cooperation should not simply focus on infrastructure projects, but look to those sectors where science, business, and society can also benefit from joint projects such as the digital industry.

11.6 Embracing the Digital Industry for a Deeper Sino-European Cooperation

A rapid and evolving market for the internet is booming. The IoT has become part of the economic and social development in both regions. ICTs bring opportunities for all sectors in society. On the one hand, mobile internet users require various types of wireless connection, higher data rate, zero latency, consistent usage under various scenarios, support of massive connections, and personalized services. On the other hand, services involve ultrahigh definition, 3D, virtual reality, cloud desktop, cloud storage, and IoT services.

In the internet age, both the EU and China are aware that they need to advance their internal conditions to adapt to the digital future and become more competitive in the sector. During the HED of September 2015, the two sides agreed to cooperate closely on investment, connectivity, and the digital economy (European Commission 2015a).

However, the EU suffers from commercial and security weaknesses in the current digital world; most of the browsers and e-commerce giants are companies from the USA. European consumers, companies, and even governments might become more dependent without direct control of big data (Prodi and Gos 2016). European policy to combat cybercrime and breaches of privacy and personal data security still requires further improvement. Existing online barriers mean that citizens lack goods and services, and that startups and internet companies find themselves handcuffed. The European Commission, aware of these constraints, decided to launch the Digital Agenda in May 2010,[10] with the aim of ensuring that ICTs, including IoT, are used to stimulate Europe's economy and help Europe's citizens and businesses to get the most out of these technologies. It is part of the "Europe 2020" strategy to foster innovation, economic and inclusive growth, and sustainable development (European Commission 2010, 2016b).

On 19 April 2016, the European Commission presented its blueprint for cloud-based services and world-class data infrastructure. It plans to create a European Open Science Cloud[11] and European Data Infrastructure[12] by interconnecting existing national research infrastructures. The European Commission intends to offer 1.7 million for research and 70 million for science and technology professionals. By doing so, the European Data Infrastructure will be leveraged with

---

[10]For more information visit https://ec.europa.eu/digital-single-market/en.

[11]For more information, see https://ec.europa.eu/research/openscience/index.cfm?pg=open-science-cloud.

[12]For more information, see https://www.csc.fi/en/-/eudat-european-data-infrastructure.

high-bandwidth networks, large scale storage facilities, and supercomputer capacity (European Commission 2016c).

Devices, applications, data repositories, services, and networks lack interoperability in all regions of the EU. Standard-setting policy, appropriate rules for intellectual property rights, and competitively priced offerings must be reviewed by the European Commission. In addition, next-generation access networks, internet access for all, and 50% of European households subscribing to internet connections above 100 Mbps by 2020 have to be in place to match world internet leaders such as South Korea. New services such as high-definition television or videoconferencing need significantly increased internet access than is generally available in Europe. To turn this ambition into reality, the European Commission's Digital Agenda is channeling a portion of its public funds into broadband infrastructure and proposes a radio spectrum plan (European Commission 2016b).

In the case of China, the flourishing of the internet in the past two decades has not yet arrived at an impasse. On the contrary, the Chinese online community has become the largest in the world. The China Internet Network Information Center (CINIC 2016) data showed that, by December 2015, there were about 688 million internet users. Despite this large number of users, China does not appear among the top 50 countries with the highest internet penetration rate. According to the Internet World Stats (IWS 2013), to be on the list, over 65% of the total country population should use the internet. China has over 50.3% penetration rate (IWS 2015). Germany is 16th with 82.7% and Spain is in 49th position with 65.6%. The new digital era has arrived at various speeds and to different degrees in China.

A digital China is strongly supported by the national government through different plans and strategies. On 19 May 2015, China's State Council unveiled their China Manufacturing 2025 strategy (中国制造2025), also known as "Made in China 2025" or the "Fourth Industrial Revolution" (第四次工业革命). This strategy aims to turn China into a leading smart manufacturing nation by encouraging innovation and digitalization, whereby production processes and speeds will be adapted to minimize costs and increase efficiency. Premier Li Keqiang has repeatedly stated that the Made in China 2025 strategy will be implemented in conjunction with Internet Plus. In this regard, the Chinese government has pledged support that will cover tax incentives and special funding for ten industrial sectors that have been identified as the core of the plan. These sectors include next-generation information technology, automated machine tools and robotics, aerospace and aeronautical equipment, maritime equipment and high-tech shipping, modern rail transportation equipment, new energy vehicles and equipment, power equipment, agricultural equipment, new materials, and biopharma and advanced medical products (PRC 2015; MIIT 2016).

Additionally, the 13th Five-Year Plan (FYP) (第十三个五年规划纲要) was adopted on 16 March 2016. The document contains a whole new chapter (Chap. 6) dedicated to expanding the space of the cyber-economy beyond the national borders (拓展网络经济空间), and chapter seven is devoted to the infrastructure required (构筑现代基础设施网络). There are two new priorities interlinked with the digital economy, innovation-driven development (创新驱动发展战略) and the new economic development system (发展新体制) (FMPRC 2016). Because the cyber-economy provides a new and promising growth path for the country, the Chinese government will update the transnational internet infrastructure and create a network for e-commerce with Arabic countries; the so-called e-Silk Road.

On Tuesday 19 April 2016, Chinese President Xi Jinping announced the new Chinese Internet Strategy or Cyber Strategy (互联网战略). He also pledged to strengthen China's internet security (中国网络安全战略) and build the nation as a strong cyber power(网络强国). President Xi, as the head of China's Central Internet Security and Informatization Leading Group (中央网络安全和信息化领导小组), reminded listeners of the ambitious objectives already described in the FYP (2016–2020) for the development of the Chinese ICT sector (Where are the current features and profound meaning of the new internet public opinion view 2016; New China internet strategy unveiled 2016). The declaration and political guidelines of the PRC came just after the adoption by the European Parliament of significant legislation for development of the European internet sector. The simultaneous actions by both partners show that they intend to adopt a more solid regulatory framework to guarantee cyber security and data privacy to foster the penetration of internet usage (New China internet strategy unveiled 2016).

On 25 May 2016, Ambassador to the EU Yang Yanyi explained that China's cyber strategy concentrates on four main tasks. First, China will build high-speed, mobile and secure modern communication networks through a new generation of high-speed fiber-optic networks; urban areas will be provided with a 1000 Mb high-speed network and about 90% of rural areas should be provided with fiber-optic networks.

Currently, China is popularizing 4G at town and village levels. The second task is to develop a modern internet industrial system, which means integrating mobile internet, cloud computing, big data, and the IoT with modern manufacturing, e-business, and internet banking, and encouraging internet-based companies to increase their presence in the international market. The third task is implementation of a national big data strategy (大数据战略规划). Big data platforms and centers are rapidly increasing at a national level to boost big data collection, storage, processing, analysis, visualization, and other key technologies; to upgrade big data technology infrastructure; and to promote big data commercialization and the development of hardware and software products for big data applications. Finally, the fourth task involves enhancing cyber security, which will be addressed by implementing a series of measures including speeding up legislation on the internet; enhancing information sharing and supervision over cyberspace; and setting up a system for protecting information infrastructure in various industries such as finance, telecommunications, and transportation (Yang 2016).

The digital economy has become a crucial driver for China's economic development. It is therefore not surprising that President Xi Jinping repeatedly emphasizes that the internet has the potential to be a driving force for economic growth, and growth should be driven by the principles of innovation, coordination, greener development, opening up to the rest of the world, and social inclusion. China's national government is encouraging Chinese internet players to innovate in core technologies and expand their businesses to overseas markets. It also intends to create a favorable environment for attracting foreign internet companies and professionals, as long as they respect Chinese regulations (Xi Jinping speech on national cyber security strategy 2014; Where are the current features and profound meaning of the new internet public opinion view 2016; Xi Jinping: Make the internet better benefit the nation and people 2016).

As indicated by European and Chinese internal policies, and internet plans and strategies, both partners wish to further improve their digitalization processes, innovative technology, and a new generation of infrastructure. The increasing importance of the digital economy is also reflected in the wider bilateral relations between the EU and China, with the topic being regularly addressed at the EU–China Summit. Moreover, since 2009, the Directorate-General CONNECT and Ministry of Industry and Information Technology (MIIT) maintain an annual Dialogue on Information Technology, Telecommunications and Information. Futhermore, since 2012 both institutions co-chair the EU–China Cyber Taskforce. This taskforce provides the framework for trade and research-related dialogues and cooperation mechanisms.[13] Taking advantage of both partner's needs, the Technical Working Group on China–EU Cooperation on Investment has exchanged views on a co-investment vehicle, developing concrete opportunities for both regions while exploiting the complementarities of each other's competitive advantages (innovative technology in Europe and a large market in China). However, up to July 2016, concrete projects have not been implemented. It seems that exchanges take place at the top level, but they do not reach the ground. Unless the private sector of both regions start to work together on their own initiative, further concrete cooperation in this field does not seem likely.

11.7   A Digital Silk Road: Starting from the 5G Market

5G is the next generation of mobile communications technology and should become standard by 2020. According to the European Commissioner Guenther Oettinger, "5G will be the backbone of our digital economies and societies worldwide" (MWL 2015). 5G is the linchpin for the IoT to offer great improvements in communication: transfer rates as high as 20 gigabytes of data per second (4G offers speeds up to 1 gigabit per second), but also other applications that connect everything to internet, such as cars, homes, health monitors, and much more (European Commission 2015c). 5G is expected to be commercially available around 2020.

However, that five-year timeframe may prove a challenge for some countries. To meet the requirements for more than a thousand-fold growth in mobile traffic in a sustainable way, to support up to 100 billion connections, and to provide a consistent experience under diverse scenarios with ultrahigh data rates requires high-speed mobile networks that can handle a huge amount of data flow. Both partners are aware that by pooling resources, the infrastructure and technology required can be

---

[13] Based on interviews conducted with European officials in Brussels during February 2016.

developed faster, while increasing competitiveness in the international digital market.

11.7.1   Background of the 5G Telecommunication System in China and the EU

Prior to signing the agreement on 5G telecommunication systems, whose commercialization is expected by 2020, the EU and China have been taking individual steps in this field.

At the end of 2013, the European Commission launched its 5G Public-Private Partnership (5G PPP) in conjunction with industry manufacturers, telecommunications operators, service providers, SMEs, and researchers. The 5G PPP was set up to deliver new generation communication infrastructure, technology, and standards for the operation of 5G.[14] A key objective is to leverage 5G research to improve competitiveness and innovation. It is expected that 5G PPP will provide solutions to some of the societal challenges identified in the Digital Agenda; for instance an optimized radio frequency usage. The European Commission will invest approximately €700 million by 2020 through the Horizon 2020[15] research and innovation program, while the European industry is set to match this investment almost fivefold to more than €3 billion (European Commission 2016d; MWL 2015). Currently, discussions concerning 5G radio access network (RAN) design aspects, particularly related to efficient integration of multiple novel 5G air interfaces, are ongoing. Under the aegis of the 5G PPP, a number of projects have ben initiated, such as METIS-II, FANTASTIC-5G,[16] mmMAGIC, and 5G NORMA.

At the 2015 Mobile World Congress, the European Commission and the European telecommunication industry presented the EU's vision

---

[14] For more information visit: https://5g-ppp.eu/.

[15] For more information see: http://ec.europa.eu/programmes/horizon2020/.

[16] The latest EU -backed research project designed to develop standards for the next generation of mobile technology is called 'FANTASTIC 5G, which was joined by 16 leading providers in July. Leading operators and vendors team up, including Nokia Networks, Huawei, Orange, and Telecom Italia, to develop a new air interface below 6 GHz for 5G networks. It will run for 2 years, with a total of €8 million in EU funding. For more information visit http://www.mobileworldlive.com/featured-content/home-banner/16-providers-join-latest-eu-backed-5g-research-project/.

of 5G technologies and infrastructure. The strategy provides a stronger voice to the EU in the global discussions related to international agreements and standards. For example, at the ICT-2015 hosted in Lisbon on 20 October 2015, Commissioner Oettinger hosted the global workshop on 5G standards and spectrum with representatives from the USA, South Korea, Japan, and China (European Commission 2015d; Liu 2016). Furthermore, at the end of 2015, the European Commission launched public consultations on the evaluation and review of the regulatory framework for electronic communications networks and services. The aim of this public consultation was to improve effective spectrum coordination and common EU-wide criteria for spectrum assignment at the national level (ETNO 2016).[17]

China wishes to become a key player in the digital world. The digital industry is developing rapidly in the country, where four of the ten largest global internet companies are evidently Chinese. Various Chinese companies have become major international players, such as Alibaba, Tencent, Huawei, ZTE, Xiaomi, Baidu, e-tailer JD.com, and travel websites such as Ctrip and Qunar (China–EU digital cooperation promising 2016). It is very likely that China will become the world's largest market for 5G technologies, products, and services. As a result, the institution of a 5G global standard is of interest to the Chinese government.

China's IMT-2020 (5G) promotion group was jointly established by the MIIT, the National Development and Reform Commission (NDRC), and the Ministry of Science and Technology (MOST) in February 2013. The aim of this group is to promote 5G technology research and facilitate international communication and cooperation. The members include the main operators, vendors, universities, and research institutions in China (IMT 2014).

According to the MIIT, China aims to develop 5G telecommunications frequency and standard for testing and trial network operation between 2016 and 2018. The national innovation internet platform (创新网络平台) serves as the basis for the exchange of ideas between industry, universities, research institutes, and the government. However, the MIIT goes further by creating a 5G technology R&D platform, which will commence from the second semester of 2016 (Jiao 2015). China has

---

[17]For more information see https://ec.europa.eu/digital-single-market/en/news/public-consultation-evaluation-and-review-regulatory-framework-electronic-communications.

already spent RMB 430 billion in 2015 to improve the nationwide internet system. In 2016 and 2017, it is expected to spend a further RMB 700 billion and RMB 140 billion, respectively, on boosting rural internet connectivity (Yang 2016).

Meanwhile, the private sector is also researching and investing to bring the vision of 5G to reality. Qualcomm, the world's largest mobile chip designer, for instance, has established a 5G research center with China Mobile. Ericsson has also started a 5G "test bed" in China, which is the first 5G prototype in the country (China at 'forefront' of 5G development 2016). During February 2016, key digital players met in Shenzhen at the 11th International Summit on 5G test and measurement instruments and 5G applications and products. Companies discussed their latest studies and research projects. ZTE Corporation, a major provider of telecommunications, presented its network architecture design concept and slice prototype system incorporating the latest generation Intel Xeon processor. All the digital players highlighted the need to develop more stable and faster networks to adapt to the requirements of multisystems, variable scenarios, and business modes. The aim is to create a future network that is more flexible, economic, and efficient (OMSI 2016).

In this context, a Sino-European agreement on 5G telecommunication systems was signed at the HED in Beijing on 28 September 2015. The agreement between the 5G PPP Association of Europe and the IMT-2020 (5G) Promotion Association is a move that aims to acquire an edge in the world's digital competitiveness, the concrete results of which remain to be seen.

11.7.2   Development of Sino-European Cooperation in the 5G Standardization Race

The industrial agreement between the EU's 5G PPP Association and China's IMT-2020 (5G) Promotion Association will enhance cooperation in this field. This agreement marks another stage in their cooperation (EU-China partnership on 5G 2015). It was based on other agreements already signed between the European Commission, Japan, and South Korea during 2015.[18]

---

[18] Interview with European official (1), 14 February 2016, Brussels.

The agreement was very opportune in the light of the countdown for the World Radiocommunication Conference 2019, because the two countries have started together in the 5G standardization race and discussions on spectrum requirements for 5G (Liu 2016).[19] Europe wants to ensure that it does not lag behind in 5G adoption by reaching deals with countries that are at the forefront of its development. China is becoming one of the major players in the development of 5G and one of the largest markets for 5G technologies, products, and services (MWL 2015). The agreement facilitates an environment for cooperation between Sino-European telecoms and ICT companies by trying to increase higher access to both markets, facilitated through development and innovation initiatives and publicly funded 5G research.[20] However, the reality is that the European market is fully open whereas the Chinese market is not. Despite official talks, there are no joint private projects between European and Chinese companies.

The areas of cooperation were defined as having five components:

1. Come to an understanding on the concept, basic functionalities, key technologies, and time plan for 5G
2. Examine the possibilities for joint research actions, including participation of enterprises on the services and applications for 5G
3. Popularize global standardization for 5G through relevant organizations such as the 3rd Generation Partnership Project (3GPP) and the International Telecommunication Union (ITU)
4. Cooperate in identifying the most promising radio frequency bands to meet the new spectrum requirements for 5G
5. Investigate the services and applications for 5G linked to the IoT (EU–China partnership on 5G, 2015)

The joint EU–China projects will be funded by a co-funding mechanism (CFM) for research and innovation for both partners. An investment of

---

[19] World Radiocommunication Conferences (WRCs) are held every three to four years. It is the job of WRC to review the Radio Regulations, the international treaty governing the use of the radio-frequency spectrum and the geostationary satellite and non-geostationary satellite orbits. For more information see http://www.itu.int/en/ITU-R/conferences/wrc/2015/Pages/default.aspx.

[20] Interview with European official (6), phone interview, 27 June 2016, Shanghai.

over €640 million from 2016 to 2020 is expected. In this regard, at the end of 2015, the MOST made its first annual call under the CFM to provide €28 million support for Chinese organizations (Huawai 2016).

Under this cooperation, it seems that many doors could be opened at all levels. Yet, at the institutional level, governments need to promote global standardization for 5G by improving infrastructure networks and facilities such as the ITU[21] and the 3GPP2.[22] This task will not be simple because some of the new spectrum requirements for 5G, such as the most appropriate radio frequency bands, are complex to achieve. This challenging situation gives rise to the possibility for Sino-European cooperation; for example, research centers and universities could work together in implementing joint research actions, and businesses could develop 5G research projects. The question is how to find those partners, sit them down together, and make them understand that by working together they could obtain better results. Even if President Xi Jinping has called on scientists, entrepreneurs, scholars, and technicians in the industry to work together toward the goal of welcoming foreign collaborations to pool together more human, material, and financial resources (New China internet strategy unveiled 2016), these actors do not know where to find potential European partners. At the same time, the European industry still has doubts about the benefits that can be obtained by sharing knowledge and expertise if local markets are still closed to them.

On the brighter side, there are wishes to jointly explore services and applications for 5G, especially in the area of the IoT, smart cities, e-health, intelligent transport, education, entertainment, and media. The case of e-banking is another significant application area because the

---

[21] The ITU is the United Nations specialized agency for information and communication technologies. It covers high speed, broadband, and internet protocol (IP)-based mobile systems featuring network-to-network interconnection, feature/service transparency, global roaming, and seamless services independent of location. For more information see http://www.itu.int/en/about/Pages/default.aspx.

[22] 3GPP2 was born out of the ITU's initiative. It involves Japan, China, North America, and Korea. It is intended to bring high-quality mobile multimedia telecommunications to a worldwide mass market by achieving the goals of increasing the speed and ease of wireless communications, responding to the problems faced by the increased demand to pass data via telecommunications, and providing "anytime, anywhere" services. For more information visit http://www.3gpp.org/, http://www.3gpp2.org/Public_html/Misc/AboutHome.cfm.

shift to a digital economy has changed the customers' use of financial tools such as e-wallets, e-payment, and touch-pay systems (Yang 2016). Moreover, Sino-European organizations, research centers, and private companies fostering cooperation in terms of reciprocity and access to 5G network research funding could provide openness in terms of market access (European Commission 2015c). European companies could increase access to and participation in China's public funds for 5G research, while Chinese enterprises are already involved in EU's 5G activities (EU-China partnership on 5G 2015; EU, China sign key partnership on 5G 2015). Yet, experience shows that these intentions have not been adopted at the time of writing this chapter.

Some Chinese and European universities are joining to prepare a formal launch of the China–EU Digital Research Center at the end of 2016.[23] This research center aims at systematically monitoring and comparing Chinese and European regulatory frameworks, e-commerce,cloud services, data protection, cyber security, 5G and future networks, copyrights, and patents to achieve better synergy between Europe's Digital Agenda and China's Internet Plus (New China internet strategy unveiled 2016). Because both the European Commission and Chinese national government are now reviewing their rules and eliminating requirements that stifle e-commerce, this type of joint project could be very complementary at the institutional level.

In contrast to the EU, which has a dedicated agency (ENISA)[24] to promote and coordinate cyber security policies, China has not yet developed a comprehensive cyber security strategy. However, as President Xi recently mentioned, cyber security will be a focal point for the national government. China's cyber security strategy builds on recent steps. Following the establishment in 2014 of the Central Cyber Security and Informatization Leading Group, the Cyber Security Association of China[25] was founded on 25 March 2016. It conforms to academic

---

[23]The China Development Research Foundation (CDRF) is a public foundation initiated by the Development Research Center of the State Council (DRC) and under the management of Cyberspace Administration of China. The president is Ma Li. Its mission is to advance good governance and public policy. For more information visit http://www.cdrf. org.cn/en/.

[24]For more information, see https://www.enisa.europa.eu/.

[25]For more information, see http://www.cac.gov.cn/english/.

institutes, individuals, and internet companies (including Tecent and Qihu360). Cyber space management and security is a prerequisite for increased internet usage everywhere. The organization aims to establish industry standards and cyber security studies, but also will promote "self-discipline" in the industry, a practice unwelcome in Europe (China launches the cybersecurity association of China 2016).

The protection of private data and the prevention of cyber attacks have become the main points in cyber security strategy in Europe and China. For this purpose, both partners wish to speed up legislation and surveillance measures to avert cyber threats (New China internet strategy unveiled 2016). This area of cooperation is described as "Cyber-Realpolitik" and is tackled by the EU–China cyber taskforce.

The success of the Sino-European cooperation for 5G standardization depends on the ability of businesses and research institutes to join forces to cooperate and implement projects together. It is also necessary for official institutions to facilitate policies, instruments, and mechanisms to carry out joint projects. At the time of writing this chapter, there was no transposition from the top level to the bottom. However, large potential avenues have been acknowledged in the digital field, particularly with the development of 5G technology.

11.8   Conclusions

As the Chinese idiom goes, 抛砖引玉 (*pāo zhuān yǐn yù*), literally meaning "cast a brick to attract jade," this chapter offers a few remarks to set the ball rolling. Similarities in the B&R initiative and the Juncker Plan have been identified. Both economic initiatives and the confident official relationship between the EU and China provide a favorable environment for develoment of the EU–China Investment Cooperation. It remains to be seen how this cooperation will play out once both initiatives have been fully developed. In the meantime, the ability to explore joint investment projects other than infrastructure is recommended to strengthen numerous opportunities for business, research, and services in both China and Europe.

The digital age is here and has not yet arrived at an impasse. Both the EU and Chinese governments are making efforts to adapt to the changing technical environment created by the internet, IT systems, and data analysis. Digital transformation is underway in both regions, which must catch up fast with the leaders of the digital world to avoid lagging behind. Research, innovation, and a new generation of infrastructure must be put in place in order to be on the frontline of the advances in cyber space and technology, as well as to adapt to the requirements of users and services.

In this regard, the EU and China have plenty of room for cooperation in the 5G market. Their intentions are still in an incipient stage but must speed up in bringing 5G to reality. Behind all the joint research projects on radio frequency bands, regulatory frameworks, cyber security, and big data, there is an ultimate idea: to keep internal markets competitive. This cooperation should focus on those sectors where science, business, and society can also benefit. Now is the moment to catch the train and adapt the ancient Silk Road into what will come to be known as the Digital Silk Road.

REFERENCES

Casarini, N. (2015a, September). China's inroads into the West. *Catham house, 71*(5).

Casarini, N. (2015b, October). Is Europe to benefit from China's Belt and Road Initiative? *Istituto Affari Internazionali, 15*(40).

Cao, X. (2015, June 26). One Belt, One Road: Europe has its own opinion, China still has an opportunity. *Southern Weekly* (in Chinese). Retrieved May 23, 2016, from http://www.infzm.com/content/110332.

China at 'forefront' of 5G development. (2016, May 5). *Shanghai Daily*. Retrieved June 7, 2016, from http://china.org.cn/business/2016-05/05/content_38387108.htm.

China launches the Cybersecurity Association of China. (2016, March 26). *Technology News*. Retrieved May 7, 2016, from http://www.i4u.com/2016/03/107716/china-launches-cybersecurity-association-china.

China-EU digital cooperation promising. (2016, May 26). *Xinhua News*. Retrieved May 30, 2016, from http://news.xinhuanet.com/english/2016-05/26/c_135389952.htm.

Chinese reactor plan fuels British security fears. (2015, October 19). *The Guardian*. Retrieved February 19, 2016, from https://www.theguardian.com/world/2015/oct/19/chinese-reactor-plan-fuels-british-security-fears.

CINIC China Internet Network Information Center. (2016, January). *The 37th statistical report on internet development in China*. Retrieved May 12, 2015, from http://www1.cnnic.cn/IDR/ReportDownloads/201604/P020160419390562421055.pdf.

Donnan, S. (2015, September 27). White House declares truce with China over AIIB. *The Financial Times*. Retrieved January 20, 2016, from http://

www.ft.com/cms/s/0/23c51438-64ca-11e5-a28b-50226830d644.
html#axzz3yP5T818m.

Emmot, R., & Taylor, P. (2015, June 15). China to extend economic
diplomacy to EU infrastructure fund. *Reuters*. Retrieved February 3,
2016, from http://www.reuters.com/article/us-eu-china-exclusive-
idUSKBN0OU0H820150615.

ETNO European Telecommunications Network Operators' Association. (2016).
Policy paper towards a new telecoms framework. Retrieved June 2, 2016, from
https://etno.eu/datas/publications/2016_Publications/2016_Summary_
TelcoFrameworkReview.pdf.

EU, China sign key partnership on 5G. (2015, September 28). *Xinhuanet*.
Retrieved June 3, 2016, from http://www.globaltimes.cn/content/944911.
shtml.

European Commission. (2010, May 19). *Digital agenda for Europe: Key
initiatives*. Retrieved May 16, 2016, from http://europa.eu/rapid/
press-release_MEMO-10-200_en.htm.

European Commission. Directorate-General for Communication. (2014,
November). *The European Union explained: Digital agenda for Europe*.
Retrieved May 5, 2016, from http://europa.eu/pol/pdf/flipbook/en/
digital_agenda_en.pdf.

European Commission. (2015a). *Investment plan for Europe goes global: China
announces its contribution to invest in EU* [Press Release]. Retrieved February
7, 2016, from http://europa.eu/rapid/press-release_IP-15-5723_en.htm.

European Commission. (2015b). *EU-China investment cooperation* [Fact sheet].
Retrieved February 3, 2016, from https://ec.europa.eu/priorities/sites/
beta-political/files/factsheet-eu-china-investment-cooperation_en.pdf.

European Commission. (2015c, September 28). *The EU and China signed
a key partnership on 5G, our tomorrow's communication networks* [Press
Release]. Retrieved June 6, 2016, from http://europa.eu/rapid/
press-release_IP-15-5715_en.htm.

European Commission. (2015d, October 20). *International workshop
on future 5G standards and spectrum*. Retrieved June 3, 2016, from
https://ec.europa.eu/digital-single-market/en/news/international-
workshop-future-5g-standards-and-spectrum.

European Commission. (2016a). *Investment plan*. Retrieved February 6,
2016, from http://ec.europa.eu/priorities/jobs-growth-and-investment/
investment-plan_en.

European Commission. (2016b, February 22). *Europe 2020 strategy*. Retrieved
May 16, 2016, from https://ec.europa.eu/digital-single-market/en/
europe-2020-strategy.

European Commission. (2016c, April 19). *European open science cloud*. Retrieved
June 3, 2016, from https://ec.europa.eu/research/openscience/index.
cfm?pg=open-science-cloud.

European Commission. (2016d, May 30). *5G infrastructure PPP: The next generation of communication networks will be "Made in EU".* Retrieved June 6, 2016, from https://ec.europa.eu/digital-single-market/en/glossary.

European Union Delegation to China. (2015). *Investment plan for Europe goes global: China announces its contribution to invest in EU* [Press Release]. Retrieved February 7, 2016, from http://eeas.europa.eu/delegations/china/press_corner/all_news/news/2015/2015092801_en.htm.

European Investment Bank. (2016, May 19). *European fund for strategic investments.* Retrieved February 7, 2016, from http://www.eib.org/efsi/.

EU-China partnership on 5G. (2015, September 28). *EU business.* Retrieved June 6, 2016, from http://www.eubusiness.com/topics/internet/5g-china.

FMPRC Ministry of Foreign Affairs of the People's Republic of China (in Chinese). (2016, March). *China's relations with the EU.* Retrieved May 23, 2016, from http://www.fmprc.gov.cn/web/gjhdq_676201/gj_676203/oz_678770/1206_679930/sbgx_679934/.

Graham-Harrison, E. (2015, May 25). China warned over 'insane' plans for new nuclear power plants. *The Guardian.* Retrieved February 19, from https://www.theguardian.com/world/2015/may/25/china-nuclear-power-plants-expansion-he-zuoxiu.

Gray, J. (2015, September 18). *Could China be Europe's savior?* World Finance. Retrieved February 7, 2016, from http://www.worldfinance.com/infrastructure-investment/government-policy/could-china-be-europes-saviour.

Guancha. (2015a, April 14). *The Belt and Road* (in Chinese). Retrieved May 3, 2016, from http://news.163.com/15/0414/06/AN5490VE0001124J.html.

Guancha. (2015b, April 28). *"The Belt and Road" roadmap* (in Chinese). Retrieved May 3, 2016, from http://www.guancha.cn/strategy/2015_03_28_314019.shtml.

IMT 2020 (5G) Promotion Group. (2014, February). *IMT vision towards 2020 and beyond.* Retrieved June 7, 2016, from https://www.itu.int/dms_pub/itu-r/oth/0a/06/R0A0600005D0001PDFE.pdf.

IWS Internet World Stats. (2013, December). *Top 50 countries with the highest Internet penetration rate.* Retrieved May 7, 2016, from http://www.internetworldstats.com/top25.htm.

IWS Internet World Stats. (2015, December). *Top 20 countries with the highest number of internet users.* Retrieved May 27, 2016, from http://www.internetworldstats.com/top20.htm.

Jiao, L. (2015a, February 12). China's white paper on 5G concept. *Beijing Morning Post* (in Chinese). Retrieved June 7, 2016, from http://news.xinhuanet.com/local/2015-02/12/c_127485619.htm.

Jing, L. (2015b, November 26). A research on the strategic coordination between "The Belt and Road" and the EU's "Juncker plan". International perspective (in Chinese). Retrieved May 15, 2016, from http://www.faob-server.com/NewsInfo.aspx?id=11562.

Liu, X. (2016, February 19). *Focus of MWC 2016: Solve technical issues in 5G technology and commercialize it.* Originally translated from (in Chinese). Retrieved May 21, 2016, from http://chinasourcing.mofcom.gov.cn/news/117/65314.html.

Lu, F. (2015, May 15). The Belt and Road: Why is it China. *Financial Times Chinese* (in Chinese). Retrieved May 3, 2016, from http://www.ftchinese.com/story/001062014.

MIIT Ministry of Industry and Information Technology. (2016). *Made in China 2025* (in Chinese). Retrieved May 3, 2016, from http://www.miit.gov.cn/n11293472/n11293877/n16553775/index.html.

New China internet strategy unveiled. (2016, April 19). *Eureporter.* Retrieved May 19, 2016, from https://www.eureporter.co/frontpage/2016/04/25/euchina-new-china-internet-strategy-unveiled.

OMSI Online Modern Scientific Instrument. (2016, February 22). *2015 5G testing and measuring technologies conference and 5G application and product exhibition—The 11th International (Shenzhen) Instrument and Measurement Automation Summit Forum was held successfully on December 18th in Shenzhen* (in Chinese). Retrieved May 27, 2016, from http://a.wangzhanhr.com/news/6/201602120827.html.

MWL Mobile World Live. (2015). *EU, China partner to make 5G a "reality by 2020".* Retrieved June 1, 2016, from http://www.mobileworldlive.com/asia/asia-news/eu-china-partner-to-make-5g-a-reality-by-2020/.

Paulo, M. (2014, March). *Opportunities and challenges of* e-Governance: A reality or science fiction of the Chinese Government? IV International electronic simposium about Chinese politics. Retrieved June 7, 2016, from http://www.asiared.com/es/downloads2/14_1s_mireia_paulo_noguera.pdf.

Pavlićević, D. (2015, July 31). China, the EU and One Belt, One Road Strategy. *China Brief,* 15 (15). Retrieved February 3, 2016, from http://www.james-town.org/programs/chinabrief/single/?tx_ttnews%5Btt_news%5D=44235&cHash=9dbc08472c19ecd691307c4c1905eb0c#.VqsM1Bh97Zs.

PRC People's Republic of China State Department. (2015, May 19). *Made in China 2025* (in Chinese). Retrieved May 16, 2016, from http://news.china.com/domestic/945/20150519/19710486.html.

PRC People's Republic of China. (2016, April 17). *Thirteenth Five-Year plan (2016–2020) on National Economic and Social Development (13th FYP proposal)* (in Chinese). Retrieved May 6, 2016, from http://news.xinhuanet.com/2016-03/17/c_1118366322.htm.

Prodi, R. & Gos, D. (2016, February 12). Digital China and its implications for Europe. *China Daily.* Retrieved May 30, 2016, from http://usa.chinadaily.com.cn/epaper/2016-02/12/content_23460202.htm.

Protests show strength of German attachment to steel. (2016, April 12). *Reuters.* Retrieved May 9, 2016, from http://in.reuters.com/article/germany-steel-protests-idINKCN0X81H7.

Steel industry calls for EU action on Chinese imports. (2015, November 15). *BBC.* Retrieved February 19, 2015, from http://www.bbc.com/news/business-34763597.

Steinbock, D. (2015, June 29). Chinese investment could energize the Juncker fund. *EU Observer.* Retrieved May 30, 2016, from https://euobserver.com/eu-china/129318.

Summers, T. (2015, September). What exactly is One Belt, One Road? *Chatham House, 71*(5).

Sykes, S. (2015, September 6). David Cameron gives go ahead to build Chinese nuclear reactor in Essex. *EXPRESS.* Retrieved February 19, 2016, from http://www.express.co.uk/news/uk/603390/China-nuclear-reactor-Essex-nuclear-power.

Tate, P. (2015, March 10). *China adopts 'Smart Manufacturing' strategy to up its game in manufacturing.* Retrieved March 21, 2016, from http://www.gilcommunity.com/blog/china-adopts-smart-manufacturing-strategy-its-game-manufacturing/.

Valero, J. (2015, October 6). China uses Juncker plan to boost involvement in Europe. *Euroactive.* Retrieved February 8, 2016, from http://www.euractiv.com/sections/euro-finance/china-uses-juncker-plan-strengthen-investment-europe-318232.

Xi Jinping: Make the Internet better benefit the nation and people (in Chinese). *Xinhua News.* (2016, April 19). Retrieved May 15, 2016, from http://news.xinhuanet.com/politics/2016-04/19/c_1118672059.htm.

Xi Jinping speech on national cyber security strategy on the internet connection and signal (in Chinese). (2014, February 28). *China News.* Retrieved May 21, 2016, from http://www.chinanews.com/gn/2014/02-28/5897947.shtml.

Yang, Y. (2016, May 25). Speech by Ambassador Yang Yanyi at ChinaEu 1st anniversary: "China-EU Partnership in the Digital Industry". *China EU.* Retrieved May 30, 2016, from http://www.chinaeu.eu/.

Wen, Z. (2015). "The Belt and Road" is a strategic concept to achieve the great rejuvenation (in Chinese). Retrieved May 3, 2016, from http://www.cnki.com.cn/Article/CJFDTotal-DQSH201504054.htm.

Wildau, G. (2015, April 20). *China backs up silk road ambitions with $62bn capital injection. Financial Times.* Retrieved May 3, 2016, from http://www.ft.com/intl/cms/s/0/0e73c028-e754-11e4-8e3f-00144feab7de.html.

Where are the current features and profound meaning of the new internet public opinion view (in Chinese). (2016, June 2). *The Journal of the Party.* Retrieved June 4, 2016, from http://theory.people.com.cn/n1/2016/0602/c40531-28406879.html.

Woetzel, J., et al. (2014, July). *China's digital transformation*. Mckinsey. Retrieved Marc 21, 2016, from http://www.mckinsey.com/industries/high-tech/our-insights/chinas-digital-transformation.

Zhou, Y. (2015, April 20). *A large "golden circle" will be formed in the area of the Belt and Road (in Chinese)*. Retrieved May 3, 2016, from http://gold.hexun.com/2015-03-20/174251626.html.

Zhu, Z. (2015, October 9). China's AIIB and 'One Belt, One Road': Ambitions and challenges. Retrieved May 3, 2016, from https://www.chinadialogue.net/article/show/single/en/8231-China-s-AIIB-and-One-Belt-One-Road-ambitions-and-challenges.

PART IV

Geopolitical Challenge in the "Belt and Road" Initiative

CHAPTER 12

One Belt, One Road and Central Asia: Challenges and Opportunities

Filippo Costa Buranelli

12.1 Introduction

Since 2013, the One Belt, One Road initiative (hereafter OBOR) has informed discussions of the infrastructure, economic, and business development of the Central Asian region. The project is seen to be the best way to develop China's commercial routes to western lands and to provide Central Asia with the necessary infrastructure, links, and connections to prosper and enhance its own economic situation. The focus of this paper is, for reasons of space and word limits, on the Belt rather than on the Road.[1] As Sect. 12.3 shows, the literature on OBOR is extensive and covers several political, economic, and infrastructural aspects of the project. Yet, despite numerous publications and reports on the OBOR project, the perspectives of the Central Asian republics are still unknown

---

[1] The OBOR project consists of two distinct, yet intertwined routes: a territorial belt cutting through the territory of Eurasia and a maritime route passing through the Indian Ocean.

F. Costa Buranelli (✉)
University of St. Andrews, St Andrews, UK

© The Author(s) 2018
Y. Cheng et al. (eds.), *The Belt & Road Initiative in the Global Arena*,
https://doi.org/10.1007/978-981-10-5921-6_12

or considered to be less important than those, for example, of China or Russia.[2]

As has been acknowledged, "the states of Central Asia have yet to make a substantial input into the project" (Gabuev 2015). Therefore, this paper aims to shed light on the political and economic context of Central Asia in order to situate better the OBOR project in the region, focusing in particular on the expectations, requests, and challenges that the Central Asian republics present China. This chapter considers three main arguments:

1. For implementation of OBOR, the economic dimension cannot be detached from political considerations. In Central Asia, politics and economics form an inextricable nexus that all external partners should take into consideration when planning business and infrastructural activities in the region.
2. Economic benefits must go hand in hand with diplomatic sensitivity and attentive, careful negotiations, both at the regional and local levels.
3. Realization of the OBOR project will depend on the consideration that China has for its Central Asian partners and on knowledge of the specifics of the social, cultural, political, and economic context. There is a saying in Uzbek, "the most important thing you can give your host is attention." China will have to pay particular attention to the requests, needs, and demands of Central Asian states and frame the project in the clearest way possible to achieve parity of information and equality during implementation of the project.

The paper is organized as follows: Sect. 12.2 reviews the OBOR project as it has been described and promoted by the Chinese government. Section 12.3 gives an overview of the state of the literature on this policy. Section 12.4 deals with the perspectives of the Central Asian republics, and sheds light on what these states expect and want from the project. This section also considers potential hurdles of the project, should the

---

[2]For the purpose of this paper, Central Asia refers to the five republics of Kazakhstan, Kyrgyzstan, Tajikistan, Turkmenistan, and Uzbekistan. Also, this paper was written when the late Uzbek President Islam Karimov was still alive. Under the new leadership of Shavkat Mirziyoyev, Uzbekistan's attitude towards regional aspects of OBOR-related projects may change.

Chinese government not pay attention to the needs of the Central Asian states as well as their socio-political and economic context. The final section recapitulates the arguments presented and offers some final thoughts on how to make the OBOR project more realistic and more detailed.

Although the OBOR project pertains to several different countries, the focus of this paper is primarily the Central Asian countries, because the intention of this research is to shed light on the perceptions of these states regarding the project.

One last point should be made on the utility of the enterprise. In other words, why focus on Central Asia within the OBOR framework? I argue that a focus on the Central Asian republics is needed because of the following points:

1. Their pivotal position in the framework of the project
2. Their sensitive security agenda
3. Their increased ability to voice and express their concerns and demands on issue of international politics and regional matters (Cooley 2012; Costa Buranelli 2014)
4. Their relations with each other, which are more often than not strained and not conducive to a good-neighborly spirit.[3]

12.2   The OBOR Project

The OBOR project was first announced in Astana, Kazakhstan, in September 2013 in the course of an official state visit of President Xi Jinping. The initiative involves an area potentially covering 55% of the world's GNP, 70% of its global population, and 75% of its known energy reserves (Colarizi 2015). In 2014, the Silk Road Fund was launched with a starting capital of US$40 billion. The management of the China Development Bank announced that by 2020 it would channel up to US$1 trillion into Silk Road projects. China needs an outlet for its excess

---

[3]This is directly pertinent to the realization of the OBOR project. The official narrative on the project does not see it as a product of good-neighborly relations between the republics, but rather as the *source* of them: "The Belt and Road Initiative is in line with the purposes and principles of the UN Charter. It upholds the Five Principles of Peaceful Coexistence: mutual respect for each other's sovereignty and territorial integrity, mutual non-aggression, mutual non-interference in each other's internal affairs, equality and mutual benefit, and peaceful coexistence." (NRDC et al. 2015).

capacity and labor force, created by the boom of the last 15 years, but which now risks being underemployed (Gabuev 2015). The project, as the name suggests, consists of two distinct but mutually reinforcing trajectories, the Silk Road Economic Belt, and the twenty first-Century Maritime Silk Road. These two vectors, alongside the secondary and parallel infrastructure, will serve as the two main commercial routes through which China will foster its own economic development by finding new export routes, but also promote, encourage, and sustain the economic development of the states and territories affected by the project (Fig. 12.1).

The project has been framed and conceived on the basis of the principles of equality and non-interference. While launching the project in Astana, President Xi Jinping also said that China respects the development paths and policies chosen by the peoples of regional countries, and will never interfere in the domestic affairs of Central Asian nations.

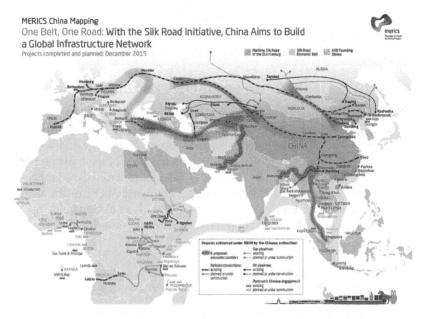

Fig. 12.1   Projects completed and planned as part of the One Belt, One Road initiative. *Source* http://www.merics.org/en/merics-analysis/infographicchina-mapping/china-mapping.html

In addition, he stated that "China will never seek a dominant role in regional affairs, nor try to nurture a sphere of influence," adding that "China and Central Asian nations should be genuine friends of mutual support and trust" (Xinhua 2013).

The project has been defined as "systematic" by the Chinese leadership (NDRC et al. 2015), and this adjective conveys the idea of creating a structure of prosperity and development, not just for China but for neighboring countries and areas as well. The wider scope of the OBOR project can be broken down into two main dimensions: infrastructure and people-to people. As I hope this paper makes clear, both dimensions have extreme importance for the Central Asian states, and both are crucial for how China deals with the Central Asian republics with respect to realization of the project.

The infrastructural dimension emphasises the construction of "a new Eurasian Land Bridge and developing China–Mongolia–Russia, China–Central Asia–West Asia, and China–Indochina Peninsula economic corridors by taking advantage of international transport routes, relying on core cities along the Belt and Road and using key economic industrial parks as cooperation platforms" (NDRC et al. 2015).

The people-to-people dimension stresses the need to "carry forward the spirit of friendly cooperation of the Silk Road by promoting extensive cultural and academic exchanges, personnel exchanges and cooperation, media cooperation, youth and women exchanges, and volunteer services, so as to win public support for deepening bilateral and multilateral cooperation" (NDRC et al. 2015). Yet, it is important to stress that the strategy for the OBOR project is, at best, vague. The bulk of the document "Vision and Actions on Jointly Building Silk Road Economic Belt and twenty first-Century Maritime Silk Road" concentrates on seven "shoulds," which does not convey a complete sense of planning. As one interviewee[4] put it, "there is a lot of paper on OBOR, lots of documents, but the strategy remains unclear, the implementation as well" (Expert 1, personal communication, 30 April 2016).

---

[4] Interviewees' names have been anonymized by request of the interested parties.

12.3   State of the Literature on OBOR

This short section provides an overview of the current state of academic and specialized literature on the OBOR project, and focuses in particular on how the Central Asian republics are seen in it. With respect to the literature on OBOR, two peculiarities are worth noting. First, there is a predominance of specialized and think-tank work on the project, rather than standard academic literature. This could indicate that a theory-informed, scholarly debate on the project is still in its nascent phase. Second, the Central Asian republics are "ossified" in their position of subaltern, passive subjects when it comes to realization of the OBOR project.

Michael Clarke discusses the importance of the OBOR project in mere geopolitical terms, stressing the power–political elements intertwined with the geographical scope of the planned infrastructure (Clarke 2016). Framed in a strong "Mackinderian" narrative, his work focuses mostly on the competition between China, Russia, and the USA on the "heartland," thus downplaying the role and position of the Central Asian states in the project. In other words, their demands, expectations, and aspirations with respect to OBOR are "exogenized."

Nicola Contessi has contributed to the academic literature on Central Asia and OBOR, emphasising the crucial role that the *topos* of "connectivity" plays in Chinese thinking on the enterprise. Again, his work tends to slightly marginalize the role that the Central Asian republics may play in realization of the project (Contessi 2016).

Alexander Cooley has made an attempt to bring Central Asia into the picture, especially from a governance perspective. He stresses that the project will face severe challenges in terms of investment management and best economic practices in what he defines as the most trade-unfriendly region in the world. However, in his work, the Central Asian republics are seen as an arena in which the project will be implemented rather than a constitutive part of it (Cooley 2015).

Colin Mackerras rightly notes that "there is still a dearth of research when it comes to Western China and its international relations" (Mackerras 2015, p. 26). Yet, his research mainly focuses on the role that Xinjiang plays in the project, and on how OBOR represents, according to him, a way to link the province to the rest of China and thus tame secessionist forces and claims to greater political, religious, and economic autonomy. Once again, how the Central Asian republics will, if ever, contribute to the realization of the project is under-researched. This is a concern shared with Raffaello Pantucci and Alexandros Petersen, who argue that there is still a need to grasp the perspectives of Central Asian states on OBOR (Pantucci and Petersen 2012).

Two recent contributions by the Royal United Services Institute, one of the world's leading think-tanks, have highlighted the role that economics and security play in China and the Central Asian republics when it comes to the realization of OBOR. These two reports stress the importance of both the security context, such as conflict over resources, radicalization, spillover from Afghanistan, and organized crime (Lain and Pantucci 2016), as well as the specification of economic planning, implementation, and incentives (Lain and Pantucci 2015). Although these two publications have the undoubted merit of focusing on the Central Asian context, they highlight only the risks and uncertainties associated with the project rather than the expectations of the Central Asian republics.

One of the very few publications dealing with the Central Asian states as actors involved in the OBOR project, and highlighting the opportunities and challenges that they present for China, is Zhang Hongzhou's report "Building the Silk Road Economic Belt, problems and priorities in Central Asia" (Hongzhou 2015). His work aptly acknowledges the specifics and complexities of the Central Asian context, such as border disputes and diverging foreign policy priorities, and analyses how these may impede or slow down realization of the OBOR project. This chapter uses his research as a base and takes it further to provide an even sharper description of the Central Asian context and its position toward OBOR.

The purpose of this short literature review has been to show that, although there is a solid ongoing discourse around OBOR and its implementation, the Central Asian republics are more often than not regarded as a territory on which the project will be realized rather than active players in its realization. The next section fills this knowledge gap and tentatively opens new avenues for research on this topic, which is of great importance for the future of Eurasia.

12.4   Central Asia and China

Before delving into the specific positions of the Central Asian republics, it is worth offering the reader a very brief overview of existing Central Asia–China relations. China constitutes one of the major economic partners, if not the major economic partner, for all Central Asian states, and its economic role in the region has been increasing significantly over the years (e.g., Laruelle and Peyrouse 2014). The Central Asian states and China are members of regional multilateral organizations such as the Shanghai Cooperation Organization and the Conference on Interaction and Confidence-Building Measures in Asia. At the governmental level, bilateral relations between Central Asian countries and China are warm, driven by the principles of respecting each other's sovereignty and non-interference, and informed by a business-oriented mindset. When the OBOR project was launched in 2013, all Central Asian states showed interest and enthusiasm. The position of each country is presented in the following subsections.

12.4.1   Kazakhstan

At the official level, Kazakhstan has been an enthusiastic supporter of the OBOR project. OBOR fits very well into two of the most important pillars of Kazakhstan's foreign policy strategies, one discursive and one "material." The first pillar is the projection of Kazakhstan on the world stage as a "bridge" or linchpin between Europe and Asia, a gateway to the West and East.[5] The second pillar is the recent "100 Steps" policy (known as *Nurly Zhol*, or "Bright Path") launched by Kazakh President Nursultan Nazarbayev in November 2014 to ameliorate the quality and quantity of Kazakhstan's infrastructure.[6] The importance of Kazakhstan for the OBOR project is indicated by the fact that President Xi Jinping decided to launch the project in Astana. In addition, the "strategic partnership" between the two countries is visible in the fact that President Xi Jinping's official visit to Kazakhstan on 7 May 2015 was the first by a head of state after President Nursultan Nazarbayev's electoral victory in the elections on 26 April 2015 (Sabayeva 2015).

Kazakhstan has warmly welcomed the launch of the OBOR initiative as a means to increase its connectivity and achieve alternative routes of transport and trade in the light of the recent financial crisis. For example,

---

[5]At the Astana Club meeting in November 2015, Prime Minister Karim Massimov and other Kazakh speakers emphasized that their country's location is ideal for the "connectivity" that the Chinese are seeking (Kirişci and Le Corre 2015).

[6]Yet, the project is now being reconsidered in the light of the recent financial crisis that has hit Kazakhstan and the tenge, the national currency (Expert 2, personal communication, 23 April 2016).

in the course of the international conference "One Belt, One Road: modern foreign policy of China," the Ambassador Extraordinary and Plenipotentiary of China to Kazakhstan, Zhang Hanhuey, announced that Kazakhstan and China had signed an agreement for 52 industrial projects worth more than US$24 billion (Kazakhstan 2050, 2016a). China and Kazakhstan also agreed to establish a free trade zone in the major cities along railways between the two countries, and to expand cooperation between enterprises.

In addition, they decided to increase agricultural cooperation and continue to strengthen relations between customs departments and the business community (AKIpress 2015). The two countries have also pledged to join forces in prospecting for solid minerals and their extraction and advanced processing; in producing copper, aluminium, and other metals and manufacturing goods from them; and in making chemicals (Xinhua 2015).

12.4.2   Kyrgyzstan

Because of the complex geoconformity of its territory, Kyrgyzstan plays a less crucial role for OBOR than Kazakhstan.[7] However, Kyrgyzstan is willing to strengthen practical cooperation with China by actively participating in building the Silk Road Economic Belt and deepening law-enforcement and security cooperation to safeguard regional peace and stability. Chinese expansion in the Kyrgyz infrastructural system is already visible in the construction of the North–South Road in addition to the already existing Bishkek–Osh route. This is a welcome move, as "in both Tajikistan and Kyrgyzstan there is huge infrastructure demand" (Expert on the region, personal communication, 24 April 2016). The route consists of three different phases:

- Phase 1 (154 km) will connect the villages of Kyzyl Jyldyz and Aral, and the village of Kazarman and the city of Jalal-Abad in the south. The cost of Phase 1 is US$400 million.

---

[7]As an example, one may consider that to cross the China–Kyrgyz border through the Irkeshtam Pass (the "smoothest" and most southern) one has to go through two border crossings, two checkpoints, and a 150-km ride (using official taxis or hitchhiking) just to change sides.

- Phase 2 (96 km) will connect Aral and Kazarman, and will build a 700-meter tunnel. The cost of Phase 2 is US$284 million.
- Phase 3 (183 km) will connect the city of Balykchi at Lake Issyk-Kul and Kyzyl Jyldyz village. The cost of Phase 3 is US$166 million (24 kg News Agency 2012).

In addition to this road, there is also the idea of building a tunnel between Kyrgyzstan and Uzbekistan, but this is far more difficult because of political and strategic concerns (Expert 1, personal communication, 30 April 2016). This issue will be discussed further in the "challenges" section of the paper (Sect. 12.6).

12.4.3   Tajikistan

Compared with Kazakhstan and Uzbekistan, and more similarly to Kyrgyzstan, Tajikistan plays a less crucial role in the development of the OBOR project because of the mountainous character of its territory. However, one year after OBOR was announced, Tajik President Emomali Rahmon "sponsored" Tajikistan as part of the project. Speaking at the Dialogue on Strengthening Connectivity Partners on 8 November 2014 in Beijing held in the framework of the APEC Forum, Rahmon stated, "Tajikistan is on the cross of the Asian roads and can play a role of the bridge between China and other countries in the region," stressing that more than 60% of bilateral trade uses the Kulma–Karasu crossing point on the Tajik–Chinese border.

Rahmon added, "Tajikistan pays a particular attention to intensive development of the network of internal and international roads and railways. We are very interested in attraction of additional funding sources for infrastructure projects. Such projects will correspond to the One Belt, One Road initiative proposed by China." He also reminded listeners that a direct flight between China and Tajikistan was launched 10 years ago.

Tajikistan is a participant in the regional project of construction of a gas pipeline from Central Asia to China, which started in September 2014. The project will bring more than US$3 billion to the Tajik economy, and will be "another opportunity for joint development, ensuring economic growth and freer movement," the Tajik President emphasized (AKIpress 2014). Tajikistan is also seeking investment from China to finance work on the highway that runs across the country, the

Dushanbe–Kulyab–Khorog–Kulma–Karokurum highway (Putz 2015). In addition to this infrastructural component, "Tajikistan would like also to see agribusiness and agriculture technology" (Expert on the region, personal communication, 24 April 2016).

12.4.4 Turkmenistan

Despite its professed neutrality, Turkmenistan is currently showing enthusiastic interest in developing an infrastructural partnership with China, and is participating in the OBOR project through construction of the Turkmenistan–Uzbekistan–Kyrgyzstan pipeline and construction of the China–Kazakhstan–Turkmenistan–Iran railroad (Kazinform 2016).

At a speech delivered at the Central Asia Regional Economic Cooperation Forum on 16 June 2015, Turkmenistan's Ambassador to China, Chinar Rustemova, stated that the One Belt, One Road initiative is a move toward promoting trade with and economic support of countries along the Belt and Road routes, as well as strengthening the infrastructure between these countries. She said that OBOR is very important for both Europe and Asia, and that Turkmenistan is actively involved in the project, hoping that it will connect Central Asia. She also reported that China and Turkmenistan are concluding large deals, particularly in the field of gas and telecommunications (Chinagoabroad 2015).[8]

12.4.5 Uzbekistan

Relations between China and Uzbekistan are warm. Xi Jinping phoned Uzbek President Karimov immediately after his re-election in March 2015, confirming the high level of mutual political support between China and Uzbekistan. Trade between the countries has increased seven-fold over the past 10 years, and for years China has been ranked among the top partners according to volume of investment in Uzbekistan. In addition, successful work on the joint construction of a number of important projects, such as the Central Asia–China gas pipeline and the Angren–Pap railway tunnel, "shows that there is ground for increasing

---

[8] It is worth noting that the China–Kazakhstan–Turkmenistan–Iran railroad communication more than halves the distance of transportation between China and Iran compared with the maritime route (Kazinform 2016; Expert on the region, personal communication, 24 April 2016).

cooperation between the two with respect to OBOR" (Chinese Embassy in Uzbekistan 2015). Uzbekistan has very high expectations about the project, the country being the geographic and territorial pivot of Central Asia. The Uzbek leadership expects the OBOR project to open up ways to reach the Persian Gulf, enabling expansion of commercial and trade routes (Expert on the region, personal communication, 24 April 2016).

As put by an interviewee, "Uzbekistan wants three main things: railway, transportation, logistics, transit for Europe and the Middle Eastern region; no free trade; move from labor-intensive to capital-intensive projects and production facilities in Uzbekistan, we would welcome joint ventures, for example in textiles. If China does not need textile anymore, why not moving production facilities to Uzbekistan and Xinjiang then?" (Expert 1, personal communication, 30 April 2016). Also, "Uzbekistan welcomes Chinese business, electronics, home-goods, machinery, mini-technology," and therefore building new transportation facilities and improving existing ones will help the country achieve that (Expert 1, personal communication, 30 April 2016).

12.5   The Central Asian Context and the Benefits for Central Asia

From the analysis presented above, it is evident that all Central Asian states have expressed favorable opinions about the project. They all foresee the infrastructural, economic, and financial benefits coming from the OBOR project, and express enthusiasm and interest. Even if Kazakhstan and Uzbekistan are, by virtue of their position, more at the pivotal center of the project, Kyrgyzstan, Tajikistan, and Turkmenistan have also expressed enthusiastic willingness to participate. The Central Asian governments expect significant benefits from the construction and implementation of OBOR. First, increased connectivity will create chances to enhance intraregional trade and commerce, which at the moment is less than 10% of the region's overall trade (Table 12.1).

Moreover, the Central Asian governments expect revenue from transit fees and investment from China. As one of the interviewees for this research stated, "all Central Asian states need roads, infrastructure and coal industry, and the major benefits will come from transit revenues and access to Chinese markets, very important in the future" (Expert from the region, personal communication, 29 April 2016). In addition to this,

Table 12.1 Indicators of intraregional trade in Central Asia

Central Asia							
Indicator	Partner	2010	2011	2012	2013	2014	Source
Intra-regional trade intensity index	Central Asia	12.78	10.96	11.38	10.78	12.07	IMF Directions of Trade Statistics
Intra-regional trade share (%)	Central Asia	6.60	6.08	6.78	6.66	7.07	IMF Directions of Trade Statistics

Source Table compiled by the author using IMF data

"Central Asian states want investments, especially in textile; special economic zones, and attention to the environment, especially in Uzbekistan" (Expert on the region, personal communication, 24 April 2016).

Advantages are not limited to transit fees and access to markets. Other potential advantages may be "self-entrepreneurship, hospitality, increased connectivity within and between countries, transit fees and import from China, but this is all to be seen" (Foreign correspondent from the region, 2 May 2016). The "all to be seen" part of the interviewee's quote is of the utmost importance to understand the complexity and multifacetedness of the Central Asian context in terms of opportunities and challenges. However, the region as a whole presents different systemic challenges that directly confront the ideas of "infrastructure" and "connectivity" on which OBOR is based and indeed founded.

12.6   The Central Asian Context and the Challenges It Presents

There are five main issues to be considered. The first is that there are intense border disputes in this region that could endanger the construction of roads and railways. Recent skirmishes on the Kyrgyz–Uzbek border, for example, and the continuous procrastination of border talks between Tajikistan and Uzbekistan will make the construction of transnational roads and infrastructure more difficult than expected. As bluntly by an interviewee, "the Uzbekistan–Kyrgyzstan railway is not going to happen" (Expert on the region, personal communication, 24 April 2016). The overall issue, in this respect, is how to develop a web of infrastructure that crosses borders by definition when several segments have not been delimited and demarcated.[9]

In this picture, broader geopolitical factors should also be taken into consideration. For example, "there is a plan to build a 90-km long tunnel in the Ferghana Valley and to conclude it by the end of 2016, but Russia is pressing the Kyrgyz government not to implement it" (Expert 1, personal communication, 30 April 2016). Therefore, "border issues are crucial, they must be resolved before engaging in every infrastructural project" (Expert 2, personal communication, 23 April 2016).

This second issue is linked to the first: mutual trust between the Central Asian leaders is not at ideal levels. Although relationships between Uzbekistan and Kazakhstan have been generally warm and cooperative,[10] relationships in the Fergana Valley are far from friendly. In this respect, China is doing well in advancing a policy of bilateralism; "In fact, China has a 'harmonizing' effect, it employs good diplomatic skills," and is capable of advancing its infrastructural agenda in the region (Foreign correspondent from the region, personal communication, 2 May 2016).

Yet, the question is to what extent this is sustainable. As noticed above, infrastructure is by definition multilateral. Although domestic projects can be easily built and pursued in the light of Central Asian demands, transnational infrastructures can be the objects of dispute and endless negotiation due to lack of cooperation (Expert 1, personal communication, 30 April 2016). In the future, especially when investment is more consistent, a balance between strong bilateralism and soft multilateralism may become ideal. At the moment, "there is still a lack of a multilateral platform to discuss OBOR, but the AIIB may become it soon" (Foreign correspondent from the region, personal communication, 2 May 2016). More on this will follow, before addressing the conclusions of this paper.

Third, there is the issue of how to bring benefits not just to governments, but also to local populations. At the moment, "effects for the

---

[9]Currently, 300 km between Kyrgyzstan and Uzbekistan are still disputed (DW 2016); half of the border between Tajikistan and Kyrgyzstan needs to be delimited (Muzalevsky 2014); and Uzbekistan and Tajikistan have only delimited 86% of their common border so far (Tajik MFA, n.d.).

[10]I was told that with Tajikistan "things are good but time [of transportation] could be better" (Expert 1, personal communication, 30 April 2016.

population are of secondary importance, because [these] are capital-intensive projects, of limited duration" (Expert from the region, personal communication, 29 April 2016). In this respect, therefore, the advantages for the common people and local employability should be emphasized, enhanced, and made clear to the Central Asian audience. Also, as noted above, there is the expectation that China will invest and bring *good* technology to countries. The local population want to be shielded from poor technology and products; the Uzbek case is indicative in this respect: "custom officials are now subject to criminal code in case they smuggle cheap and poor technology in the country; before, it was an administrative case" (Expert 1, personal communication, 30 April 2016).

One additional element to take into consideration is the disposition of Central Asian people toward Chinese workers and, more generally, Chinese economic penetration. It is no secret that in Kazakhstan, Kyrgyzstan, and Tajikistan there are hostile attitudes toward Chinese, albeit at different levels. As a local interviewee conveniently put, "fear is proportional to GDP" (Expert from the region, personal communication, 29 April 2016).

In Tajikistan, despite the strong demand for infrastructure and investment, "there is a general aversion to China"s capitalistic *modus operandi*," especially because of the traditional imprinting of society (Expert from the region, personal communication, 29 April 2016).

In Kyrgyzstan, although there is a general tolerance toward Chinese presence in the country, recent events suggest the contrary. The scandal of Junda Petrol Company in January 2016, when Yu Shan Lin, the director of the company, was accused of evading 54 m som (US$716,000) of taxes, was unusual in the country in terms of publicity and resonance (Foreign correspondent from the region, personal communication, 2 May 2016).

In Kazakhstan, the population's suspicious attitude toward the Chinese has been present for a while,[11] but was recently exacerbated by the proposed reform of the Land Code, granting permission to foreigners to lease land for 25 years instead of the existing 10-year period. Protests spread all over the country, from Atyrau to Uralsk to Almaty, with people

---

[11] All my interviewees confirmed this. Yet, the question as to whether Chinese immigration constitutes a threat to Tajikistan is still debated in Kazakh academia. For interesting perspectives on the topic, see Svetlana Kozhirova and Bakyt Ospanova (2014) and Yelena Sadovskaya (2015).

demonstrating against the reform. One protester said "We came to the square to tell our regional administration that we don't want to give out our native land for rent to anyone, especially the Chinese" (The Conway Bulletin 2016). Even if not related to OBOR, agri-business "says a lot about attitudes toward China. It elicits nationalism, but why is China the threat? Can you believe it, there were protests in Atyrau, 5000 km away from China! This is a blow to China's PR activities" (Foreign correspondent from the region, personal communication, 2 May 2016).[12]

Fourth, there are important legislative factors regarding protection of local employees. As an interviewee stressed, "Uzbekistan requires local workforce in every contract, although in the country there is no Sinophobia, Uzbeks are more pacific than others. Also, in whatever projects, the Chinese can be only in the top-management" (Expert 1, personal communication, 30 April 2016). The Turkmens require a minimum of 70% of local population employed in every project (Expert on the region, personal communication, 24 April 2016).

It is important to keep in mind that Kazakhstan, Kyrgyzstan, and Tajikistan are all members of the World Trade Organization (WTO) and therefore may not benefit from fixed regulation with respect to local employment: "WTO regulations do not foresee fixed employability terms for the local population, therefore [the possibility to employ a vast majority of local employees] will be left to the good will of the governments" (Foreign correspondent from the region, personal communication, 2 May 2016).

Even wider economic implications should considered. For example, China should be aware that countries such as Kyrgyzstan and Tajikistan will have serious difficulties in repaying loans if not over a very long term. The impact of delayed (re)payments on the overall budget for the project should therefore be taken into account.

With Uzbekistan, the problem is not with loans but with how to view trade and commerce *as a practice* overall. Uzbekistan's scepticism toward open free trade with neighbors is notorious, and this is also true for China. One interviewee made this clear, saying "free trade would be unacceptable [for Uzbekistan], there would be unfair competition,

---

[12] In this respect, it is also of utmost importance to remember that between 1999 and 2002, Tajikistan, Kyrgyzstan, and Tajikistan all ceded portions of land to China in the course of border negotiations. For more details, see Bruce Pannier (2016).

[Uzbekistan and China] cannot compete at this stage. OBOR should be for more trade, but not free trade, at least not yet" (Expert 1, personal communication, 30 April 2016).

Fifth, there is the need to stress the agency of Central Asian states, while at the same time keeping in mind their idiosyncrasies. In other words, China needs to ensure that the OBOR project does not appear as "overimposed" and decided without consulting the interested parties and respecting their sovereignty. President Xi recognized this in 2013 when launching OBOR, arguing that China respects the development paths and policies chosen by the peoples of regional countries, and will never interfere in the domestic affairs of Central Asian nations (Xinhua 2013).

Yet, this means that China needs to be more specific, and more precise, in explaining the project. As one of the interviewees acknowledged, "at the moment there are no clear benefits, there are no details in the document; we do not have the exact routes! There is the need to tackle vagueness, and this can be done by inviting proposals from countries benefitting from the project" (Expert 1, personal communication, 30 April 2016; Lain and Pantucci 2015).

This, of course, has implications for how China and Central Asian states see each other as partners in this framework of action. Recent research has shown that, despite the obvious imbalances in economic development and international political clout, Central Asian states want to be seen as equals (Costa Buranelli 2015). This pertains to both demands (what Central Asian states want and expect from the project) and negotiations (how Central Asian states want to talk about the project). While "Central Asian states are developing assertiveness" (Expert on the region, personal communication, 24 April 2016), the Chinese "are very respectful, they listen, we feel it" (Expert 1, personal communication, 30 April 2016).

However, this could also mean that there is a plurality of voices to be heard, complicating the whole scenario: "the relationship is asymmetric, but Central Asian states are not accepting everything; there are elites' interests, especially in Tajikistan" (Expert on the region, personal communication, April 24, 2016). Moreover, "in Kyrgyzstan it is even worse, as there is the problem of multiple elites," at the national, regional, local, and even border level (Expert from the region, personal communication, April 29, 2016).

Table 12.2 Ease of doing business in Central Asian countries

Economy	Ease of doing business rank
Kazakhstan	41
Kyrgyzstan	67
Uzbekistan	87
Tajikistan	132

Source Data taken from http://www.doingbusiness.org/rankings. Table obtained by filtering data for the region

It has been noted that "Beijing is deeply worried by Kyrgyzstan's volatile political environment, as a 'democratic oasis' subject to frequent political reversals, surrounded by totalitarian regimes. Chinese concerns have grown, especially after insistent voices began to point out an unusual radicalization among the most marginalized fringes of Kyrgyz society" (Colarizi 2015). In addition, as a local interviewee stressed, China has to remember that compared to Kazakhstan, Uzbekistan, and Turkmenistan (and Tajikistan to a lesser extent), "in Kyrgyzstan there is not a vertical structure of government" (Expert from the region, personal communication, 29 April 2016).

In other words, China must keep in mind that realization of the OBOR project depends on a series of relations with national and subnational elites, whose interests may be opposing, contradicting, and therefore detrimental to the project. Corruption is the natural result of such dynamics. Although not the only one, Central Asia is famous for these practices: "On the road Almaty–Bishkek, even if there is not dramatic relationship at all [between Kazakhstan and Kyrgyzstan], I do not drive anymore; this because the leaders do not care, and officials on the ground want to make money. There is competition for corruption, this is anecdotal evidence" (Expert from the region, personal communication, 29 April 2016).[13] Therefore, even if dealing with Central Asian states implies playing according to "local rules" (Cooley 2012), ensuring transparency will be crucial (Table 12.2).

It is evident that China needs to consider these factors in the implementation of the OBOR project. The argument advanced here is that

---

[13] In this respect, it may be interesting to consider that China and Kazakhstan have signed a memorandum of understanding on cooperation between the customs departments of the two countries. See AKIpress (2015).

it is not just an economic or a trade-related consideration, but also and especially a normative one, which can have resonance at the intraregional and the international levels.

In other words, thoughtful, considerate, and people-oriented implementation of the project would be beneficial not just to the economies of China and Central Asia, but would also favor China's image in the region and at the international level. This would perfectly fit China's discourse on its "peaceful rise." By playing according to the rules of international society, China can show how this project can contribute to the role of a responsible great power in a developing area (Buzan 2010). There are several aspects to this, as discussed next.

First, by incentivizing best economic practices, such as transparency of contracts, reduction of corruption, and favoring local economies by bringing them into OBOR-related projects, China will show other actors in international society that it takes globally shared economic norms seriously, thus following the rules of the game. In this respect, as noted by an interviewee, "China needs to be more responsible, as this would enhance its legitimacy" (Expert on the region, personal communication, 24 April 2016).

Second, by focusing on people and not just on states and governments, China would appear more inclusive and calm possible fears of "inadvertent empire" (Pantucci and Petersen 2012). An article in *Forbes* pointed out that the OBOR project still has difficulty in being known by people "on the ground," saying that "it is hard to find business executives [...] who are either aware of the policy or understand its potential implications" (Simpfendorfer 2015). As recognized by some of the interviewees for this research project, "the narrative at the governmental level is that it is good to do business with China, but the socio-cultural aspect of diplomacy, the people-to-people part is rather cold, not well developed; there is no information in Central Asia, it is not much talked about, it's an underground topic."

"Also, there is no significant engagement between the Chinese and Central Asian populations, you will not see adverts, the project is too sensitive, the leaders do not want this; furthermore, there is no effective integration, even if more and more Chinese are studying Russian" (Foreign correspondent from the region, personal communication,

2 May 2016).[14] Joint discussions are needed with partners that are inclusive to avoid characterizations of "inadvertent empire" and that respect the norms of sovereignty and non-interference. This is particularly relevant if we keep in mind that, although an infrastructural project is multilateral by definition, the current low level of trust between the Central Asian republics does not easily lend to multilateral frameworks for cooperation.

Although this distrust is prevalent between the elites, it can be overcome at the level of experts and professionals. One way to do this is encouragement of multilateral forums for discussion, and institutes on the model of China's OBOR Strategic Research Institute at the Beijing International Studies University or the China Institute of International Studies in Beijing. In other words, involvement of governmental officials as well as scholars, professionals, and technical experts from the Central Asian republics could lead to better understanding of the project and to better specification of its suggested implementation and effective viability. A good example of this is the fact that it was decided to deepen contacts between the political parties of Kazakhstan and the Communist Party of China, in addition to the joint forum with participation of representatives of small and medium-sized enterprises of the two countries (Kazakhstan 2050, 2016b).

Furthermore, tourism can also help the development of warmer relations between people. Kazakh Ambassador to China Shakhrat Nuryshev recently noticed how 2017 was declared the Year of Chinese Tourism in Kazakhstan and how in the short term there are plans to sign an agreement on group tourist trips from China to Kazakhstan (Kambarov 2015).

12.7   Conclusions

This paper has highlighted the position of the Central Asian republics with respect to the OBOR project. The demands and contextual difficulties, and the ways in which China can deal with them, have been

---

[14]Also, one may consider as an example that the Irkeshtam Pass, which serves as entrance gate for Chinese goods from Kashgar to Karasuu bazaar in Kyrgyzstan's part of the Fergana Valley, snoozes surrounded by high mountains. Although officially it should be finished by 2020, so far the Kashgar's Special Economic Zone is little more than a white elephant project on the outskirts of the city, which only a few people know how to reach.

explored, thanks also to the words of experts who are familiar with or even from the region and extremely knowledgeable about the project.

The overall conclusion that can be drawn from the research is that the OBOR project is certainly welcome in the region. It meets the favor of Central Asian states and can enhance the connectivity of different regions across Eurasia for economic and social purposes. Yet, paradoxically, establishment of OBOR will be long and not necessarily smooth. It will be up to the Chinese leadership to listen carefully to the demands of the Central Asian governments and, more importantly, of the people.

In particular, effective public relations and multilevel diplomacy (interstate and state–people) are the best strategies to make the project comprehensible, understood, and thoroughly explained. In other words, "the Chinese need to do effective and more PR, otherwise OBOR will seem overimposed. The question is: how ready, willing is China to do PR?" (Foreign correspondent from the region, personal communication, 2 May 2016). Furthermore, such engagement will give the Chinese leadership the possibility to address some of the deeply rooted nationalistic fears that permeate, albeit in different ways, Central Asian societies. It has been said that "China will have to change its way of doing business" (Expert on the region, personal communication, 24 April 2016) and, most of all, "will need patience" (Expert from the region, personal communication, 29 April 2016).

If OBOR pertains to the construction of roads and infrastructure to connect countries and markets, it must also be thought of as connecting spirits and minds. Only in this way can China enhance its legitimacy in Eurasia and in international society.

REFERENCES

24Kg News Agency. (2012, January 27). Kyrgyzstan starts construction of alternative North-South road. Retrieved from http://www.eng.24.kg/bigtiraj/170022-news24.html.

AKIpress. (2014, November 10). Tajikistan can bridge China and other countries of region—Rahmon. Retrieved from http://akipress.com/news:551120/.

AKIpress. (2015, May 28). China, Kazakhstan sign MOU on customs cooperation. Retrieved from http://akipress.com/news:559718.

Buzan, B. (2010). China in International Society: Is 'Peaceful Rise' Possible? *The Chinese Journal of International Politics, 3*(1), 5–36.

Chinagoabroad. (2015, June 17). Turkmenistan's Ambassador to China: Turkmenistan to Actively Participate in the "One Belt, One Road" Initiative. Retrieved from http://www.chinagoabroad.com/en/article/

turkmenistan-s-ambassador-to-china-turkmenistan-to-actively-participate-in-the-one-belt-one-road-initiative.

Chinese Embassy in Uzbekistan. (2015, May 6). Посол КНР в РУ Сунь Лицзе:Китай и Узбекистан идут по пути совместного строительства "одного пояса и одного пути". Retrieved from http://uz.chineseembassy.org/rus/slfy/slxw/t1261160.htm.

Clarke, M. (2016). Beijing's March West: Opportunities and Challenges for China's Eurasian pivot. *Orbis, 60*(2), 296–313.

Colarizi, A. (2015, August 11). China and Kyrgyzstan: So near, yet so far. *The Diplomat*. Retrieved from http://thediplomat.com/2015/08/china-and-kyrgyzstan-so-near-yet-so-far/.

Contessi, N. (2016). Central Asia in Asia: Charting growing trans-regional linkages. *Journal of Eurasian Studies, 7*(1), 3–13.

Cooley, A. (2012). *Great game, local rules.* Oxford: Oxford University Press.

Cooley, A. (2015). New Silk Route or Classic Developmental Cul-de-Sac? *PONARS Eurasia Policy Memo, 372*, 1–7.

Costa Buranelli, F. (2014). May we have a say? Central Asian states at the UN General Assembly. *Journal of Eurasian Studies, 5*(2), 131–144.

Costa Buranelli, F. (2015). International Society and Central Asia (Unpublished doctoral dissertation). London: King's College.

DW. (2016, March 24). Border dispute riles Kyrgyzstan, Uzbekistan. Retrieved from http://www.dw.com/en/border-dispute-riles-kyrgyzstan-uzbekistan/a-19140776.

Gabuev, A. (2015, November 12). China's Silk Road Challenge. *Carnegie Moscow Center*. Retrieved from http://carnegie.ru/commentary/2015/11/12/china-s-silk-road-challenge/ilrk.

Hongzhou, Z. (2015, May). Building the Silk Road Economic Belt, problems and priorities in Central Asia. *Policy Report*. Singapore: Rajaratnam School of International Studies.

Kambarov, B. (2015, December 15). Kazakhstan, China Sign $50 Billion Worth of Deals in 2015, Ambassador in Beijing Says. *Astana Times*. Retrieved from http://astanatimes.com/2015/12/kazakhstan-china-sign-50-billion-worth-of-deals-in-2015-ambassador-in-beijing-says/.

Kazakhstan 2050. (2016a, January 20). Kazakhstan, China signed agreement for $ 24 bn—Chinese Ambassador. Retrieved from https://strategy2050.kz/en/news/30784.

Kazakhstan 2050. (2016b, February 25). China intends to strengthen party-to-party ties with Kazakhstan. Retrieved from https://strategy2050.kz/en/news/32380.

Kazinform. (2016, April 26). China-Kazakhstan-Turkmenistan-Iran railroad presented in Beijing. Retrieved from http://www.inform.kz/eng/article/2897009.

Kirişci, K., & Le Corre, P. (2015, December 18). The great game that never ends: China and Russia fight over Kazakhstan. *Brookings.* Retrieved from http://www.brookings.edu/blogs/order-from-chaos/posts/2015/12/18-china-russia-kazakhstan-fight-kirisci-lecorre.

Kozhirova, S., & Ospanova, B. (2014, May). Chinese Migration in Kazakhstan: Implications for national security. *European Scientific Journal,* 482–486.

Lain, S., & Pantucci, R. (2015, November). The Economics of the Silk Road Economic Belt. Workshop Report, London: Royal United Services Institute for Defence and Security Studies.

Lain, S., & Pantucci, R. (2016, February). Security and stability along the Silk Road. Workshop Report, London: Royal United Services Institute for Defence and Security Studies.

Laruelle, M., & Peyrouse, S. (2014). *The Chinese question in Central Asia.* London: Hurst.

Mackerras, C. (2015). Xinjiang in China's foreign relations: Part of a New Silk Road or Central Asian Zone of Conflict? *East Asia, 32*(1), 25–42.

Muzalevsky, R. (2014, August 1). Border disputes in the Ferghana Valley threaten to undermine regional trade and stability. *Jamestown.* Retrieved from https://jamestown.org/program/border-disputes-in-the-ferghana-valley-threaten-to-undermine-regionaltrade-and-stability/.

National Development and Reform Commission, Ministry of Foreign Affairs, and Ministry of Commerce of the People's Republic of China. (2015). *Vision and Actions on Jointly Building Silk Road Economic Belt and 21st-Century Maritime Silk Road.* Retrieved from http://en.ndrc.gov.cn/newsrelease/201503/t20150330_669367.html.

Pannier, B. (2016, May 2). Central Asian Land and China. *RFE/RL.* Retrieved from http://www.rferl.org/content/central-asian-land-and-china/27711366.html.

Pantucci, R., & Petersen, A. (2012, November-December). China's Inadvertent Empire. *The National Interest.* Retrieved from http://nationalinterest.org/article/chinas-inadvertent-empire-7615.

Putz, C. (2015, September 3). Tajik leader in China, building roads. *The Diplomat.* Retrieved from http://thediplomat.com/2015/09/tajik-leader-in-china-building-roads/.

Sabayeva, G. (2015, May 18). Border does not divide Kazakhstan and China, but brings them closer, says Kazakh Ambassador in Beijing. *The Astana Times.* Retrieved from http://astanatimes.com/2015/05/border-does-not-divide-kazakhstan-and-china-but-brings-them-closer-says-kazakh-ambassador-in-beijing/.

Sadovskaya, Y. (2015, January 7). The mythology of Chinese migration in Kazakhstan. *CACI-Analyst.* Retrieved from http://www.cacianalyst.org/

publications/field-reports/item/13112-the-mythology-of-chinese-migration-in-kazakhstan.html.

Simpfendorfer, B. (2015, November 24). How China's Silk Road policy is shaping up in neighbouring countries. *Forbes.* Retrieved from http://www.forbes.com/sites/bensimpfendorfer/2015/11/24/kazakhstan_china_onebeltoneroad/#445639cc1a23.

Tajik MFA. (n.d.). Tajik-Uzbek state border. Retrieved from http://mfa.tj/en/border-issues/tajik-uzbek-state-border.html.

The Conway Bulletin. (2016). Kazakh President scraps land reforms after protests spread. Retrieved from http://theconwaybulletin.com/blog/2016/05/06/kazakh-president-scraps-land-reforms-protests-spread/.

Xinhua. (2013, September 7). Xi suggests China, C. Asia build Silk Road economic belt. *Xinhuanet.* Retrieved from http://news.xinhuanet.com/english/china/2013-09/07/c_132700695.htm.

Xinhua. (2015, May 7). China, Kazakhstan to align development strategies for common prosperity. *Xinhuanet.* Retrieved from http://news.xinhuanet.com/english/2015-05/08/c_134219458.htm.

CHAPTER 13

Is Afghanistan in the Way or on the Way of the New Silk Road?

Péter Marton

13.1   INTRODUCTION

To offer a realistic assessment of the question posed in the title of this paper, one may look into the past to examine the existing record of daring ambitions and investments related to developing connectivity in Afghanistan. Based on such an overview, starting with a look at Pakistan's plans in the mid-1990s to turn Afghanistan into a corridor of trade with Central Asia, it is hard to conclude that the country might play a significant role in the realization of the One Belt, One Road concept. Working toward conflict resolution or at least to mitigate problems in Afghanistan is going to remain crucial in containing spillover effects that could disrupt the New Silk Road elsewhere.

13.2   PAKISTAN THINKS BIG

Afghanistan's troubles stem largely from the period starting at the turn of the 1960s and 1970s. In the course of 1969–1972, a major drought destroyed livelihoods in rural areas of the country (Ruttig 2013, p. 2). It

P. Marton (✉)
Corvinus University, Budapest, Hungary

© The Author(s) 2018   231
Y. Cheng et al. (eds.), *The Belt & Road Initiative in the Global Arena*,
https://doi.org/10.1007/978-981-10-5921-6_13

shook the foundations of the political system, contributing to the 1973 fall of the Afghan monarchy, and affected southern areas of Afghanistan particularly badly. Some hundreds of thousands of deaths may be attributed to the crisis as a result of climate-induced scarcities.

For the economic and political crisis to turn into a fully fledged intrastate conflict, Pakistan's use of the Afghan Islamist opposition's various elements was crucial. Pakistani Prime Minister Zulfikar Ali Bhutto's Afghan affairs advisor, Naseerullah Babar, set up armed training for the members of two key factions opposing the secular government in Kabul: one led by Ahmed Shah Massoud from the north of Afghanistan (the Panjsheer valley) and the other led by Gulbuddin Hekmatyar (Abbas 2007). In 1975, an uprising was instigated against the Afghan government in a prelude to what was to come post-1978. Once Afghan Communists of the People's Democratic Party of Afghanistan (PDPA) overthrew President Mohammed Daoud Khan's regime in the Saur Revolution, the forces of the Soviet-backed Communist leadership as well as, eventually, Soviet troops came under attack by the same Islamist factions. Training continued to take place in Pakistan, and by this time on a much larger scale than before.

Although Pakistan was, in the 1980s war against the Soviet-backed regime in Afghanistan, by no means alone in supporting Afghan guerrillas, it was in a pivotal position in this respect, providing access to Afghanistan that was available from nowhere else in a politically convenient way. Pakistan's motive stemmed from the conventional strategic thinking in Islamabad that emphasized concern over possible encirclement (a pincer move) by India and any Afghan leadership that was not dependent on Pakistan (Pande 2013). In the event of war, in Pakistani strategists' minds, this could translate into an actual attack on Pakistan from two directions. They feared the motives of the Afghan leadership partly because of the disputed border line between the two countries, the Durand Line, whose Pakistani interpretation was never accepted by any Afghan government (ironically, even the Taliban's internationally unrecognized government made no concessions in this regard) (Rubin and Siddique 2006, p. 2).

When the Soviet Union left Afghanistan, Naseerullah Babar was still around, this time on the side of Benazir Bhutto's government, as interior minister. Both Bhutto and Babar wanted to "market Pakistan internationally as ...the crossroads to the old silk roads of trade between Europe and Asia" (quoted by Steve Coll [2004] who interviewed

Bhutto on 5 May 2002, p. 290). In fact, they considered Pakistan as being at the crossroads, with the function of gate-keeper. With reference to Pakistan being the gateway to Afghanistan (in the form of the Khyber and Bolan Passes) Bhutto said "control of the trade routes is a way to get my country power and prestige" (Coll 2004).

It was in this context that the Pakistani leadership witnessed the rise of the Taliban in southern Afghanistan. The latter started out as a small militia of former madrasa students (hence the name "taliban" or students). Many of them were veterans of the 1980s war (including Mullah Omar, leader of the Taliban for over two decades). They hailed from small settlements to the west of Kandahar, had their founding meeting in Sangisar, and established their first road checkpoint at Hawz-e-Mudat. They were seeking justice related to atrocities that local warlords were committing against the population of the area. Southern Afghanistan's political landscape was extremely fragmented at the time, with dozens of different armed groups controlling a large number of checkpoints along the Herat–Kandahar–Spin Boldak/Chaman route up to the Pakistani border (Zaeef 2010, pp. 65–72). Kandahar's merchant class lent its support to the group when the Taliban were able to defeat a lesser warlord in their area, seeing in this the success of religious mobilization against one of the local strongmen who impeded trade along the road to Pakistan. Taliban ranks began to swell, and they eventually grew capable of clearing the road up to the crossing at Spin Boldak/Chaman, taking control of Kandahar as well in the meantime (Zaeef 2010). These developments attracted the attention of Bhutto's government, who began to provide support to the group, including setting up a telephone network and a wireless communication network in southern Afghanistan specifically for the Taliban, repairing roads, and generally sending aid through the Trade Development Cell of Pakistan's interior ministry (Rashid 2001, pp. 184–185). The Pakistani secret service, Inter-Services Intelligence (ISI), was at first skeptical but eventually lent its own support to the policy. This came once the Taliban defeated the forces of their client Gulbuddin Hekmatyar for control of a key supply base in Spin Boldak (on the Afghan–Pakistani border) (Coll 2004, p. 291).

From then, the Taliban's rise led to its control of over 90% of Afghanistan's territory by the year 2000. This required significant external support by the Pakistani military, members of the Arab jihadi movement (in the framework of al-Qaida's 055 Brigade), Kashmiri militant groups (e.g., Lashkar-e Tayba), and anti-Shi'a Pakistani militant groups

(Lashkar-e Jhangvi, Sipah-e Sahaba). Earlier, up to around the autumn of 1997, even some in the West (and in the US administration of President Bill Clinton) considered that the Taliban might provide stability for free trade and the development of the economy in the region. However, the group's intolerant views and draconian principles began to express in ways visible even from half a world away, resulting in the impression that working with this faction as a legitimite representative of Afghanistan was a non-starter in terms of basic human values. Female members of the US administration, such as Madeleine Albright and, to some extent, even Hillary Clinton (as First Lady and not a formal member of the administration), made the difference initially but then the negative assessment of the Taliban's role became more widespread (Coll 2004, p. 352).

Thus, ironically, it was Pakistan's interest in opening up a trade corridor toward Central Asia in Afghanistan, combined with its interest in creating a client Islamist Afghan government, that brought about the increased isolation of Afghanistan and significant deterioration of the general prospects there. It was a country taken over bit by bit by a force that had no realistic chance of becoming an internationally recognized government and no real intention of serving as a bridge between East and West.

13.3   TAPI: The Trans-Afghan Pipeline

The Trans-Afghan pipeline, at times optimistically called the Turkmenistan–Afghanistan–Pakistan–India (TAPI) pipeline, originated as a plan from the context of the 1990s, in the wake of the dissolution of the Soviet Union and the independence of former Central Asian Soviet Socialist Republics.

Turkmenistan's gas reserves were an enticing natural resource for companies seeking to expand into new areas and, although the relationship between the West and Russia was much better in those years, securing access to these gas reserves via a non-Russian route seemed to offer strategic benefits to the West.

Major oil companies, however, did not make a move, given the inconvenience of the situation in Afghanistan at the time. The first half of the 1990s saw a major round of civil war between the forces holding Kabul (the Rabbani government supported by, among others, Ahmed Shah Masoud's and Rashid Dostum's respective militias) and the key Pakistani-supported challenger, Gulbuddin Hekmatyar and his Hizb-i-Islami faction.

The south of the country was left to itself in a state of hyperfragmentation with dozens of armed groups in control. However, this part of the country was vital in any plan because the best pipeline route seemed to follow the arc of the Afghan ringroad from Herat to Kandahar.

An Argentinian company, Bridas, was the first to attempt negotiations on building a pipeline. It secured the Pakistani government's willingness to support the project. A lesser US firm, Unocal, soon followed and realized that key advantages were to be attained by getting consent from local players in Afghanistan, specifically in the south. By 1994–1995, the Taliban were already in the ascendancy in the south, and a representative of Unocal, Marty Miller, flew there to negotiate directly. He constantly informed US government circles about any advances made. Unocal mobilized a considerable lobby machinery to secure bipartisan support for the project in the USA, and obtained vocal endorsements from across the political spectrum, from members of the Clinton administration to Henry Kissinger (former National Security Advisor and Secretary of State in Republican administrations) and Zalmay Khalilzad (the Bush administration's ambassador to Afghanistan and later its envoy to the United Nations). However, this eventually was of no avail because the Taliban's reputation soon made them impossible partners. Unocal remained interested up to 1997–1998, but then had to discard its project (Coll 2004, pp. 338–339).

It took over one and a half decades before serious thinking about this project recommenced, showing the level of difficulty and risk involved. News reports at the end of 2015 accounted how construction of the pipeline eventually began in Turkmenistan (near the Galkynysh field that will supply the TAPI pipeline). Yet, the same reports did not fail to add that "Although it is backed by hydrocarbon resources, the TAPI project faces several risks, such as the deteriorating security situation in Afghanistan and lack of clarity about its financing" (Reuters 2015). The Turkmen government has managed to put together only a framework agreement with a consortium of interested Turkish and Japanese companies, whose involvement may speak more about Turkey's cultural diplomacy and Japan's interest in foreign aid in Asia, respectively, than about the actual vitality of the project.

13.4   The Experience with the Aynak Copper Mine

Simple narratives of the investment of two Chinese companies, the Metallurgical Corporation of China (MCC) and the Jiangxi Copper Corporation (JCCL), in copper mining at the Mes Aynak site in

Afghanistan often speak of this as "China free-riding on security provided by the West in the country" (formulated from a perspective critical of the statement by Downs 2012). To anyone familiar with the conditions on the ground this is a laughable proposition.

First, the chance to invest came at a cost and hence was not "free:" the two companies had to win a tender in competition with other firms, including US and Canadian companies. They offered a high royalty rate, bonus payments (conditional upon necessary developments such as the approval of a feasibility study), and an infrastructure development package to the Afghan government. The latter included the building of roads, a railway connection to the mine, and a thermal power plant with accompanying coal mine. The Chinese companies' return on the prospective investment is made rather uncertain by significant risks. The latter stem not only from political instability but also from the fluctuation of the price of copper on the world market. Some commentators have talked of the "100 billion dollars" in revenue that the MCC and JCCL are set to make with their US$3 billion investment. In fact, price drops coming at inconvenient times may reduce the prospective revenues considerably. A major price fall in 2008, connected with the worldwide economic slowdown and the decrease in demand, may well be responsible for slowing down development at the Mes Aynak site to a critical extent.

Second, the area is not exactly "secure" and this is the other form of risk that needs to be kept in mind. The Mes Aynak site is in a region that sees frequent movement by insurgent factions operating in eastern Afghanistan, who may need be paid off for the sake of security, as often happened in the case of other major investments and even lesser development projects in Afghanistan over the years (MacKenzie 2009).

It is small wonder, therefore, that the investment that some commentators speak of as a "done fact" has not really taken off in almost a decade since the contract was awarded to the two Chinese firms. It is not only that the promised roads, railway, and thermal power plant are still waiting to be built, but the feasibility study has not yet been completed, either.

The lesson is, regrettably, that infrastructure development proves extremely challenging in Afghanistan, even when for-profit ventures are at stake and even when these enjoy a degree of political support from the investors' home countries (in this case, China).

13.5 THE AFGHANISTAN RING ROAD

Afghanistan's modern surfaced road network has its origins in the time of the Soviet presence (in the 1980s). The "Ring Road" connecting Kabul in the center with Kandahar in the south, Herat in the west, and Pul-i-Khumri and other cities in the north, forming a 2200-km circle, was constructed in that period. Other roads were built as well, but once Soviet forces left and civil war ensued, there were little to no resources devoted to maintenance and the roads fell into a very poor, in places unusable, condition. Post-2001, the international community undertook to re-create an extended road system of regional highways (including the ring road), national highways (connecting provincial capitals to the ring), and provincial roads (connecting provincial capitals to district centers) (Amiri 2013). The United States Agency for International Development (USAID), the Japanese International Cooperation Agency (JICA), the Asian Development Bank (ADB), and the World Bank were the key donors. The Louis Berger Group (LBG) was the biggest contractor involved, mostly related to the USAID-financed section of the Ring Road.

Even the development of this basic infrastructure was, however, in many ways (when viewed in light of the ambition of re-booting Afghanistan's economy) under-resourced—handled as an economy-of-force mission. There were frequent complaints about price overruns caused by lengthy subcontractor chains. In reality, price overruns and subcontractor chains are often also seen in developed countries in the field of road construction.

The results were as expected. After the initial investment and eventual completion of the ring road in 2013 (the Saudi-financed section was completed last), maintenance was again left to the Afghan government, which is not able to generate the kind of revenue or political/territorial control that would be required for the results of these efforts to be sustainable. The existing roads are already in a bad condition, as a 2014 *Washington Post* article accounts in graphic detail:

> They look like victims of an insurgent attack — their limbs in need of amputation, their skulls cracked — but the patients who pour daily into the Ghazni Provincial Hospital are casualties of another Afghan crisis. They are motorists who drove on the road network built by the U.S. government and other Western donors — a $4 billion project that was once a symbol of promise in post-Taliban Afghanistan but is now falling apart. (Sieff 2014)

Insurgents are also causing deterioration of the available infrastructure; their improvised explosive devices (IEDs) regularly damage the road surface, leaving large craters behind.

Yet, the key challenge is the lack of a central government with the capacity and integrity to take matters fully into its own hands, coupled with fast-decreasing international interest in Afghanistan's development.

13.6   Conclusion

As this brief paper has shown in its discussion of Pakistan's plans in the 1990s to open up an Afghan trade corridor toward Central Asia, the plans for the TAPI pipeline, China's mining investment related to the Mes Aynak copper deposit, and the Afghan ring road network, there are practically insurmountable obstacles in the way of integrating Afghanistan into the OBOR initiative.

These stem first from Pakistan's desire to be a gateway and a gatekeeper to Afghanistan which, given its ideological preferences, has unfortunate consequences for political stability and the quality of governance on the other side of the Durand Line. Second, with some of the same issues, the TAPI pipeline is another spectacular indicator of problems in that it shows the lack of confidence by profit-driven investors. Third, the Aynak copper mine project, although simultaneously hailed by some as "China's buying into Afghanistan's future" and criticized by others as "China free-riding on security provided by the West," is in many ways a similar indicator. Because the Chinese leadership's strategic calculus was behind the project, its failure may show that even investors that are not purely profit-driven do not have the ability to move forward with projects on a large scale in Afghanistan. Fourth, road building has taken place in two major waves in Afghanistan's history but, with no local capacity and capability for road maintenance, these achievements cannot realistically be expected to last.

The reason why Afghanistan remains of interest for the OBOR initiative is because it can disrupt its operation via spillover effects. Militant groups who find harbor in Afghanistan's areas outside central government control can pose a threat directly or indirectly in the wider region, from Central Asia to Pakistan. In the case of the former, the Islamic Movement of Uzbekistan's forays into the Central Asian republics in 1999 and 2000 could be a demonstration of this. With regards to the latter, numerous past incidents of attacks on Chinese and other interests in Pakistan illustrate this point.

Mass movements of refugees, through movements of migration, can also contribute to knee-jerk government reactions, for example in the European Union: a (prospective) general hardening of borders may slow down the movement of goods as well. If the latter scenario were to play out fully, it would also have regrettable implications for the New Silk Road. Inasmuch as Afghanistan (together with Syria) is a key source of refugee flows, the country's conditions are felt through their political implications in the context of some of the key markets that the OBOR initiative is interested in connecting.

REFERENCES

Abbas, H. (2007). Transforming Pakistan's frontier corps. *The Jamestown Terrorism Monitor*, 5(6), retrieved from https://jamestown.org/program/transforming-pakistans-frontier-corps/ (accessed: May 4, 2016).

Amiri, M. A. (2013). Road reconstruction in Afghanistan: A cure or a curse? *International Affairs Review*, XXII(2), Spring 2013, retrieved from http://www.iar-gwu.org/sites/default/files/articlepdfs/Road%20Reconstruction%20in%20Afghanistan%20-%20Mohammad%20Abid%20Amiri.pdf (accessed: May 6, 2016).

Coll, S. (2004). *Ghost wars: The secret history of the CIA, Afghanistan, and Bin Laden, from the Soviet invasion to September 10, 2001*. New York: Penguin Books.

Downs, E. (2012).China buys into Afghanistan. *SAIS Review*, XXXII(2), retrieved from http://www.brookings.edu/~/media/research/files/papers/2013/02/21-china-afghanistan-downs/china-buys-into-afghanistan-erica-downs.pdf (accessed: May 5, 2016).

MacKenzie, J. (2009, August 13). Who is funding the Afghan Taliban? You don't want to know. *Reuters/Global Post*, retrieved from http://blogs.reuters.com/global/2009/08/13/who-is-funding-the-afghan-taliban-you-dont-want-to-know/ (accessed: May 4, 2016).

Pande, A. (2013). Reality or paranoia: Why is Pakistan afraid of India & Afghanistan ties? Hudson Institute, September 2, 2013, retrieved from http://www.hudson.org/research/9708-reality-or-paranoia-why-is-pakistan-afraid-of-india-afghanistan-ties- (accessed: May 3, 2016).

Rashid, A. (2001). *Taliban: Militant Islam, oil and fundamentalism in Central Asia*. New Haven: Yale University Press.

Reuters. (2015, December 23). Turkmenistan starts work on gas link to Afghanistan, Pakistan, India. *Reuters*, retrieved from http://uk.reuters.com/

article/turkmenistan-gas-pipeline-idUKKBN0TW05Q20151213   (accessed: May 4, 2016).

Rubin, B., & Siddique, A. (2006). Resolving the Pakistan-Afghanistan stalemate. *USIP special report 176*, October 2006, retrieved from http://www.usip.org/sites/default/files/SRoct06.pdf (accessed: May 5, 2016).

Ruttig, T. (2013). How it all began: A short look at the pre-1979 origins of Afghanistan's conflicts. *Afghanistan analysts network occasional paper* 01/2013, retrieved from http://www.afghanistan-analysts.org/wp-content/uploads/downloads/2013/02/20130111Ruttig-How_It_All_Began_FINAL.pdf (accessed: May 3, 2016).

Sieff, K. (2014, January 30). After billions in U.S. investment, Afghan roads are falling apart. *The Washington Post*, retrieved from https://www.washington-post.com/world/asia_pacific/after-billions-in-us-investment-afghan-roads-are-falling-apart/2014/01/30/9bd07764-7986-11e3-b1c5-739e63e9c9a7_story.html?utm_term=.4ce30bd1f26d (accessed: May 8, 2016).

Zaeef, A. S. [Mullah] (2010): *My Life with the Taliban*. London: C. Hurst & Co. Publishers Ltd.

CHAPTER 14

China in Central Asia and the Balkans: Challenges from a Geopolitical Perspective

Junbo Jian

14.1   INTRODUCTION

China and the Central Asian countries are geographical neighbors. Clearly, their relations have a complicated history, including the fact that parts of Central Asia once belonged to ancient China and now many Chinese ethnic groups live in Central Asia. Regardless of the history of their relations, a close economic relationship is now being shaped.

China has invested heavily in this region, including investments in manufacturing, agriculture, high technology, energy, and commodities. The engagement of China in Central Asia is not only to sell manufactured goods and invest in this region, but also to obtain oil and other natural resources, while stabilizing the region to improve the environment for Chinese economic prosperity. In recent years, Central Asia has become an inevitable and pivotal partner of the China-initiated Silk Road project, just as it was part of the ancient Silk Road.

Although China did not leave the Balkans after the end of the Cold War, their bilateral relations have strengthened remarkably in recent

J. Jian (✉)
Fudan University, Shanghai, China

© The Author(s) 2018   241
Y. Cheng et al. (eds.), *The Belt & Road Initiative in the Global Arena*,
https://doi.org/10.1007/978-981-10-5921-6_14

decades, especially after the China–Central and Eastern Europe Summit ("Sixteen plus One") was inaugurated in 2012 and the New Silk Road (One Belt, One Road or OBOR) was initiated in 2013. This does not mean that more natural resources such as oil or minerals have been found in the Balkans (although these resources are now necessary to feed China's growing economy) or that the Balkan market has suddenly enlarged; instead, it means that the two sides have found more common ground for enhancing their relations. For China, the Balkans, like a bridge, are becoming increasingly important for promoting Beijing–Brussels relations and bolstering the new Silk Road initiative. For the Balkans, China is increasingly becoming one of the key investors for their economic development. Scholar Valbona Zeneli argues that, "The interest of China's engaging in the Balkans appears to go beyond markets – in fact, the Balkan markets could be considered insignificant for trade... It also seems to go beyond the need to secure a source of commodities, although the Balkans are rich in natural resources. Rather, it appears that China is focused on infrastructure and access to Western European markets" (Zeneli 2014). China's increasing engagement in the Balkans is mainly to support the OBOR initiative and bind China more closely with Western Europe, consolidating the Sino-European strategic partnership economically and politically.

However, both Central Asia and the Balkans have been used historically in the competition between great powers. Traditionally, the EU and its large partners, the USA, Russia, and Turkey, are players in the Balkans. Russia, the USA, Turkey, Europe, and even India are now actively involved in Central Asia. Beijing always states that the OBOR (and the 16+1 platform) is only an economy-related initiative and a cross-border project, focusing on sustainable development and a win–win situation, and that engagement in these regions is only to strengthen China's relations with countries there and to benefit them economically. However, many scholars and politicians of the above-mentioned powers view OBOR as a form of expansion of China's influence. Namely, China's increasing engagement in Central Asia and the Balkans is to some extent regarded by the West and other related powers as part of a geopolitical competition with them in these two regions.

This chapter argues that China's involvement in Central Asia and the Balkans is facing geopolitical challenges, regardless of Beijing's words and deeds. In addition, Beijing should take some appropriate steps to cope with these challenges and try to translate the potential geopolitical competition into comprehensive cooperation with related countries and powers.

14.2   Challenges of China's Engagement in Central Asia and the Balkans

As Beijing increasingly engages in Central Asia and the Balkans economically, some serious challenges are arising. These challenges are a result of the inevitable geopolitical competition, domestic political disputes in the countries of Central Asia and the Balkans, and China's own problems such as its awkward form of engaging in geopolitical arenas.

14.2.1   Domestic Issues in Central Asia and the Balkans

As one part of the former Soviet Union and a region surrounded by multiple cultures and religions, there are many domestic issues in Central Asia, and these issues and social disturbance create risks for Chinese investment. After 2003, and especially after 2010, the security situation in Central Asia underwent a great change. Penetration of the Taliban and the "Islamic State" is increasing and imposes pressure on Central Asia's security.

On 30 August 2016, the Chinese Embassy in Kyrgyzstan was attacked by a car bomb. This attack was carried out by members of the East Turkistan Islamic Movement, which was identified in September 2002 by the United Nations as a terrorist organization. As early as 1998, members of the terrorist group East Turkistan Liberation Organization set off bombs in Osh, Kyrgyzstan; in 2000, an official delegation from Xinjiang, China, suffered a terrorist attack in Bishkek, the capital of Kyrgyzstan; in the same year, the East Turkistan Liberation Organization implemented an openly armed robbery of the World Bank office in Almaty, Kazakhstan; and in 2003, a bus full of Chinese was burned after a terrorist attack on the road over 200 km away from Bishkek.

In recent years, many terrorists from Afghanistan have entered the Fergana valley in Central Asia through Tajikistan. This trend is increasing, especially after withdrawal of the USA from Afghanistan.

Apart from terrorism and local disturbances, the distrust of local people in Chinese engagement is another challenge. Although bilateral relations are kept well at the central government level, officials at the local government level and the common people do not have enough trust in

Chinese investment. They worry that China's investment in their countries may make territorial disputes with China more complicated and bring about environmental deterioration, cultural conflicts, and so on. For example, Kazakhstan is worried about the excessive influence of Chinese investment and wants to limit the flow of investment and subsequent immigration. Kyrgyzstan wants to promote relations with Russia to balance the influence of Beijing.[1]

In the Balkan countries, there is also some suspicion of China's involvement. For example, in January 2015, when Syriza (a coalition of radical left parties in Greece) came to power, they swiftly declared that the previous administration-initiated privatization of enterprises was illegal and should be re-examined. This directly attacked the operation of China-invested Piraeus Port. In the early privatization of Hellenic state-owned assets after the debt crisis broke out in 2008, Chinese companies, mainly the COSCO Group, acquired the franchise for Piraeus container terminals 2 and 3. When the privatization was frozen by the new Tsipras-led administration, Chinese investment in this port quickly faced serious challenge (Korybko 2015). Although this disturbance over the privatization or nationalization of Piraeus port was finally resolved (China still keeps its rights), it illustrates how China's engagement can be challenged by the domestic affairs of host countries. A similar challenge for Beijing is very possible in the Balkans in the future.

Moreover, interior political disputes in Balkan countries can give rise to attack on China's investment there. For example, In October 2014, the government of Montenegro signed an agreement with the Chinese Exim Bank on a US$1 billion loan for construction of a stretch of a highway through Montenegro, to be built by the China Road and Bridge Corporation. However, this cooperative project was highly questioned by the opposition parties of Montenegro, which claimed that the loan would enormously increase the already high public debt and potential corruption.

Political crisis in Macedonia poses another challenge for China's cooperative projects with this country. The mass antigovernment protests on 5 May 2015 and a violent and deadly clash between the police and a

---

[1] US media: Central Asian countries worry about the Belt and Road, Chinese investment limited. (2015), Retrieved from http://military.china.com/news2/569/20151230/21044790.html.

militant group in the city of Kumanovo threatened the stability of the country and stimulated tensions in this region. Clearly, China-supported construction of a logistical network in this region via a high-speed railway and a port in the Mediterranean Sea would be seriously challenged by Macedonian domestic turbulence, because Macedonia is at the center of the Balkans, lying at the intersection of this transportation network (Vangeli 2015).

Other regional issues, such as disputes between Greece and Macedonia over "national" naming and Albania's nationalism and radical leftism could also destabilize this region and, consequently, undermine China-supported projects.

Meanwhile, the relatively low efficiency of governance in Balkan countries is also a long-term challenge for Chinese investment there. Compared with other European countries, especially Western European countries, the governance level in Balkans is far below EU standards. The low efficiency of this governance is reflected by corruption, gray economy, and insecurity. The disordered tax management and imperfect legal systems are unable to resolve economic disputes, chaotic rental market, the nontransparency of policies, and so on.[2]

14.2.2   Power Games in Central Asia and the Balkans

The Balkans and Central Asia have always been hotly contested spots in international power games in history, and today is no exception. As China increasingly engages in these regions, it encounters complicated geopolitical competition and even rivalry with some other powers. Because of the huge interests that some powers have in these regions, China's engagement will be primarily challenged or opposed by the EU, Russia, Turkey, and the USA.

The European Union's Suspicions
After the collapse of Soviet Union, the EU/European Community strengthened relations with five Central Asian countries through several policy instruments. In the 1990s, the EU signed Partnership and

---

[2] Macedonia and Albania are listed as the least desirable investment destinations in the Balkans. (2009). Retrieved from http://www.mofcom.gov.cn/aarticle/i/jyjl/m/200912/20091206668429.html.

Cooperation Agreements (PCAs) with Central Asian countries. The agreements mainly focused on economic cooperation and trade with post-Soviet states and paid only secondary attention to good governance and democratic rule. The central instrument for Brussels to strengthen economic cooperation with Central Asia within the framework of the PCAs was the Technical Assistance to the Commonwealth of Independent States (TACIS) programme, launched in 1991.

In 2002, the EU advanced its policy toward the five Central Asian countries by issuing the separate Regional Strategy Paper (RSP). Based on this policy, the EU Special Representative to Central Asia was appointed in 2005 (Kavalski 2007).

In June 2007, the European Council approved a German-drafted new strategic policy toward Central Asia—the EU and Central Asia: New Partnership Strategy. This was the EU's first comprehensive and systematic Central Asia policy, indicating that the EU would be more actively engaged in Central Asia at multiple levels. However, because of the situation in Afghanistan, a neighbor of Central Asian countries, and Russia's action in this region, trade and investment were less important in this stategy than energy and security in EU–Central Asian relations. For example, military cooperation with Kyrgyzstan and Uzbekistan became vital for EU members involved in Operation Enduring Freedom, because they needed access to military bases in the region (Hoffmann 2010). Prompted by the new strategy, the two sides had held several meetings regarding security. For instance, in September 2008, the EU and Central Asian countries held a conference on security in Paris and issued a joint declaration on security cooperation.

Through these efforts, the EU gradually became a very important presence in Central Asia, and is now the second most important trade partner of this region. To enhance their strategic relations, the EU plans to provide more aid and offer more investment in the region, according to Federica Mogherini, the EU's High Representative for Foreign Affairs and Security Policy.[3]

Central Asia is considered a strategic partner for EU for several reasons. It is a key region for Europe in countering the threat posed by Russia, constructing more friendly relations with the Muslim world by

---

[3] The EU and the Five Central Asian Countries Discussed Economic Cooperation and Anti-terrorism Issues. (2015, December 22). *Xinhua News*.

building good relations with Central Asian countries that are relatively moderate Muslim countries, fighting against trans-border terrorism, spreading European norms and soft power, and constructing a stable neighborhood. However, China's engagement in Central Asia will not only make the EU face economic competition, but also reduce the reliance of Central Asian countries on the EU, thereby reducing the EU's international influence and level of leverage against Russia.

For Europe, the Balkans are not an alien region, they are in Europe. Thus, the Balkans are always significant for the EU, militarily, politically, and economically. The importance of the Balkans for European security was especially revealed by the interior conflict of the former Yugoslavia in the 1990s, which evolved into a cross-border conflict and humanitarian disaster, forcing several international powers including the USA and Russia to become involved. This case showed that the Balkans, although there had been a long peace before the crisis, was a key region that could threaten the security of the whole of Europe.

Considering energy security, the Balkans form an important corridor for pipelines to connect Europe with gas suppliers. They are also "the main axis by which a massive transfer of Middle Easterners is taking place nowadays with an estimated 1.5 million people using the so-called 'Balkan route' between early 2015 and early 2016" (Michaletos 2015). Thus. the Balkans as a migration corridor is more and more significant for European stabilization. The Balkans are also part of the European economic system, especially as a manufacturing base and resource supply for Europe. In general, the Balkans are part of Europe and are becoming more and more important for the EU and European countries in many aspects.

EU policy toward the Balkans, especially the Western Balkans (Eastern Balkan countries Bulgaria and Romania are Member States of the EU), is based on its enlargement policy. About three-quarters of Balkan countries are members of the EU, and the others are framed into its Association Policy. Some countries in the Western Balkan (Serbia, Montenegro, Macedonia, and Albania) are EU candidate states, and others (Bosnia and Herzegovina and Kosovo, whose nationality is controversial) are potential candidate states.

All of the Western Balkan countries are eager to access the EU, and they are regularized and normalized by the EU's Stabilization and Association Process (SAP), launched in 1999, and the Thessaloniki Agenda adopted in 2003. Within the SAP framework, all Western Balkan

Table 14.1 The EU Stabilization and Association Process in the Western Balkans

Countries	Negotiations started	Initialed	Signed	Entry into force
Albania	2003	2006	2006	2009
Bosnia and Herzegovina	2005	2007	2008	2015
Kosovo	2013	2014	2015	2016
Montenegro	2005	2007	2007	2010
Serbia	2005	2007	2008	2013
Macedonia	2000	2000	2001	2004

countries have signed Stabilization and Association Agreements (SAA) with the EU at a bilateral level, aiming to help Western Balkan countries reach the accession threshold of the Copenhagen Criteria by financial assistance, political dialogue, trade relations, and regional cooperation (Table 14.1).

In June 2016, a "new strategy" of the EU was issued that reaffirmed the weight of the Balkans in its global strategy and external relations. The strategy indicates that the EU needs the Balkans to deal with many issues, from energy security to terrorism:

Within the scope of the current enlargement policy, the challenges of migration, energy security, terrorism and organized crime are shared between the EU, the Western Balkans and Turkey. They can only be addressed together. Yet the resilience of these countries cannot be taken for granted. The EU enjoys a unique influence in all these countries. The strategic challenge for the EU is therefore that of promoting political reform, rule of law, economic convergence and good neighborly relations in the Western Balkans and Turkey, while coherently pursuing cooperation across different sectors.[4]

With this background, the Balkans have strong economic links with the EU. The EU is the Western Balkans' largest trade partner, accounting for over 75% of the region's total trade, although the region's share of overall EU trade was only 1.1% in 2014.

---

[4]Shared Vision, Common Action: A Stronger Europe A Global Strategy for the European Union's Foreign and Security Policy, June 2016.

Because the EU has such strong links with the Balkans, any Chinese engagement in this region is sensitive for the EU. In the EU's opinion, China's presence in Balkans would undermine the dominance of the EU. For example, it is well known that China envisages a transport network of China-financed express railways and highways through the Balkan countries. Nevertheless, the EU also planned to integrate the Balkans into the EU geographically via railways. In 1994, on the Greek island of Crete, the second Pan European Transport Conference defined the Pan European Corridors. The tenth corridor was proposed after the end of hostilities between the states of the former Yugoslavia. "Corridor 10" was to be a 2300-km long run between Salzburg in Austria and Thessaloniki in Greece, passing through Austria, Slovenia, Croatia, Serbia, Macedonia, and Greece.

The China-supported transport network in the Balkans is similar to the EU-proposed Pan European Corridor 10 passing through the Balkans. After the debt crisis in 2008, the Pan European Corridor 10 is facing a stalemate, although originally planned to be finished in 2015. In comparison, China has the funds to develop the transport network in this region, and projects regarding transport construction seem to be progressing smoothly.

Undoubtedly, China's engagement in transportation and other fields is affecting the EU's dominance and the authority of agenda-setting in the Balkans. It was commented that "Investments by Chinese state-owned companies on the periphery of the EU have not only given China an indirect say in European affairs; they have also signaled to the U.S. and the West that Beijing is ready to advance its own agenda in the region" (Poulain 2011).

Furthermore, China's engagement is also regarded as an attack on the EU's soft power in the Balkans. Because of China's increasing investment there, countries in the region have more choices of finance for their domestic construction and economic development, and are able to be more independent economically and financially. In the EU's eyes, more independence of Balkan countries would be considered as more dependence on China. François Godement and his colleagues in the European Council on Foreign Relations, a think-tank based in Brussels, worried that "Central and Eastern European Member States such as Bulgaria and Hungary, which were already vying for Chinese investment, are now seeing European flows of investment drying up and are thus increasingly dependent on China" (Godement et al. 2011).

The increase in independence endorsed by Beijing callenges the EU's policy on China to some extent. For example, some Balkan countries are strong supporters of lifting the arms embargo on China, although the embargo is widely agreed policy at the EU level. In the EU's eyes, economic independence of the Balkans endorsed by China encourages the independence of these countries in politics, which not only undermines the EU's policy toward the Balkans, but also its policy toward China (Pavlićević 2014).

Meanwhile, the EU also worries that China's investment might undermine their influence as a "normative power" in the Balkans. From the EU's perspective, the SAP as a primary EU instrument to integrate and regularize Western Balkan countries is challenged by China's non-conditioned loan policy. Because some Balkan countries are not EU members, Chinese investment in them is not restricted by EU policy. For Europe, the Balkans are "a gateway to the European Union but not yet in the EU and the EU rules do not apply."[5] The "danger for Europe is that there will be a kind of 'China lobby' of smaller Member States within the EU" (Krauthamer 2012). Thus, for the EU, Chinese investment means that its enlargement policy toward the Balkans would not function as planned. However, the ineffectiveness of the enlargement policy not only undermines the EU's Balkan strategy, but also affects its global strategy, especially toward Russia and the Middle East, because the latter two affect European security and are adjacent to the Balkans geographically.

In addition, because China's trade relations with non-Balkan countries are not restricted by EU regulations, and the Balkan countries and the EU have signed a free trade agreement, China can use the membership of some Balkan countries to circumvent EU trade barriers and indirectly export products to European markets.[6] This indicates that the EU regulations are not as effective as imagined regarding China–EU trade relations.

Last but not least, China's investment is, to some extent, competitive with European companies for business contracts with Balkan countries. Without Chinese competition, European companies could monopolize

---

[5]China seeks gateway to EU via cash-strapped Balkans (2014, 16 December), EurActiv. com, Reuters.

[6]Japanese Media: China's gamble is aimed at Western Europe market via Balkans (2014). Retrieved from http://oversea.huanqiu.com/article/2014-12/5248561.html.

the Balkan investment market; now however, intensive competition with China is inevitable.

Russia's Worries

For Russia, Central Asia is a region that cannot be dominated by other powers. Its interests in this region can be traced back to the Cold War era when Central Asia was part of the Soviet Union. Russia still has a diaspora (ethnic Russians) in Central Asia of approximately 9.5 million people. Thus, in terms of history, blood, and culture, Central Asia is of particular interest to Russia. For Moscow, Russian domination in Central Asia should be the core target of its policy toward this region.

Russia has established military bases in Kyrgyzstan and Tajikistan, and pressed Uzbekistan to shut down the US Air Force base in that country. It signed a collective security treaty with Central Asian countries and took a series of initiatives to strengthen its military presence in this region.

Economically, Russia has the dominant position in the energy system in this region. Through cooperation with Central Asian countries, Russia controls the exploitation and transportation of a large part of the energy in Kazakhstan, Turkmenistan and Uzbekistan. Meanwhile, several million people from Kyrgyzstan, Kazakhstan, and Uzbekistan work in Russia and are suppliers of these countries' foreign exchange, which gives Russia an important influence in these countries.

To strengthen ties between Russia and Central Asia, Moscow has proposed some multilateral arrangements such as the Eurasian Economic Community signed by leaders of Belarus, Kazakhstan, Kyrgyzstan, Russia and Tajikistan in October 2000. In 2011, Russian Prime Minister Putin proposed establishment of the Eurasian Union between Russia and some states of the former Soviet Union. In May 2014, leaders of Russia, Belarus, and Kazakhstan signed the Eurasian Economic Union treaty. The Eurasian Union was officially launched in 2015, and the aim is to ultimately realize an economic union similar to the European Union.

China's involvement in Central Asia affects Russia's agenda in this region. For example, China's "growing energy footprint in Central Asia perhaps gradually undercut Russia's political leverage and economic influence over its Central Asian neighbors" (Danchenko 2010). If the dependence of Central Asian countries on China's investment and trade increased, Russia would feel the competitive challenge to its dominance there. For example, Tajikistan will replace its Russian aircraft with Chinese aircraft and the gas that was mainly exported to Russia from

Central Asia is now also exported to China. This long-term trend poses serious challenges to Moscow (Younkyoo et al. 2013).

Historically, Russia and the Western Balkans are linked by Slavic kinship and Orthodox tradition. The Balkan countries were part of Russia's sphere of influence in the Cold War era, and now act as a buffer zone between Russia and the West, especially NATO. This implies that the Balkans form a key region for Russia's security. From this perspective, Russia never wanted Balkan countries to be members of the EU nor members of NATO.

However, some Balkan countries are now members of both the EU and NATO, and others are only EU members or only NATO members. Only Serbia, Bosnia and Herzegovina (BiH), Montenegro, Macedonia, and Kosovo are neither EU members nor NATO members. Clearly, in terms of security, the key role of Russia's foreign policy toward the Balkans is to try to prevent these countries from being members of NATO, if unable to prevent them from becoming EU members (Dempsey 2014).

Commonly, in international relations, influence penetration starts from economic engagement; Russia's engagement in the Balkans is no exception. Namely, Russia has deep economic involvement in the Balkans. It invests in this region in diversified areas, including infrastructural construction and manufacturing. For instance, Russia has a large number of investments in Serbia. The state-run Russian Railways is upgrading a 350-km stretch of track in Serbia; Gazprom, Russia's state-owned energy giant, has a majority stake in Serbia's natural gas supplier; and Lukoil, another giant Russian energy company, holds almost 80% of Beopetrol, a Serbian gas-station chain (Dempsey 2014). Serbia is Russia's main partner in the Western Balkans. Since 2013, the two countries have maintained a strategic partnership.

Russia also maintains close relations with the Republika Srpska in BiH. This constituent republic is seeking secession from the state. Russia can greatly influence BiH via supporting the republic. Montenegro, independent from Serbia since 2006, is also strongly dependent on Russian investment and, meanwhile, Russia exercises political influence in this country via the opposition parties and the Serbian minority.

It can be said that all Western Balkan countries, especially Serbia, Bosnia, and Macedonia, depend significantly on Russian natural gas. For instance, more than 75% Serbia's gas is from Russia (Bieri 2015).

In consideration of Russia's long-term and deep engagement in the Balkans, China's involvement is not welcomed. Beijing has projects in the Balkans to similar to Russian projects, which means they are in competition in this region. For example, China has made large investments to establish a transport network in the Balkans, with Serbia as an axis, for enhancing trade links between China and Central and Western Europe. Meanwhile, Russia plans to build an energy line through Balkan countries, also with Serbia as axis, via Turkey. The Russia-supported line is called the "Turkey Stream" (replacing the previous "Southern Stream" that was declared by Russia to be ineffective in 2014). The China-financed Balkan high-speed railways and highway networks are competing for the Balkan countries' favor and strengthening the "independent decision-making capabilities of their transit partners and guide them toward multipolarity" (Korybko 2016).

Although Beijing is only aiming at doing business in Balkan countries, its investment can make these countries (viewed by Russia as its backyard) more independent economically and, thus, politically. Economic competition in the Balkans will prompt emergence of a multipolar system, preventing hegemony in the region, which does not meet Russia's strategic interest.

Furthermore, as mentioned, both Beijing and Moscow consider Serbia as the key Balkan state and wish to strengthen relations with this state as an important step in strengthening relations with the whole Balkan region. When Chinese President Xi visited Sebia in June 2016, the two countries enhanced their relationship into a "comprehensive strategic partnership" to replace the "strategic partnership" built in August 2009. During President Xi's visit, both sides signed a number of commercial agreements regarding diversified fields such as energy, infrastructure, military industry, science and technology, culture, and media.[7]

Undoubtedly, to some extent Belgrade–Moscow relations are like an alliance. In 2013, in a meeting in Serbia, Serbia's President Tomislav Nikolić said to Russia's President Vladimir Putin, "I would like you to know that Serbia is Russia's partner in the Balkans...Serbia loves you. And you deserved this love by the manner you rule Russia."[8] President Nikolić also argued that the EU should not bring sanctions against

---

[7] The relationship between China and Serbia (2016). Retrieved from http://wcm.fmprc.gov.cn/pub/chn/gxh/cgb/zcgmzysx/oz/1206_34/1206x1/t257882.htm.

[8] Helsinki Committee for Human Rights in Serbia 2013 (2013), *Helsinki Bulletin*, No.93, 4.

Russia because of the crisis in the Ukraine. He said that Serbia could not tolerate worsening relations with Russia.[9] These two countries are closely linked by Slavic kinship and Orthodox culture. Since 2009, the "strategic partnership" coordinated their positions in the fields of politics, defense, energy, and economics.

Thus, it can be predicted that China's deepening relations with Serbia will cause Russia's jealousy and hidden hostility, which would cast a shadow on China–Russia bilateral relations and challenge China's presence in Serbia and the Balkans.

Turkey's Competition

Central Asian countries are neighbors of Turkey and they have deep ties in history, religion, language, culture, and kinship. In addition, from the perspective of Turkey, strengthening relations with Central Asia is an important step in improving the status of Turkey in the West, because once Turkey becomes the region's leader Europe can never neglect Turkey in international relations. The collapse of the Soviet Union gave an opportunity for Turkey to realize its ambition. Just like its views on the Western Balkans, because of the Ottoman legacy and the links of religion and language with Central Asian countries, Turkey considers itself the natural dominant power in Central Asia. Simultaneously, by virtue of the "model of Islamic state with democracy," it also thinks of itself as the leader of Central Asian countries.

Based on this identity and position, Turkey has adopted various policies to enhance its cultural, political, economic, and social relationships with Central Asian countries. For example, Turkey is promoting Turkish cultural penetration in Central Asian countries by donating books, helping reform textbooks, supporting student-exchange programs, and providing free broadcast and television programs by satellite, and so on.

Economically, Turkey provides financial aid to influence Central Asia. Especially in the early years of independence from the Soviet Union, these Central Asian countries lacked sufficient fiscal capacity and Turkey's aid was a timely support. With the aid provided to Central Asia, Turkey

---

[9] Serbia's President: worsening relations with Russia cannot be tolerated (2016, 10 March), *Global Times*.

influenced social and economic reforms, and much more investment from Turkey flowed into this region.

Apart from the competition and suspicion described on the part of the EU and Russia, some other powers also pose challenges for China's engagement in Central Asia. The USA has great geopolitical interests in this region, especially after the war in Afghanistan in 2001. The USA enhanced its presence in Central Asia by taking advantage of the war against terrorism. Additionally, India became an important player in Central Asia by fostering strong bilateral contractual ties with some of the Central Asian states (in particular Kazakhstan and Tajikistan) in order to carve out a space for its stakes in the region (Kavalski 2007).

Historically, Turkey has a long-standing involvement in the Balkans because of the legacy of the Ottoman Empire, which ruled the Balkan region for several centuries. Thus, Turkey and Balkan countries have some shared history, ethnics, and culture, which makes Turkey a natural partner of the Balkan countries (Gayle 2015).

Contemporary Turkey's ruling party, the Justice and Development Party (AKP), adopts a foreign policy of "zero problems with neighbors," actively developing relations with the Balkan countries that belonged to the former Ottoman Empire, especially when its endeavor for accession to the EU faced deadlock.

Economically, Turkey is increasingly a remarkable investor in the Balkans and is even dominant in foreign direct investment (FDI) in some Balkan countries. For example, in recent years, it is one of the biggest investors in Albania, especially in areas of telecommunication, finance, and architecture. It is involved in infrastructure projects – mainly highways – in Kosovo, Serbia, Montenegro, and Albania, worth hundreds of millions of euros. It has established a strategic partnership with Slovenia and the trade volume reached about 400 million euros in 2013. It was the first country to sign a Bilateral Investment Treaty (BIT) with Kosovo, and is helping to build a gas pipeline from the Black Sea to Greece, in cooperation with Russia. These examples show that the Balkans represent an important investment destination for Turkey. In 2009, its investment in the Balkans stood at US$4.6 billion, accounting for 16% of total Turkish investments abroad.

The Balkan countries are not only Turkey's economic partners, but also targets of its foreign and cultural strategy. As a would-be multicultural center (moderate Islamism, Turkic language-speaking people, and Ottoman successor), Turkey is expanding its soft power to the Balkan countries and deeply influences the people in this region. Because Turkey considers itself a multicultural center, it believes it can attract the Balkan people culturally. For a long time, Turkey has seen itself as a moderate Islamic state and believes that it can be a model for Balkan countries.

As the then Turkish Prime Minister Bülent Ecevit stated in 1999, "Turkey is, I believe, a model for Islamic countries (...) I believe that Turkey's example has played an important role in this respect, because the Turkish experiment has proven that Islam can be compatible with modernity, with secularism, and with democracy" (Benhaïm 2015). This is called the "Turkish model," a balanced mix of Islam, democracy, free market, and modernity. In reality, Turkey has taken a "charm offensive" in culture and achieved some success.

For example, various Turkish soap operas broadcast throughout the Balkans influence views and opinions on Turkish lifestyle and society. Turkey also funds universities and schools in BiH, Kosovo, and Albania; provides free Turkish language courses in Albania; helps renovate Ottoman-era monuments in Serbia, Albania, Kosovo, Macedonia, and BiH; builds Islamic cultural centers in Romania, Albania, Kosovo, and BiH; and supports Turkish minorities and culture in Bulgaria, Greece, Kosovo, and BiH. (Nagy 2012).

In summary, Turkey was and is an important engager in Balkan countries, and has deep and wide economic, strategic, and cultural interests in this region. In this context, China will inevitably meet Turkey while engaging in the Balkans and this meeting could result in potential cooperation, or perhaps conversely, in conflict.

The Turkish government does not openly criticize or doubt China's engagement in the Balkans, because its relation with the Balkans is not similar to that of the EU. The EU considers the Balkans to be part of Europe and is very sensitive about its security. Turkey views the Balkans as part of its sphere of influence, not a region with sensitivity for its national security. However, in consideration of its deep engagement in investment and trade, and in cultural fields, it would be unsurprising if Turkey came to consider China as a big competitor economically, or even strategically, especially considering that these two countries are emerging economies with similar interests in investment in the Balkans.

14.3   APPROACHES TO DEAL WITH THESE CHALLENGES

Although Beijing's engagement in the Balkans and Central Asia is viewed with suspicion by several powers and related countries, the challenges should not be overestimated. Some of the suspicion is just illusion. For example, the EU values its rules and norms highly and worries that China's engagement would make these rules and norms become ineffective in the Balkans. This could be true in some Western Balkan countries that are not EU Member States and in which EU rules are not enforced. However, in practice, China takes a serious attitude to investment abroad and emphasizes that Chinese companies should abide by local laws and regulations to ensure that the investment is successful and to improve the management level of Chinese enterprises. China does not have the desire to change the domestic situation in the Balkans and Central Asian countries, nor to threat other players' strategic interests in these regions. However, Beijing should take some measures to reduce suspicion of China's engagement and, meanwhile, keep its own interests appropriately.

14.3.1   Soft Involvement in Domestic and Regional Affairs

Non-interference as a doctrine in Chinese diplomacy has been kept by all generations of Chinese leaders. This doctrine is embedded in a more comprehensive Chinese diplomatic principle, the Five Principles of Peaceful Coexistence, which was jointly advocated by China, India, and Myanmar in 1953–1954. Through this policy of non-interference, China has applied "sovereign equality" and "mutual respect" in its diplomatic relations with other countries and, simultaneously, defended its own domestic authority and sovereign integrity. Although non-interference is debated and some Chinese scholars argue it should be replaced by some more ambitious approaches, it is still affirmed by Chinese leaders and insisted on as a principle of diplomacy.

Notwithstanding, it should be admitted that active engagement to undertake international responsibility and not only to make money in Central Asian and CEE countries means that some new approaches should be used. China should insist on non-interference, but develop new approaches to adapt to the current situation, which is very different from that when the Five Principles of Peaceful Coexistence were advocated in 1953, and the new requirement that Beijing undertake more international responsibility.

Accordingly, some active engagement policies should be used, while insisting on non-interference. This does not mean putting new wine into old bottles, but taking new measures to insist on non-interference (not only respect for sovereign independence), and also providing some public goods and accepting some obligations. Active engagement includes active mediation, connecting grassroots, and connecting through multilateral organizations (as discussed next).

First, Beijing should actively engage in the domestic affairs of related countries, although these affairs do not have a direct impact on Chinese interests. They can, however, have an indirect impact, considering the fast internationalization of Chinese interests. This active engagement, such as mediation to help to calm a worsening domestic situation, should be commonly accepted by both or all sides concerned in rivalry in a county. In recent years, China has been increasingly active in helping to resolve other countries' domestic affairs, for example, sending representative on African affairs to handle problems in Darfur, South Sudan, and Syria. As another example, China has invited opposition groups of countries that have fallen into disturbance and civil war, such as Sudan and Libya, to visit Beijing, persuading them to participate in truce negotiations.

Second, Beijing should deepen contact with the grassroots of the countries along the new Silk Road, although many of these countries are not Western-style democracies. Nowadays, by means of the internet, the grassroots in each country has increasing influence on domestic political processes. This implies that to obtain the friendship of countries along the Silk Road, the first step should be to get the friendship of those grassroots. Of course, some bottom-up approaches to communication with individuals and groups in civil society is needed.

Third, Beijing should use the UN and the Shanghai Cooperation Organization (SCO) to engage legitimately in other countries' affairs. On a global level, the UN has enough authority, and at the regional level, the SCO has full legitimacy, to engage in Central Asian affairs, if necessary.

An active, yet soft, engagement in Central Asian and CEE countries is necessary for Beijing, not only to deal with issues that impact regional security but also to undertake international and regional responsibility, by which Beijing would gain more trust and friendship from these countries.

14.3.2 Inviting Powers to Engage in the Projects of the Silk Road Proposal

The China-initiated new Silk Road is not China's individual initiative or even a bilateral cooperative project between China and some countries along the Road. It is an initiative concerning China, countries along the Road, and some powers that have great interest in the countries of Central Asia and CEE.

In terms of this perspective, the Silk Road initiative should invite some relevant powers, such as Russia, the EU, Turkey, and the USA to participate. For Beijing, this invitation can send a friendly message directly to competitive counterparts in these regions, reducing their doubts and increasing their trust in Chinese involvement. On the other hand, according to different endowments and based on the division of labor, a triangular and multilateral cooperation in Central Asia and CEE can benefit not only the destination countries, but also the corporations of China and other related powers.

For instance, Russia, an important actor in Central Asia and CEE, should be invited to participate in the Silk Road Economic Belt, especially in the areas of energy and security Fortunately, two state have started to cooperate under the frameworks of the China-initiated Silk Road and Russia-initiated Eurasian Economic Union. This means that Beijing and Moscow support each other's trans-border strategic projects and will try to make them harmonious and mutually beneficial. In May 2015, the heads of the two states signed and issued a joint statement on "cooperation on the construction of the Silk Road Economic Zone and the construction of the Eurasian Economic Union," according to which the two sides will start dialog on extensive economic cooperation.

In Central Europe, China's involvement cannot neglect the EU's views and positions. As the deepest involved and most important stakeholder in this region, the EU and key members cannot not be excluded from China-initiated projects regarding economic and social development. In the economic arena, both sides have the will to promote economic prosperity in CEE countries and maintain stability, especially in the Balkans. Thus, China's logistic construction in the Balkans should be accepted by the EU if the EU plays some role in the construction; for example, if some European corporations are invited and some EU rules are applied and respected.

If Chinese engagement in countries along the Belt can benefit these countries and related powers, geopolitical competition can be translated into an exciting economic cooperation, which no power would oppose.

It is said "Give a man a fish and you feed him for a day. Teach him how to fish and you feed him for a lifetime." Thus, Chinese engagement should be accompanied by Chinese-supported capability building for countries along the Belt. Through cooperation in multiple levels and multiple fields, the industrial technology and reserve of talents in concerned countries should be promoted. Accordingly, Chinese engagement should include construction of special economic zones for technological transfer, educational communication, and financial aids for capability building. If Chinese engagement is accepted and welcomed by concerned countries along the Belt, it could not be opposed by other powers in these regions.

14.4   CONCLUSION

In this era of globalization, goods and capital flow freely in the world. Therefore, as an emerging economic giant, China's increasing investment in Central Asia and the Balkans is easily understandable. Consolidation of this economic relationship includes the enhancement of diplomatic relations with the countries in these regions based on the principle of non-interference. From this perspective, China's engagement in Central Asia and the Balkans can be considered more a capitalist-style competition than a new geopolitical competition. Based on this, the competition between China, Russia, Turkey, the EU, the USA and others in Central Asia and the Balkans should not be transformed into rivalry, but into cooperation and coordination within the framework of capitalist economy.

REFERENCES

Benhaïm, Y., & Öktem, K. (2015). The rise and fall of Turkey's soft power discourse, Discourse in foreign policy under Davutoğlu and Erdoğan, *European Journal of Turkish Studies*, issue 21.

Bieri, M. (2015). The Western Balkans between Europe and Russia, Center for Security Studies (CSS), N0. 170.

Danchenko, I., Downs, E., & Hill, F. (2010). One Step Forward, Two Steps Back? The Realities of a RisingChina and Implications for Russia's Energy

Ambitions, Brookings Institution Policy Paper 22 (Washington, DC: Brookings Institution, 2010), p. 5.

Dempsey, J. (2014, 24 November). The Western Balkans Are Becoming Russia's New Playground, Carnegie Europe.

Gayle, A. V. (2015). How China successfully adjusts its policies towards the western Balkans—An analysis of the role, experience, and potential impact of key stakeholder. *European Studies* (Beijing), Vol 6.

Godement, F., Parello-Plesner, J., & Richard, A. (2011). The scramble for Europe, The European Council on Foreign Relations (ECFR), July 2011.

Hoffmann, K. (2010). The EU in Central Asia: Successful good governance promotion? *Third World Quarterly, 31*(1), 87–103.

Kavalski, E. (2007). Partnership or rivalry between the EU, China and India in Central Asia: The normative power of regional actors with global aspirations. *European Law Journal, 13*(6), 839–856.

Korbko, A. (2015). How China's Balkan Silk Road Can Resurrect South Stream, Oriental Review.

Korybko, A. (2016). Hybrid Wars: Breaking the Balkans. The Russian-Chinese Strategic Partnership Goes To Europe (Part II), Retrieved from http://www.globalresearch.ca/hybrid-wars-breaking-the-balkans-the-russian-chinese-strategic-partnership-goes-to-europe/5525029.

Krauthamer, K. (2012, February 18). China in the Balkans: Invasion of the Voleex? Transitions Online.

Michaletos, I. (2015). Balkans lose geopolitical importance, RIMSE, 2015-10-7.

Nagy, G. (2012). Turkey—A welcome return to the Balkans? TransConflict, Retrieved from http://www.transconflict.com/2012/01/turkey-a-welcome-return-to-the-balkans-031/.

Pavlićević, D. (2014). China's Railway Diplomacy in the Balkans. China Brief, *14*(20).

Poulain, L. (2011). China's New Balkan Strategy, Central Europe Watch, Volume 1.

Vangeli, A. (2015). Macedonia's crisis: A challenge for the New Silk Road? CritCom.

Younkyoo, K., Blank, S., & Bed, S. (2013). Different dreams: China's 'peaceful rise' and Sino–Russian rivalry in Central Asia. *Journal of Contemporary China, 22*(83).

Zeneli, V. (2014, December 15). China's balkan gamble: Why is china investing so much in the debt-burdened balkans? *The Diplomat.*

INDEX

© The Editor(s) (if applicable) and The Author(s) 2018   263
Y. Cheng et al. (eds.), *The Belt & Road Initiative in the Global Arena*,
https://doi.org/10.1007/978-981-10-5921-6

CPSIA information can be obtained
at www.ICGtesting.com
Printed in the USA
BVOW08*2203041217
501911BV00015B/672/P